Fighting Back

Also by Janet Bode

View from Another Closet:
Exploring Bisexuality in Women

Fighting Back

*How to Cope with the
Medical, Emotional, and
Legal Consequences
of Rape*

by JANET BODE

Macmillan Publishing Co., Inc.
New York

Macmillan Publishing Co., Inc.
866 Third Avenue, New York, N.Y. 10022
Collier Macmillan Canada, Ltd.

Library of Congress Cataloging in Publication Data
Bode, Janet.
  Fighting back.
  Bibliography: p.
  Includes index.
  1. Rape. 2. Rape victim services. I. Title.
HV6558.B62   362.8'8   78-17166
ISBN 0-02-512050-6

First Printing 1978

Printed in the United States of America

Grateful acknowledgment is made to the following for permission to
reprint material from copyright sources:

From the book, *Sex and the Law*, by Morris Ploscowe. Copyright
1951 by Prentice-Hall, Inc. Published by Prentice-Hall, Inc.,
Englewood Cliffs, New Jersey.

Excerpt from the article "Forensic Psychiatry: Profiles of Two Types
of Sex Offenders" by Fritz Henn, Marijan Herjanic, and Robert
Vanderpearl from the *American Journal of Psychiatry*, vol. 133, no. 6,
pp. 694–96, 1976. Copyright 1976, the American Psychiatric
Association. Reprinted by permission.

To My Family

Contents

Acknowledgments

Never do you feel so alone and isolated as when you have been raped. My emotional recovery was speeded because of the love and support offered by many friends. I wish I could reciprocate with more than a few words of thanks. Deep appreciation goes to my family, as well as to Joanne Althoff, Joan Doherty, Kay and Bill Franey, Betsy and Al James, Michael Mendelson, Judy Pollock, and Austin Scott.

Writing a book is also a solitary experience. I would like to thank the following people for their continual understanding and encouragement: Barbara Althoff, Sandee Bonham, Jeannie Dougherty, David Fechheimer, Audrey Kavka, Jean Naggar, Joanie Oaktree, David Rich, Edmund Shea, and Victoria. Special praise goes to John Brinck, David Chesnick, Robin LaFever, Carole Mayedo, Catherine Sollecito, Terry Tomaselli, and Barbara Zaun.

This book would not have been possible if the women interviewed had remained hidden behind a wall of silence. We hope that by sharing our stories, other women's burdens will be lightened.

Fighting Back

1: *No Longer Silent*

A kid, he looked about twelve, walked toward my car as I unlocked the door. In the darkened university parking lot, he asked for help. "My uncle's run out of gas. He needs a ride to a station. It'll only take a few minutes." As he disappeared, an older man came over. I had had a good day. It was only nine-thirty. Do a favor. A human kindness.

Nothing seemed unusual as we talked and drove away. But I was set up. Do you know what it does to you when a knife is pushed to your side? While a man's arm is locked around your neck? He said he would kill me if I didn't follow his instructions. The pain of the blade was reinforced by threats of a gun. I wanted to live.

The trap proved insidious, for he traveled with friends. The surrounding woods yielded a second man. And then a third, patiently waiting his turn to rape. I still remember my distorted words, "My God, how many are there?"

As one finished, the next began. Chantlike they chorused, "We'll kill you. Kill you. Do what we want or you'll be dead." Three to one. Night. Deserted. No lights. I scanned the tree-tops somberly waving in unison, the patterns the clouds made as they glided soundlessly past the moon.

They used and abused me. Physically. Emotionally. My transformation from person to object was complete. After violating my body, they turned on my soul. They trampled my dignity. Kicked my spirit when my guard was down.

I really thought I was going to be murdered. Death seemed so close, I could reach out and touch it. Evil hung stagnating in the air. That night a part of me did die—my faith, openness, trust. In an hour's span they altered all that, and left with warnings of vileness if I were to tell anyone. I was supposed to exist being thankful they spared my life.

Their laughter echoed through the darkness as I picked myself up from the dirt and stones. Slowly, I moved back to my car. They had stolen my money, my jewelry, my freedom from terror. The drive home was in stunned silence. I had no idea what to do. I had never reported a crime to the police. The assailants' words wrapped themselves around my mind.

"Forget. Forget," I told myself. "Protect those I love." My anguish ran too deep. I had to let it out.

I called my sisters. As days slid by, I told a few close friends. They wanted to help, but no one could remove memories of humiliation. The fear. Pain. Ugliness. Knives. Arms. Hands.

And then I knew I had an obligation to protect other women. I could not let the men succeed again. My gullibility must not be repeated. Ten days later, I went to the police.

"Of course we can't do a thing, " the officer said, "until you take a polygraph test. That's required even if you'd had medical proof of intercourse and came to us that night." Delay in reporting. My word alone. I was separated from my husband. "I personally don't think it's worth the effort," the detective replied.

The men struck again. Same method. Same location. This time there were five matched against one woman. I felt hollow. I had failed once more.

Back and forth to the station. Interviews. Formal statement. Mug shots. To the crime scene. Standing on the very ground where I had been raped only days before was horrifying. Fight the tears. Fight the images. Fight the questions. Why? Why had they done that?

The other victim's immediate report resulted in the men's apprehension. At four in the morning I was called to view more photographs. I shuddered at the awesome responsibility. These were faces I had been erasing, not memorizing. Systematically I shifted them across the desk top. I watched my hand write on the back of each picture, "I identify this man as one of those who raped me on October 5, 197—."

As I began to leave, the officer drew me aside and asked, "Did you know that each man must have an individual trial?"

"No," was my weak response.

Days of fear. Nights of restlessness. Peace was nowhere. I was afraid at work, on the street, in my car. I paced around my home. It had to end. I had to become whole. I am a survivor.

Postpone the trial. Wear down the witness. Maybe she'll change her mind, drop the charges. The weeks lengthened to months, until I could not contend with the reminders. Because of that night, those men, that event, I quit my job, packed, and moved 3,000 miles away.

It helped. I improved. My smiles returned. Ten months later, a trial date arrived. Intellectually, I believe in protecting the rights of the accused. I know a defendant must be in the same courtroom with the witness. I realize his lawyer's position is to convince the jury to render him not guilty. But mind and emotions do not always mesh. During the days of the trial, they rarely intersected.

After I was guided through a description of the assault, the cross-examination began.

"Didn't you approach those three men, tell them you were separated from your husband and hadn't had intercourse for a long time?"

"No."

"In fact, you know you suggested going into the woods for some fun," the attorney continued.

"That's not true."

"Well then, isn't it correct you approached the man, the uncle, and suggested you drive him to a gas station?"

"The man came to me with the request...."

"Isn't it right you invited him into your car?"

"You're playing with words. I didn't 'invite' him. After he said he was out of gas...."

"Hearsay, hearsay. I object, your honor," he interrupted.

"Didn't you even bring a blanket from your car into the woods for comfort sake?"

"No, I didn't even have one."

"While you were supposedly being raped, you looked at the trees and sky instead of closing your eyes in terror. Everyone knows when something hideous is happening you close your eyes. Kindly explain that."

"I felt the only way I could endure the experience was to mentally remove myself from it. I searched for something calming to view, so I wouldn't have to think about what was happening."

"How far away from you was this man while you were making love?"

"Inches," was the only thing I could answer.

The lawyer looked at me, turned to the jury, and said, "This isn't a young girl, but an older woman who had abandoned her husband." With a whirl, he once again walked toward me. "If all you claim is true, why didn't you fight to save your honor? Where were your bruises of resistance?"

This was near the end of my testimony. I had been on the stand for several hours. Every detail of the case had been examined and reexamined. My initial composure had been steadily eroded. I no longer cared if I were held in contempt of court.

"This was the third man to rape me. I didn't know how many more there might be. Look at him. He's six feet tall and weighs over two hundred pounds. I'm barely five five, and my weight is 105. They told me they would kill me if I didn't obey. They were armed. I wasn't. No one was within screaming or running distance. I didn't know the area. I could see no lights. He raped me! You should pray your wife or any woman you love never has to experience a similar night. I wish they never have to decide to fight and possibly be killed, or submit in hopes of living. Be glad you've never had to make that choice yourself."

The judge glared while reprimanding me for my rambling

response. After I was dismissed, character witnesses trooped forward to defend their friend.

The last person to testify was the boy who had waited by their car during the attack. He revealed how they had planned the event, selected the location, and watched for the parking lot to empty. When it was over, they had returned to their hidden automobile and told him, "Hey, we just raped some lady!"

The trial was over, with the decision resting with the jurors. Two women. Ten men. Mostly middle-aged. With no emotion in his voice, the foreman rose and read the verdict to the charges. Kidnapping. Not guilty. Forcible rape. Guilty. Armed robbery. Guilty.

The remaining assailants? One pled guilty. The second was found guilty in the other woman's case. The criminal justice system had performed its duty. That pointless night had permanently changed my life and now the rapists', none for the better.

A body that has been raped heals. The mind's recovery is a more gradual process. It has been five years since the assault. The details have blurred. No longer do they invade my daily thoughts. Yet, in quiet times, I know the most bitter truth. It can happen again. While acknowledging this fact, I live in a world of mental gymnastics. I know the reality of rape. I survived once. I do not know if I could find the inner strength to do it again.

I am not alone. As you are reading this chapter another woman is being raped. By the time you finish, the total will be even higher.

This book evolved from a meeting for victims that I attended. As six of us compared our thoughts, one mentioned she had written poetry as an outlet for her anger. Another had done a short story.

I contacted crisis centers and women's organizations in the United States and Canada, requesting other manuscripts. I taped interviews. For two years I worked with San Francisco Women Against Rape, a community-based advocate group. This is a compilation of that research.

Most who speak through these pages wish to remain anonymous, although they want to be heard. Therefore the names used are fictitious.

These women are unanimous on one point—they will no longer be silent.

2: *Facing the Facts*

Irene and I take a shortcut through a wooded block in our suburban neighborhood. A man approaches us. "Raise your skirts and pull down your panties," he tells us. We run. Our parents have told us not to use that path. We are five years old. Guilt. Confusion. Fear. I still remember.

I am riding the subway. A man sitting next to me begins intentionally pressing his leg against mine. At the next stop, I change cars. I am fourteen. Embarrassment. Confusion.

On a sunny afternoon, Joanne and I are running errands. A businessman carrying a briefcase walks toward us. As he passes, he moves the briefcase. His fly is unzipped, his penis exposed. We run. We are eighteen.

Barbara, her two-year-old daughter, and I are sunbathing at the beach. A fully-clothed man surveys the area, then sits twenty feet from us. He smiles while he begins masturbating. We gather our towels, lotions, books, and snacks. We go to the far end of the beach, nearer other people.

It is 2:15 A.M. The phone rings. Half-awake, half-asleep, I think the voice is a friend's. I provide the information I know seconds later I should not have. "I'm home . . . alone. . . ." I leave and spend the night at a friend's.

Passing a construction site, we are met by hoots and calls from the workers. We cross to the other side of the street to avoid the confrontation.

Men drive by yelling, "Hey, honey, wanna lil' fun? How 'bout a piece of ass for us? What's the matter? Too good to talk to us?" We turn around, walk in the opposite direction from which they are driving.

These are the "little" rapes. Whenever a person intrudes on your privacy—pressing unwanted, uncalled for, unsolicited direct or indirect intimacies on your being—that is a little rape.

Women are beginning to tell themselves they will no longer tolerate these little rapes, these constant reminders of men's power over them.

These situations are not the limits to which men push women. They are merely the hints, preliminaries, previews, of men's ultimate potential. They miss by a mile the legal concept of this act which has evolved through our common law system, a system in which judges make individual, case-by-case determinations of what constitutes the crime.

Legally, under common law, rape is unlawful carnal knowledge of a woman, not one's wife, by force and against her will. Any penetration by the penis of the vagina, however slight, is enough to complete the crime when there is also force by the assailant and resistance by the victim. Other forms of sexual assault, such as oral and anal contact, and use of objects, while not included in this traditional definition, are encompassed in most states' revised legislation.

Society has added other ideas, preconceived and emotional, of what rape is. A rape is an isolated happening, carried out by a stranger who is mentally ill. Leaping from a dark alley, he forces intercourse on a young, attractive woman because he is overwhelmed by an uncontrollable sexual arousal.

Society must consider an accusation of rape with special caution. It is well known that women can be vindictive, hysterical, and untruthful. They make rape accusations to retaliate against men who have spurned them or to explain a pregnancy.

And, of course, all women fantasize about being raped. Some may have difficulty separating their daydreams from reality.

In the early 1970s, when a few women began discussing and organizing around this topic, they realized the absolute necessity of cutting through this stranglehold of myths. Despite several years of education by women's groups, outreach programs, and the media, many people have not progressed past these stereotypes.

Those involved in the initial battles had little research to back up their feelings. They began by proving that rape, even when limited to the legal definition, is not a series of isolated incidents affecting only a small number of women.

Yearly, the Federal Bureau of Investigation prepares the *Uniform Crime Reports,* a compilation of offenses reported across the country. In 1976 there were 56,730 reported rapes, one every nine minutes. This was an increase of 105.4 percent since 1967. The southern states accounted for 32 percent of the total, while the western states had 26 percent, the north central states 24 percent, and the northeastern states 18 percent.[1]

Even these appalling figures are extremely conservative. As the FBI points out, "This offense is a violent crime against the person and, of all the Crime Index offenses, law enforcement administrators recognize that this offense is probably one of the most underreported crimes, due primarily to fear of victims of their assailants and the sense of embarrassment over the incident."

What the FBI does not note is that their statistics exclude those rapes that end in death for the victim. These are added to the murder tally. The statistics also exclude a specific category for statutory rape, both consensual and forced intercourse with a minor. Without listing a definite number, the FBI puts that type of rape under the heading of crimes against chastity, common decency, and morals.

The estimates of rapes reported versus rapes committed range from a high of nearly all rapes committed being reported to a low of only one out of ten being reported. A study by the Minnesota Department of Corrections proposed that 25 percent of rapes committed came to the attention of some law enforcement agency.[2] A study in California cited a rate of approximately 20 percent of those that occurred.[3] The National Opinion Research Center of the University of Chicago stated 27 percent.[4] Two Washington, D.C., surveys gauged the rate from three and a half to nine times the number actually reported to the police.[5]

In the early 1970s the Law Enforcement Assistance Administration (LEAA) made an extensive survey of reporting rates of various crimes in the nation's five largest cities.[6] Their findings for rape: Chicago, 53 percent reported to the police; Detroit, 55 percent; Los Angeles, 46 percent; New York, 61 percent; Philadelphia, 55 percent. They followed this with a survey of Atlanta, Baltimore, Cleveland, Dallas, Denver, Newark, Portland, and St. Louis. In these locations, a little less than half of all rapes committed were reported.

And some victims who refused to summon police might be equally hesitant to record this information on a form given them by a branch of the Department of Justice. This probability can be extrapolated from murder statistics. In major cities, such as New York, 75 percent of murders committed are by nonwhites against nonwhites. It is extremely likely that a high number of unreported rapes take place within this same population. Richard Harris, in a *New Yorker* article,[7] further suggested that low-income people from all racial backgrounds refrain from calling police because that can translate into more trouble. He stated that some ethnic groups view reporting as a betrayal of one of their own race. Police cause hardship, rather than alleviate it.

Although the crime occurs most frequently in cities with populations over 250,000 few areas escape reported cases. Travel around the country—Alamogordo, New Mexico; Ashtabula, Ohio; Butte, Montana; Cartersville, Georgia; Coeur d'Alene, Idaho; San Clemente, California; Wausau, Wisconsin; on through to Zion, Illinois—all these cities had reported rapes. It takes only a minute to count the few towns that did not have this entry on police ledgers.

Isolated occurrences? No. At least half a million women

could be victims this year, and the numbers go up every year. Many divorce themselves from this crime by assuming that rapists are rare, and those few who exist are mentally ill. They can be classified as to type and their actions explained away by specific causes.

This belief in the rapist as a sick individual was reinforced by the initial investigators. Alfred Kinsey et al at the Institute for Sex Research provided data from their studies in the late forties and early fifties.[8] This work involved categorizing rapists. Convicted rapists were divided into five personality types: (1) The assaultive variety, who used violence and threats. His aim was to punish and/or harm his victim. (2) The amoral delinquent, who was egocentric and expected to receive immediate gratification of all his desires. (3) The drinker, whose capacity for self-control was seriously impaired by alcohol. (4) The explosive rapist, whose actions were inexplicable and unpredictable. (5) The double-standard rapist, who lived by the conviction that there were two types of women—the good ones you married and the bad ones you could rape.

Another study was conducted at the Center for Diagnosis and Treatment of Sexually Dangerous Persons in Bridgewater, Massachusetts.[9] After examining one hundred convicted rapists, they discerned three general categories. The aggressive personalities wanted to degrade, defile, and humiliate their victims. Women in the abstract they held in high regard, but the women they met were contemptible, conniving, and untrustworthy. The second type were those men with a combination of low sex drive and unresolved homosexual feelings. The last classification were the psychopaths, brutal, sadistic, and explosive.

Other investigators looked for additional clues to discern and understand rapists' behavior. Members of the University of Minnesota Medical School launched a study at Sing Sing Prison, now known as the Ossining Correctional Facility. Their conclusions, published in the *Science Digest,* September 1957, were that none had normal personalities.

Drs. E. G. Hammer and Bernard Glueck, Jr., supervised a series of projects over a five-year period of two hundred convicted sexual offenders.[10] They added more ammunition by determining that men raped because of sexual confusion in their formative years. Thirteen percent of the men had mothers who had been actively hostile toward them. Forty-four percent had slept in the same bed with their mothers, either frequently or occasionally. The mothers behaved in a sexual manner toward their male children. In some instances, the men had a dominating mother and an ineffectual father, or the reverse—an overprotective mother and a tyrannical father.

Rapes occurred more frequently when self-control was lessened by alcohol or a combination of temptation and frustration. On these occasions, the men's consciences were overcome by a rage response, and an aggressive outburst took place.

After further investigation, Hammer and Glueck stated, "In many cases, rape may be related unconsciously to early incestuous desires and the fury aroused by the Oedipus complex. . . . The victim may be a substitute for the criminal's mother, who would naturally resist the attack by her son."[11] They felt that only a victim's resistance made the rapist potent.

Other researchers, such as Drs. Manfred Guttmacher and H. Weihofen, administered Rorschach tests to incarcerated rapists. The results of those interpretations, published in 1952 in *Psychiatry and the Law,* revealed much conflict and internal disharmony hidden beneath a surface of outward calm. The men tended to be overcontrolled. A theme of violent and forced penetration became apparent from the manner in which they analyzed the blots.[12]

The author of the article "The Sex Offender," published in December 1962 in *Police Chief,* offered a different slant. He felt that the rapist was the true victim, because his emotions and passions were uncontrollable. He had unexplained urges and fierce desires that were impossible to halt after they had been aroused.[13]

All this data was culled from examining the exceptions, rather than the rule. Convicted rapists were questioned and tested, as opposed to the vast majority of rapists who were never apprehended, incarcerated—or even reported. Any research based on such a skewed sample is highly open to question.

As the number of reported rapes soared, and women's cries of pain turned to cries of anger, a more varied group of investigators entered the field. These current researchers still include many psychiatrists, but the Freudian influence—which is strongly biased against women as well as viewing much of one's life in terms of repressed sexuality—has decreased among them. The range has widened to lay people, psychologists, criminologists, sociologists, and lawyers, blending and balancing their technical expertise and training. Although these researchers, too, are studying imprisoned offenders, they are asking questions more relevant to the times. Methodology and diagnostic devices have improved. These factors combine to make their data more accurate than previous studies.

The information they have gathered is destroying some of the myths. This process has been expedited and given firmer direction by recent historical investigations and by studies based on victims' statements about their reported and unreported rapes. The emerging profile of the rapist, his actions, and his victims is very different from the old stereotype.

The belief that only men who are mentally ill rape is not true. Some rapists are, but the majority are not. If a typical rapist exists, he is most likely the sane, average male living next door. He wants what he wants when he wants it. He has been raised with the concept that a woman is a man's possession. If she happens to be single, not protected by another man, she is especially fair game. Women can be used and/or abused at will.

The vast number of rapists are men who pushed women into feeling they had to acquiesce to sex out of duty or obligation or because of the threat of real physical harm. If you were to survey a group of a thousand men, it would become clear that the rapists' attitudes are by no means isolated beliefs. Evaluate the men's responses to such questions as: Did you ever force, coerce, or intimidate your female partner into having intercourse even though you knew she did not want to? Did you ever demand that your bed-partner simulate resistance because sex is more exciting to you that way? Did you ever take sexual advantage of a woman who had consumed too much alcohol or drugs? Did you ever demand your "rights" as a husband and have sexual intercourse against your wife's will? Did you ever use your role as an authority figure (such as employer) to manipulate a woman (an employee) into having sexual intercourse? Did you ever participate in a "gang bang" or "train"? Did you ever force sexual intercourse on a woman because you were angry at someone else? Did you ever rape in a situation of war, where as a member of the invading army you considered that part of your reward? As the litany of questions continue, you might be surprised how many men would answer yes to one or more of them.

Camille E. LeGrand, a California lawyer, has examined the topic of rape. In a *California Law Review* article in 1973, she wrote that the hostility of men toward women is growing because women are increasingly equal and have more freedom. Rape is an exceedingly effective way of consciously or unconsciously "keeping them in their place," by showing men's continued strength and power over women.[14]

In the book *Our Bodies, Ourselves,* the authors state that a rapist is not generally a disturbed person, but "one who sees women as people to be used, . . . or a man with a history of getting what he wants."[15]

Menachem Amir, a lecturer at the Institute of Criminology at Hebrew University and former visiting professor at the University of California, Berkeley, is the author of *Patterns in Forcible Rape,* 1971. This book was one of the first comprehensive examinations of the subject. After researching 646 cases, he concluded that "studies indicate that sex offenders do not constitute a unique or psychopathological type; nor are they as a group invariably more disturbed than the control groups to which they are compared."[16]

A San Francisco policewoman with fifteen years experience on the force, the last four with their special sex detail, said she certainly would not categorize rapists as mentally ill.

Drs. Fritz Henn, Marijan Herjanic, and Robert Vanderpearl, in a study published in *The American Journal of Psychiatry*, examined the records of 239 men charged with sexual offenses and referred by the courts to Malcolm Bliss Mental Health Center, St. Louis, Missouri, from 1952 to 1973. Even though these assailants were sent for evaluation with a bias toward finding some type of psychiatric disorder, major mental illness among the sample was rare. The main diagnosis for rapists was "anti-social tendencies"; for child molesters, "sexual deviation," with no other mental disorder. The authors concluded that "the myth of the 'crazy rapist' seems to apply to the extreme exception. . . . Psychosis does not appear to be associated with either of these sexual offenders."[17]

A federally and privately funded research project was conducted in 1975 by the Queen's Bench Foundation at Atascadero State Hospital, California, which specializes in treatment for sex offenders. The interviewers questioned seventy-three rapists about what they were seeking when they raped. Most cited such objectives as dominance and power over their victim, control of the victim, and/or humiliation and revenge. They offered such "explanations" for their actions as lack of self-confidence, unsatisfying family life, negative self-concept, poor social interaction, inability to develop interpersonal relations, lack of understanding of women, lack of communication outlet, feeling of inadequacy. Not one said he raped because he lacked a sexual outlet.[18]

A study done by the Rape Crisis Center in Pueblo, Colorado, of ninety convicted rapists produced the same general response. Their main objective was, again, power and control—not sex.[19]

Dr. Richard Rada has conducted studies on the relationship between alcohol and rape. After interviewing seventy-seven convicted rapists, he discovered that 50 percent of the men had been drinking at the time of the offense, with 43 percent of that total drinking "heavily." For purposes of his research, "heavily" was defined as ten or more beers or the equivalent. Using stringent criteria, he furthered determined that 35 percent were alcoholics. A second study by Rada in 1974 of 122 committed rapists revealed that 57 percent admitted to drinking immediately prior to the assault, 35 percent drinking heavily.[20] For the nonalcoholic, the drinking might have been used to overcome fear or timidity. Studies tend to indicate men drink not to lessen anxiety, but to feel stronger. The reader is reminded that drinking and/or alcoholism and rape is not necessarily a cause and effect relationship.[21]

Other professionals, such as Drs. Gene Abel, David Barlow, Edward Blanchard, and Donald Guild, turned their attention elsewhere.[22] They examined "The Components of Rapists' Sexual Arousal" by using a device to measure the erections of nonrapists and rapists during audio descriptions of nonrape and rape sexual scenes. One encounter involved a mutually enjoyable intercourse; the other used the same partner and surroundings but depicted a man forcing himself on the woman. They discovered, on the basis of their erection measures, that nonrapists did not achieve erections when listening to rape scenarios, while rapists did. They concluded that the dangerous rapist is more sexually aroused by the act of rape itself than by the victim of it.

The subjects of these studies are, of course, the exceptions, the men who were caught and then convicted. What about the respectable man next door, or in your own home, who answered yes to one or more of the questions on page 16, and whose victim for one reason or another could not or would not report him? In many cases, the offender is not the stereotype stranger. He is known to the victim, as neighbor, date, uncle, stepfather, father, or friend. Once again, we can extrapolate from murder statistics. Crimes of violence, anger, and power occur most often between people who know each other. It is not farfetched to conclude that rape, another crime of violence, anger, and power, frequently takes place between acquaintances.

The late Dr. Joseph J. Peters, of Philadelphia General Hospital, supervised one of the most thorough examinations of rape victims and the circumstances surrounding their attacks.[23] The project, known as "The Philadelphia Assault Victim Study," was funded by the National Institute of Mental Health. The findings revealed that, of children who were victims, 80 percent knew their attackers, and 32 percent of the known attackers were either extended or nuclear family members. In the case of adolescents, age thirteen to seventeen, 60 percent were at least acquainted with the assailants. Among adults eighteen and over, 40 percent of the victims knew their attackers. These figures represent only those cases brought to the attention of the police. It certainly seems likely that cases in which the victim knew the rapist are the cases least likely to be reported to the police.

It is not only the young, attractive female who is victimized by men. Women in their eighties and infants of a few months have been sexually assaulted. Women of all degrees of beauty, the mentally retarded, the blind, and the physically disabled have been raped as well.

Much energy is spent warning women about dark alleys and dead-end streets. They are told this is where the men will be lurking. The fact is that indoors is an equally dangerous place.

In the Philadelphia Assault Victim Study for victims, regardless of age, as many as two-thirds of the attacks took place inside. For children and adult victims, over a third of the attacks occurred in the home. This was true in approximately 20 percent of the cases involving adolescents.[24]

According to Amir's study, a total of 67 percent of the rapes were indoors.[25] Another project, conducted by the Denver Anti-Crime Council, revealed that nearly 60 percent of reported rapes took place inside. The second most frequent crime scene was the automobile, involved in 18.5 percent of the incidents.[26]

The Atlanta Regional Commission came up with a different percentage, but it too refutes the belief that the sole place a woman has to be cautious is the unlighted pathway. That survey indicated victims were raped in residences half the time, in open areas 41 percent, and in cars, commercial businesses, and public buildings the remainder.[27]

Some studies have further refined the statistics as to time factors and peak days of the week. Jodi Tasso and Elizabeth Miller, psychologists at Edgecliff College, Cincinnati, examined the influence of the full moon on human behavior. For one year they gathered data in a large metropolitan area. Rape and seven other categories of crime occurred significantly more frequently during the full moon phase than at other times of the month.[28]

Our society's racism brings forth an added layer of erroneous, emotional reactions. It is a widespread belief that rape is an interracial crime, with mainly black men attacking white women. The facts reveal the opposite—it is predominantly intraracial.

A nationwide survey completed in 1967 by the National Commission on the Causes and Prevention of Violence found that, in seventeen cities, blacks raped whites in 10 percent of the reported cases.[29] The Center for Rape Concern in Philadelphia recorded that 16 percent of the rapes in that city were committed by black men against white women. Statistics from 1973 in Atlanta revealed that blacks were victims in 62 percent of the reported cases. Blacks raped whites in 25 percent of the incidents, blacks raped blacks in 61 percent of the complaints, whites raped whites in 13 percent, and whites raped blacks in one percent of the reported cases.[30]

The Battelle Memorial Institute Law and Justice Study Center, Seattle, Washington, polled prosecutors across the country for statistics regarding rape cases presented to them for prosecution.[31] The statistics were broken down by county

21 : Facing the Facts

size: small, 25,000 to 100,000; medium, 100,000 to 1,000,-
000; large, above 1,000,000. Victims and accused were then
classified as either white or minority, including not only
blacks, but Latinos, etc. Even after this tremendous winnow-
ing-out process, rape remains primarily intraracial.

	County size		
	Large*	Medium	Small
Both white	27%	50%	63%
Both minority	34%	24%	25%
Accused white/minority victim	10%	6%	3%
Accused minority/white victim	20%	20%	9%

(*No explanation as to why this does not total 100 percent.)

Many police officers admit that when the rapist is a minority member and the victim white the chances of reporting
increase. When the reverse is the situation, the tendency to
report is minimal.

Racism adds even more burdens to minority victims, especially blacks. Some whites theorize that rape is not as damaging for black women. They say that black women are more
sexually active than white women. Black women have a tradition of being strong under stress. Violence is an accustomed
fact of their daily lives, because the majority live in ghetto
areas where crime is rampant. Therefore they can assimilate
a rape experience more readily than white women.

Because of these specially-tailored myths, black women
suffer doubly. The ability to cope with life traumas does not
increase with practice. Rape rates rise with the density of
population, but if this crime were reserved for ghettos, the
general public's concern would probably not have grown to
its current high level.

Rape is more than one man spontaneously attacking a lone
woman and forcing her to submit to a single act of intercourse. Amir discovered that force was used in 85 percent of
the cases he examined. Additional sexual humiliation (fellatio, cunnilingus, etc.) existed in 27 percent of the incidents.
Forty-three percent of the victims were raped by two or more

men. Ninety percent of all group rapes (three or more men raping the victim) involved advance planning, as did 83 percent of pair rapes and 58 percent of single rapes.[32]

Planned rapes often involved detailed preparations, learning the habits of a specific woman, deciding how to entice her to a safe location, and, when more than one man was participating, even who would be first to rape her.

The Rape Prevention Program, Violence Research Unit, at the Denver General Hospital studied assaults by strangers in 1974. In these cases, 59 percent of the rapists were armed. Sixty percent began with physical force or restraint. Ninety-three percent of the victims endured continual physical force during the attack. Fifty-nine percent were threatened with further physical injury or death to themselves or someone close.[33]

The Queen's Bench Foundation research project revealed more facts about planned rapes. A little over half of the rapists interviewed stated they had been explicitly looking for a woman to rape. Approximately three-quarters were feeling frustrated, angry, and/or rejected prior to planning and committing the attack. Nearly 80 percent had been observing their victim before approaching her. Almost 70 percent had a weapon with them, even though originally they did not intend to use violence. Fifty-five percent stated the injuries they inflicted on their victim were intentional, but not because they wanted to hurt her—they did so because their "expectations" were not being met.[34]

The Philadelphia Assault Victim Study noted these results.[35] Force was an integral part of the attack. Over half the victims were threatened with bodily harm. Twenty percent were intimidated by the offender's violent, physical gestures. More than a third of the assailants were armed—27 percent had a gun, 47 percent a knife, and another quarter used a weapon such as a chain, a broken bottle, or a club. "Actual physical force was applied by the offender in 81.8 percent of the cases." While child victims were the least likely age category to suffer physical force, nearly half experienced some type. Among adolescents, 80 percent endured a wide range of force, from pushing to slapping, kicking, slashing, choking. Add to that information the fact that for these teenagers the average number of attackers was 2.7. In cases where the victim was eighteen or above, 90 percent of the incidents involved the use of at least one type of physical force. The average was 1.5 attackers per victim. For rapes of victims of all ages, in nearly 20 percent of the cases there were others present who did not participate in the sexual assault but added implied force, intimidation, and brutality.

Rape can be accomplished while leaving no outward scars, no medically verifiable proof to show society. Often rape includes much more than forced intercourse. There is fellatio, cunnilingus, rectal intercourse, and repeated acts of sexual invasion. In some cases foreign objects are forced into the vagina and/or anus. Victims have been urinated upon, burned, tortured, and mutilated. Some have been killed.

This is what rape is about. Yet society retains a blind fear of the vindictive, untruthful woman. Victims know this, and it is one of numerous reasons that many decide not to report. They realize they might not be believed. They could be classified as one of those hostile, deranged females who race to the police station reporting fantasized rapes that never occurred.

What about all those women who want to retaliate against their boyfriends? The women who said, "Yes," and then changed their minds? Or the women who want the notoriety generated by their charges, who are basically amoral? Don't forget the prostitutes; their tricks run out without paying and they scream rape. Think about those countless men already languishing in jail because of hysterical conniving females who trumped up charges against them.

The FBI statistics aid in reinforcing this myth. According to their recording system, when a law enforcement agency receives a complaint of any criminal matter and the follow-up investigation discloses no crime occurred, it is marked "unfounded." Then these unfounded complaints are eliminated from the crime counts. The problem is that too many people erroneously think "unfounded" and "false accusations" are synonymous. Unfounding a rape charge has evolved at the local level as police officials' method of ridding themselves of what they consider legally weak cases. It does not mean the crime was not committed, merely that they have chosen to advise against prosecution.

The FBI statistics for 1976 state that 19 percent of the rape complaints were unfounded with no differentiation between unprosecutable cases and false accusations.[36] Most of the cases marked in this manner involved one or more of these factors: (1) The victim delayed before reporting the crime to the police.[37] (2) The victim refused to submit to a medical examination.[38] (3) There was evidence the victim was intoxicated at the time of the attack.[39] (4) The assailant was known to the victim.[40]

Serious doubt and often an "unfounded" decision applies to any sexual assault occurring in an automobile.[41] Some police forces automatically dismiss all date rapes in cars.[42] Further research and interviews with victims revealed that police officers frequently list cases as unfounded if they decide the victim is too young, afraid, emotionally upset, or embarrassed to cooperate fully with an investigation. When the victim happened to bathe or douche before reporting, the police can claim she failed to preserve necessary physical evidence, and they will not pursue the case.

Other jurisdictions require the submission of an unfounded rape complaint under these two circumstances: (1) When patrol officers respond to a call, arrive at the stated location, and there is no victim present. (2) When an injured victim goes to a hospital, receives medical treatment, and the hospital staff summons the police without her being willing to press charges.[43]

When the victim has placed herself in what some define as a compromising situation, such as hitchhiking, going to a man's apartment, inviting a man to hers, or meeting at a party, courts can claim victim "precipitation." The case is tremendously weakened or lost. The police often label these unfounded as well.

What matters to the police is not whether the rape took place, but whether there is sufficient evidence of that rape which could be used to obtain a conviction in court. Police already feel pressured because of the low number of rape apprehensions and convictions, without adding these extra cases.

In reality, the rate of false accusations as opposed to unfounded cases is very low. Lieutenant Julia E. Tucker, formerly with the New York City Rape Analysis Squad, stated that the number of false complaints in their jurisdiction was about 2 percent. That is the same unfounded rate as for all felony complaints.[44]

Detective Sergeant Rinaldo of the Washington, D.C., Sex Squad was questioned whether that police force had encountered many women bringing false rape complaints. "There's a small amount," Rinaldo said. "Usually it's found out before the arrest. It's not a big problem at all."[45] Social workers at Philadelphia General Hospital estimated that only one percent of the victims they treated had possibly fabricated their stories.[46]

It is not only the police who worry about women making false claims. Various professionals have supported this fear and distrust of female accusers. Morris Ploscowe wrote in *Sex and the Law* that many experts in the field of legal medicine believe "rape cannot be perpetrated by one man alone on an adult woman of good health and vigor. . . . Medicolegal experts therefore tend to regard all accusations of rape made under such circumstances as false."[47]

Dr. Manfred S. Guttmacher, who before his death headed the psychiatric clinic attached to the Baltimore courts, and who wrote *Sex Offenses: The Problems, Causes and Preventions,* explained "Women frequently have fantasies of being raped." Dr. Karl A. Menninger said such fantasies might almost be said to be universal. And in a hysterical female, these fantasies are all too easily translated into actual belief

and memory falsification. It is fairly certain that many innocent men have gone to prison on the plausible tale of some
innocent-looking girl because the orthodox rules of evidence
(and the chivalry of judges unversed in psychiatry) did not
permit adequate probing of her veracity."[48]

Because of this kind of "evidence" and attitudes toward
women, many victims decide against reporting. In fact, one
begins to wonder why any sane woman would even consider
summoning the police. Too often that call may involve her
in countering all the myths while reporting the crime. For the
victim, her emotional burden is multiplied, her actions futile.
Her chances of convicting a guilty man, let alone an innocent
one, are minimal.

The notion of women's universal rape fantasies is another
myth used to deny the reality of women's experience. Some
women may daydream about "rape," but in terms much
different from the real event. Hollywood might have convinced them a tall/short/dark/blond/stranger/friend will
come into their lives, swoop them up, and carry them off.
While quietly protesting, because of remaining societal
mores, their cries of "no" will slide into sighs of "yes." That
occasional fantasy has nothing to do with the actual horrors
of the crime.

Psychiatrists from Sigmund Freud to Helene Deutsch have
asserted that the tendency for victimization and masochism
is also a universal female condition. Less widely known
theoreticians, such as L. Eidelberg, have further proposed
that all women share a wish to be raped.[49] Ralph Slovenko
and C. Phillips in an article for the *Vanderbilt Law Review*
carried this supposition a step farther.[50] Because rape is now
so prevalent, women may be employing a "riddance mecha-
nism." They intentionally place themselves in dangerous situations to become victims and thereby be rid of their anxiety
of the experience. By doing the very thing that is feared, the
victim yields to being raped in order to "get it over with."[51]
After following this sequence then, the woman will be able
to deal with rape in a more rational manner.

Did the seventy-five-year-old woman who was raped and robbed of $1.39 while on her way to church fantasize and then employ the riddance mechanism? Three months later she committed suicide because of the trauma of the event. A seventeen-year-old west coast victim killed herself two nights after being raped by five motorcyclists. A teenager received a scholarship which included a trip to a foreign country and admission to a school outside her community. When a local gang learned this, they raped her. Fantasy events? Riddance mechanism?

What about the child victims? Society does not instruct us as to what age these fantasies begin to simmer in female minds.

The final absurdity society has imposed on women is the conflicting advice on how to react when rape seems inevitable. Some say that a victim must fight to the death to preserve her honor and chastity. Others, that she should not resist, but rather "lie back and enjoy it."

Neither tactic shows any understanding of the realities of being raped. Both are demeaning to women, cruel, narrow-minded, stupid. And both lead women to judge their own responses to rape in a totally inappropriate, detrimental way. The end result being that one after another of the victims I spoke to talked about their feelings of guilt and inadequacy over the way they had handled themselves during the incident.

Women's lives are changing. They are commencing sexual intimacies at younger ages. Virginity is less frequently saved for the wedding night. Their "chastity" does not seem something for which to sacrifice their lives. Even if they feel they should fight, they seldom have the physical prowess or training to fight effectively. They are shorter, lighter, and weaker than most men, and they have never been encouraged to develop their physical potential. Adolescent and adult women of today have taken few physical education courses. Those that were required included mainly warm-up exercises, perhaps basketball (girls' rules) and a little volleyball.

When they find themselves about to become rape statistics, they do not know their strength or capabilities to defend themselves, or even how fast and far they can run. And how does an unarmed woman, however fit, protect herself against guns, razor blades, knives, broken bottles, multiple attackers, beatings, or terror?

If a woman decides not to fight, does that mean she should give in and "enjoy it"? It is not human nature to enjoy doing anything you do not want to do. Who enjoys being robbed of material goods, let alone emotional? Rape is not "making love." It is a repugnant, degrading, inhuman, painful, horrifying occurrence.

Firmly implanted, preconceived ideas about the crime of rape will take more years to uproot and change. As documentation of the reality of rape increases, the myths will disappear. And yet, recent years have produced examples of their continuation.

Winter, 1976. A news item concerning the attempted rape of an eight-year-old was reported on WABC-TV in New York City. Tex Antoine, the station's weather announcer, reminded viewers, "Confucius once say: 'If rape is inevitable, relax and enjoy it.' " After enough protest calls were logged, Antoine was required by station officials to offer a public apology. He said he regretted making the statement, because he did not realize the victim was only a child.

Gallant Greetings Corporation, Chicago, Illinois, produced and distributed a birthday card. On the front was a disheveled woman with a wide grin. The inscription read, "Birthdays are like rape," then you opened the card, and the message continued, "When it's inevitable/Enjoy ... Enjoy...." There was space to sign your name, and then the final phrase, "Happy Day."

On September 25, 1977, the San Francisco *Sunday Examiner* ran a front-page story based on an interview with a convicted rapist. The headline proclaimed, "He Calmly Tells You 'Why Men Rape.' " His explanation was because "they see ... girls walking around braless with their nipples sticking through their dresses, and short dresses, and it drives them nuts. . . . They try to talk to these girls, they try to reach out, and, man, they get rejected right and left. After a while they don't know what to do. Maybe you want to kick her teeth in, and maybe you don't. They're walking around showing themselves off like that. . . ." Police believe this man raped fifty or more women, and possibly killed as many as five. These offenses occurred during a six-month period while he was on parole because he had testified against two convicts accused of attacking a guard.

A Harris Poll conducted in the fall of 1977 revealed current attitudes.[52] Eighty-seven percent believed that "rapists are sick and perverted males who commit crimes against women that these women often can't fully recover from." Eight percent disagreed with the statement. Seventy-two percent agreed that the rape of any woman is a violent crime that can not be justified by suggesting the victim caused the event by the way in which she dressed. A 64 to 24 percent majority rejected the hypothesis that in many rape cases it was probably the woman who initially led the man on. But a 68 to 18 percent margin of those polled accepted the theory "some women carry on sexually, and then get scared and unfairly call it rape."

But still, after the years of education and research, after thousands of women suffered the reality of rape, the poll showed the basic ambivalence about rape remains for the American public. In the same poll, 49 versus 45 percent believed that "with women appearing in ads in newspapers only scantily clad, with stories about prostitutes in the papers and on TV, with bars that have nude dancing and women dressing in revealing clothing, it is no wonder that men think women want to carry on sexually."

Myths die slowly. Remember the facts.

3: *Cry Pain, Cry Anger*

Rape is an act of power and violence. It is a person or persons totally subjugating another. It is humiliating, brutal, terrorizing, and aggressive. Although rape is not sexual, an overlay of sexuality remains attached to it, and therefore people continue to make moral judgments. Rape is a total attack that affects both the mind and the body, one's self-concept and societal attitudes. It is a complete invasion coupled with an absolute deprivation of control.

Have you ever entered your home to discover you had been burglarized? Do you remember your reactions? Shock. Fear. This is a violation of your property, your privacy, and, to an extent, yourself.

A victim of armed robbery suffers as well. Freedom of movement, control, independence, are temporarily suspended. It is a frightening, threatening, horrifying event which underscores one's vulnerability. Assault and battery victims readily recall the physical and emotional upheaval they endured. Their scars are external, yet internal ones develop.

The rape victim is forced to contend with the emotional culmination of those other criminal acts, with an additional burden. Not only is she the victim of an ultimate violation of self, but she is also thrust into a category no other crime victims combat—moral judgments, taboos, evaluations, and edicts as to *her* behavior.

For these reasons alone, the rape victim would find herself in a uniquely isolated and disadvantaged position. But there are more. One must consider her prerape mental health, the specific circumstances of the attack, and her postrape response. It is only recently that any investigators, let alone health professionals, turned their attention to examining the victims' reactions to sexual assault. The problems of child victims had received some attention in studies completed in 1937,[1] 1955,[2] and 1969.[3] The sole recommendation for adolescents and adult victims was that people should be sensitive to their emotional needs.

Sandra Sutherland Foxe and Donald Scherl interviewed and assessed postrape reactions of a small, homogeneous sample of adult victims who had sought help at a community mental health center.[4] Their findings, published in 1970 in the *American Journal of Orthopsychiatry,* revealed that although no two victims nor their rape experiences are alike, there are certain behavior patterns. They divided these into three categories. For each they listed the potential emotional reaction and its duration. These were further refined with recommendations for ways in which friends, family, and counselors could provide aid.

The initial feeling is one of acute shock, dismay, and disbelief. As with any terrifying event, some victims may become hysterical, begin shaking, or appear restless. Others try to mask their feelings, using great effort to present a calm facade. Many show signs of fearfulness and anxiety. This stage can last from twenty-four hours to a week, during which time the victims often want to talk about their experience and are receptive to help.

The next stage is defined as outward adjustment, or pseudoadjustment, lasting from a few weeks to many months. Victims attempt to resume normal activities. Many deny feelings expressed earlier. At this time, the women subdue some of their anger and appear less depressed. Some rationalize the incident, attributing it to blind chance. It could have happened to anyone. On occasion, they accept many of the myths and search for excuses for the rapists' actions. Frequently, people inaccurately assess the degree to which the victims have adjusted to their experience.

Phase three, integration and resolution, calls for accepting and dealing with the impact of the event and any believed complicity in it. This final step is accompanied by the deterioration of emergency defenses and the onset of depression. The timing might be activated by a specific reminder of the attack—a police lineup, a diagnosis of venereal disease, or a glimpse of a man who resembles the attacker. Many begin dwelling on details of what happened, the total dimensions of the event. Eventually, there should be a realistic evaluation, the return of self-reliance and esteem, and an integration of the experience.

Ann Wolbert Burgess, associate professor of community health nursing, and Lynda Lytle Holmstrom, associate professor of sociology, both at Boston College, are two of the leaders in the field of current rape research. In their first work, using basically a sociological approach, they concentrated on adult victims.[5] After surveying nearly one hundred victim participants at the Boston City Hospital, they discerned two periods—one of disorganization, followed by one of reorganization. During the initial response, victims stated that self-blame and fear were their predominant emotions. Besides these were varied elements such as embarrassment and anger. Bodily changes observed included headaches, gastrointestinal complaints, altered appetite, erratic sleep patterns, etc. Victims coped with these in either an expressed or controlled manner. Some became very verbal and revealed many signs of crisis. Others appeared composed, suppressing their feelings.

Reorganization, the second period, involved adjusting to the ramifications of the crime. Some moved, changed jobs, turned to others for support, expressed conflicts about their sexuality or relationships, and so forth. This was the time for putting their lives back in order. Rape is a stressful life crisis and should be treated as such.

An even more comprehensive study, mentioned in the previous chapter, was that initiated by the Philadelphia General Hospital Center for Rape Concern.[6] With Dr. Joseph J. Peters, principal investigator; Linda Meyer, research sociologist; and Nancy Carroll, research assistant; this extensive project covered a one-year period and examined the somatic and psychological reactions of victims. They recorded responses for child, adolescent, and adult victims of sexual assault and also offered suggestions for family members. They concluded that, for all victims, it was the aggression, not the "sex," that was most traumatic. Fear and lack of control combined to make the attack a crisis situation.

The following data, divided according to victims' ages, are a combination of material from the Philadelphia report and interviews I conducted while preparing this book. Where my information differs is in the long-range effects of this crime. I talked with women days and months, as well as years, after their attacks. They offered a perspective none of this previous research had provided—what has happened to them after the one year anniversary of the assault.

Children

Rape recognizes no age limits for victims. Although more are between fourteen and twenty-four, babies and young children have been sexually assaulted. For the age bracket up to twelve years old, the attack does not always meet a strictly followed legal definition of the crime, but from the standpoint of the assailant's purpose and the victim's well-being, it *is* rape. There might have been manual penetration of the vagina and/or anus, oral intercourse, rectal intercourse, penile/vaginal contact without penetration, manipulation of external genital area, and so forth. Some children are unclear regarding the specifics of the act, because they understand neither their own sexuality nor the implications of what occurred.

When children are victims of sexual assault, we tend to cloud the facts by substituting terms. We call the perpetrator a child molester, or a pedophile. If a battered child is brought to the attention of authorities, there is sometimes a sexual component. This aspect is ignored, while efforts focus on external medical complaints.

Prior to the late 1960s, many people refused to admit that children could be raped. In the cases that were noted, the child frequently received the blame. The child was seeking affection, flirting, behaving in a provocative manner; young children were accused of being the cause of the event. What was ignored was that the offender, not the child, initiated the sexual assault.

Often when children are raped, no one ever finds out about it because they are less likely than adolescents or adults to have been raped by sheer physical force, therefore less likely to display external physical injury. They have often been tempted, coerced, or ordered to participate. Equally true, the young victims, being confused, scared, and intimidated, are less likely to tell anyone about it.

Phyllis was barely five when two neighborhood teenagers raped her on several separate occasions.

She recounted, "They conned me into going to their house under pretense of favors. They enticed me. I'd tag along, and they'd make me submit. Afterwards they'd threaten me with disaster if I were to tell anyone. At the time I didn't even know what they were doing to me."

In many cases the child is assaulted by an authority figure. The physical damage may be less, but the emotional scars run deeper. This is especially true when the child liked, respected, and trusted her attacker. To compound the problem, when victim and attacker share the same residence, she can be raped repeatedly over an extended period of time. The same techniques of entrapment appear—enticing and tempting, followed by threats to maintain their secret.

I listened to women's accounts of incestuous rapes by their fathers, stepfathers, uncles, and brothers. These men ranged from unemployed laborers to professionals highly regarded in the community. While in private practice, Dr. Peters treated thirteen women who were victims of childhood rape. The attackers included a minister, a judge, and an architect.[7]

Generally the women I met merely acknowledged the incident, leaving it at that. A few touched on brief thoughts and unanswered questions:

"How could I tell my mother her new husband was attacking me?"

"My uncle was supporting us. What good would it have done if I had let anyone know he was sneaking into my room at night?"

"The whole family thought Uncle Charlie was great with kids. He'd baby-sit for me when my parents went out. From the time I was seven until I turned twelve, he raped me on a regular basis."

When the victim is assaulted by a nuclear or extended family member, or a close friend, the difficulties multiply. If the child speaks up, sometimes she is not believed. She comes to symbolize divided family loyalties and love. Confusion, bewilderment, guilt, and ambivalence on the part of family members surface. In cases where the rapist is the father or stepfather, the mother must question herself about priorities.

When the attacker is a stranger, one facet of the dilemma is simplified. The family can unite around the child. Their emotions of dismay, anger, or rage can be channeled toward the outside offender. The victim is more easily supported.

The researchers at Philadelphia General Hospital recorded numerous preliminary reactions of youthful victims. When parents said their children had adjusted well, that is showed no behavior problems or changes, they might have been observing the period of outward adjustment.

Although children exhibited fewer alterations than did adolescents or adults, there were noticeable differences. Immediately following the rape, and for varying duration, parents stated marked changes in the children's eating and sleeping habits. Nightmares occurred in 20 percent of the incidents. Mothers often noticed that the child cried out while sleeping. Nearly a third revealed negative feelings for men they knew and slightly more for strange men. Almost half feared being outdoors. Ten percent stopped going to school entirely. These changes decreased, except when the attacker remained in the home or when the child realized that a court appearance or other rape-related event was approaching.

It is difficult to chart changes in children, because many may be attributed to general maturing rather than direct results of the event. The most frequently cited personality changes were anxiety or tenseness. The victims and their families were revisited three, seven, and eleven months later. At those times, additional reactions were compiled. Every child did not experience all of these reactions, but they were prevalent in many.

1. Social withdrawal: refusal of adult help, seclusiveness, lack of motivation for play, less verbal communication.
2. Guilt, self-reproach, self-punishing actions.
3. Aggressive fantasies.
4. Repression.
5. Imagined aggression.
6. Excessive clinging and dependence on the mother.
7. Projection of guilt, sadness, and/or fear.
8. Dissociative behavior.
9. Denial of feeling, depression of affect.
10. General depression.
11. Easily distracted, fidgeting, restlessness.
12. Lowering or loss of self-esteem.
13. Compulsive washing, cleaning.
14. General fears, concerns, nightmares.
15. Compulsive avoidance/attraction with offender.
16. Bed-wetting.

Many women I talked to who had been child victims of rape were plagued by guilt and self-blame. Frequently they believed they had done something wrong. Their fears carried them as far as thinking that they would be punished. Often these emotions had been suggested to them by the attacker.

Thus, many shouldered their attack and its effects in silence, either temporarily or permanently. One child's parents did not discover what was occurring until she developed difficulty urinating. Because she was so young, her vagina had been damaged by the recurring forced penetration. A doctor discovered the cause of the complaint.

Children are keen observers. They recognize signals from those around them, and often mirror those reactions. If parents feel guilt, the child may duplicate that emotion. The same holds true for fear, anxiousness, and so on. If parents and other important people in the child's life pretend that nothing out of the ordinary has taken place, the victim will be confused. She may feel equally rejected and unprotected.

This crisis affects both the child and her family. On occasion, parents must seek help in coping with their reactions. Ms. Sherry Hallet of Anchorage, Alaska, discovered the horrors that can come to a family when her nine-year-old daughter was viciously attacked. The girl, who weighed fifty-four pounds, was drugged, choked, beaten, raped, and forced to commit fellatio. Ms. Hallet wrote to me that her little girl "has been handled delicately with help from doctors, a child psychologist, and various school personnel." But the mother required counseling as well. While searching for an outlet for her anguish, she helped establish a rape crisis center.

The rapist had been paroled from a Colorado prison after serving two years for the rape of a twelve-year-old. He had been indicted for raping a young, pregnant woman and was free on bail awaiting sentencing. Even though Ms. Hallet's daughter identified the man, the district attorney stated she would be an unreliable witness because of her age. Thus there was no trial. Whether the extra emotional intrusion of a trial would have been worthwhile, is hard to determine. Ms. Hallet reported that the longest sentence for rape in Anchorage at that time was one year.

Many parents believe that if they do not discuss the incident, it will be better for the child. She can more readily forget what occurred. But children do not forget. Being the victim of a sexual assault is traumatic. The child must have the opportunity to discuss her emotions. Love and support, especially from the mother, must be freely offered. The victim must learn she was not at fault.

The key for family members is not to be judgmental. When the child withdraws, or hesitates to mention the event, that does not mean she is unaffected. Rather, she is continuing to interpret adult cues. Open-ended, broadly worded questions, in terms the child can understand, should be asked. The duration of this ventilation period varies with each separate case. If parents feel confused about proper support, they should call on outside help. They can contact a hospital staff or a rape crisis center for suggestions. Group discussions for family members have been instigated at Philadelphia General Hospital, and these could be duplicated in other locations.

After an attack, parents must battle for a balance between overprotection and allowing their daughter to resume her normal activities. When a child breaks a bone or is hit by a car, parents react in a particular manner. They offer love, support, concern, and precautions against it happening again. The same response should follow a rape. If the child is discouraged from playing with friends, attending school, and maintaining the same daily schedule, she will conclude that something very wrong indeed has taken place.

This advice is a starting point. Important people in a victim's life know her best. There is such limited data on the effects of such an occurrence that even professionals often feel their way in offering recommendations.

When Alicia, twenty-seven, was a child, her father deserted the family. Because her mother was incapable of supporting them financially, she placed her daughter in a foster home. Alicia was ten. Her words detail the event, present her emotions now, and portray the many levels of this experience.

"Soon after I began living with my foster family, the father began troubling me. He'd plunk me down on his lap while he fondled me. For that he'd give me a penny or nickel. At that age I didn't understand the gravity of his actions, but I recall it made me feel dirty. I wasn't sure what was happening or why he was doing it, although I guessed there was something wrong about his behavior. Other times he'd peek in when I was bathing, make me kiss him when I didn't want to.

"I was confused, but I knew I had to stay there. I couldn't bring myself to complain. Who could I have turned to anyway? What could I have said?

"It was as if I were in slow torture with his constant, petty assaults wearing me away. Sometimes I believe his advances were even more gruesome than what eventually took place. After I'd been there awhile, their sixteen-year-old son decided to follow in his father's footsteps. I've wondered since then if this isn't how some men who rape begin, emulating what they see in their own homes. Adult males toying, pawing, humiliating the females around them.

"What his father initiated, the teenager fulfilled. He'd sneak up from behind, jab and poke at me, try to torment me. One day, when all of us youngsters went for a walk, somehow the boy and I became separated from the others. I have no idea whether he intentionally singled me out, led me away from the rest, but we were very much alone. I remember the fear, his pulling down my pants. He threw me on the ground and began humping me. Again, I was unclear what was happening. I didn't know how to get him to stop. I never told anyone. I sensed something evil had gone on, but my emotions didn't go far beyond that.

"During the coming school year, my mother decided I could live with her again, but I'd have to return to the family for summers. About a week before I was to leave for home, everyone was out of the house except me and their boy. I stayed in my room until I had to go to the bathroom, which was downstairs.

"As I left my room, I saw him scrubbing the steps. Even though I wished I could creep by him unnoticed, I knew he was staring at me. He hadn't done anything or said a word, but terror was there. While I edged down the last two steps, he grabbed me from behind. I was just ten, so small. He carried me to a bedroom and raped me.

"When my foster sister returned home, I told her what happened. She informed her parents when they arrived. The father decided to examine me to see if it were true. I felt like I'd been turned over from one attacker to the next. He said I was lying, so there I was.

"The next week is a complete blank. I have no idea how I existed in that house until my mother came. All I know is I felt ashamed and guilty about everything. In some twisted way, they'd made me feel I'd done something wrong. In retrospect, I wonder about my foster mother. I have almost no memory of her appearance or character. She must have known some of what was going on, but maybe she was afraid of her husband and son.

"I didn't tell my mother. I wasn't ever going to let her know, until she said it was time for me to return to that family. If you wanted to see an example of a child in absolute, absorbing panic, you should have been around. 'Please let me stay home,' I'd beg my mother. She'd say no. It wasn't possible.

"There wasn't a method to convey the enormity of my fear. I diluted and translated my emotions into an accusation that they were mean people. Describing what the son and father had done was beyond me. Finally, a week before I was due to leave, I wrote her a letter. I had such a fragmented knowledge of what sex was about, but somehow I must have known that intercourse could make me pregnant. Even now I remember the words in my note, 'Dear Mother, I know how people get pregnant. I know because. . . .' And I put it under her pillow while she was asleep.

"I woke up in the middle of the night. As I walked past my mother's room, I saw her sitting on her bed just bawling. My letter was on her lap.

"We never talked about it after that. Her main admission of the note was that she taught me a little bit about sex and having periods. I didn't even know about menstruation. I stayed home that summer. That was all. My mother and I are very close now, but we've still not discussed it.

"The rape is something I hadn't thought about for years. Sometimes I'd tell people I was raped when I was a kid, but I never went into any elaboration. The first time I did was only two weeks ago, when I launched into the story without realizing how it would affect me. By the time I finished, I was shaking and could hardly get the words out. Maybe because I'd always said it so casually. I convinced myself an event that happened long ago had no right to shape any of my feelings or reactions at my present age.

"It hit me this morning that one of my outstanding memories was that I couldn't believe how big his penis was. It was just horrifying to me that he was going to put such an enormous thing into me. I screamed and cried. The boy threatened if I kept yelling he'd ram a hairbrush up at the same time. That scared the daylights out of me. The fear is still too real.

"I've been trying to figure out how the incident has affected me. It's hard to divide what in my life has caused me to behave in a certain manner and what other factors might have been at work. For instance, I don't know if my sexual responses are normal compared to other women who didn't go through that. I don't share my sexual history with others. I have a feeling I put too much emphasis on sex. I've been married nine years and have had affairs. Most have been one or two time things. It seems to be something I'm driven to do.

"On the other hand, I know basically I'm hostile to men, other than relating to them sexually. I don't trust men, don't have much respect for them. My choice of clothes may be part of a sexual hang-up. I tend to dress provocatively, even though I'm a feminist and obviously don't want to be raped again. I guess I'm going to be the way I am, in spite of the presence of rape. I believe those reactions may come from my rape experience. I consider every male a potential rapist.

"My daughter is six years old. I lie awake nights being

frightened for her innocence. The other day I tried to explain a few things to her. I put a great deal of thought into it, since I didn't want to create faceless monsters for her. My approach was introducing the idea that her vagina was a private place and just her own. If anybody ever touched her there, I'd like her to tell me. But I don't know if she would, because I can understand someone saying 'This is our secret.' So I worry for her, and myself as well."

Adolescents

The adolescent years from thirteen to seventeen are times of turmoil. Physical and emotional growth accelerate. Conflicts swell within the family as the teenager strives for increased independence. Communication with adults is strained on any issue. Peer group approval becomes more vital than parental approval. An awareness of herself as a sexual being develops. And then she is raped.

The victims' immediate reactions during the first two days are similar to those described in the Sutherland and Scherl study discussed at the beginning of this chapter. The person is in shock which may be manifested by agitated speech, uncontrollable crying, nervousness, and verbalized anxiety to outer calm and quietness.

The response of one interviewee, Sandra, fell in the latter category. Because of this, she was further victimized. As she said, "We're taught all females become hysterical in crisis. I didn't. I pulled into a protective shell and behaved rationally. The result? Everyone thought I was lying."

As the first weeks pass, the young women who were badly beaten had physical pain as well as emotional. Many experienced symptomatic changes that were often the same as those noted for child victims. These included general tension, erratic sleep, recurring nightmares, and numerous gastrointestinal and urinary problems.

At age fourteen, Pat was raped by three classmates. Her menstruation had begun at twelve, stabilized by thirteen.

"After being raped, aside from spotting, I didn't menstruate for almost a year," she explained. "First I panicked, thinking I was pregnant. When that proved untrue, I was tremendously relieved. The last blood I saw was the evening I was raped. I think I subconsciously wanted to erase any evidence of the sexual side of me."

Others reported similar decreases and increases in their menstrual flow.

General and specific fears were cited. The majority had been threatened by the attacker(s) with retaliation if others learned of the rape. Whether or not the external physical results were obvious, this fear was present. Some victims of gang rapes subsequently joined the same gang for protection against future attacks. The fear of possible pregnancy was prevalent, especially among those maintaining silence about their rapes. They reported to no medical facility, so what questions they had remained unanswered. Many expressed concern about contacting venereal disease, a valid possibility. Because of their marginal knowledge on this subject, they repeatedly felt unclean and contaminated for long periods after the attack. This occurred even when they had been tested and had received preventive medication.

Their fears went even beyond these. A large number recalled being afraid not only of strange men, but of male friends as well. They persistently worried about future relationships with men in general, the sexual aspect in particular. One young woman believed she would never be able to marry because she considered herself "damaged." Often there was a frantic longing for a location that would bring peace and safety. They felt vulnerable outside on the streets, but this pressure was not alleviated when at home. They were uneasy if surrounded by friends or family, frightened when alone. No place or person could serve as a refuge for their emotional havoc. Many remembered a decrease in their social lives for these reasons. They felt isolated, and that reaction caused bitterness. It was not unusual for those fears to grow to phobias.

Not all victims could check off every one of these responses, but all experienced at least several. When the weeks lengthened to months, many had additional problems. They lacked self-confidence and self-esteem. Their ability to concentrate was diminished. Routine tasks, homework, learning new skills, came slowly or not at all. Troubled sleep combined with nightmares did not disappear. A general restlessness continued. Many remembered they wished they could move. Some changed schools. Others quit entirely.

Some kept the event a secret, trying to survive mentally as best they could. When the attack was obvious, because of their battered appearance, they offered edited versions of the event. Those confiding in friends received mixed messages. Because many adolescents were raped by peers, the attackers were known to their circle of friends. Their loyalties were challenged. Pressure not to inform police or any adult was prevalent. The sexual connotations, the retaliation threats, joined in bringing inadequate support. Even those who might have wanted to help lacked the emotional tools. They were unprepared when presented with a crisis situation.

In a few cases, friends helped significantly. They allowed the victim the opportunity to talk about her feelings. This need to ventilate was essential. Because many victims felt closer to friends than to their family, this was where they sought advice and solace.

When parents learned of the event, their reactions were also varied. As with the parents of child victims, when the attack was at random by a stranger they were more likely to gather together against the outsider. Because many were raped by friends when social situations escalated beyond the teenagers' control, too often parents accused their daughter of being at fault.

One woman, Cathy, reported her parents lectured her for weeks. The essence was, "We told you so. We warned you not to hang around with that group of kids. You were out on the streets when you should have been home. That's what happens when you don't listen to us." The tension increased until she ran away from home. Later, she returned to an improved environment, but the emotional violence her parents had done her remained with her for years.

Cathy's parents, and others like them, placed an additional burden on their daughter by forcing her to contend with the emotional impact of the crime, while also blaming her for causing the attack. Frequently the parents felt embarrassed. The rape represented their loss of control over their offspring. Their concerns included the community's reaction. They acted as if they had been victims, instead of their daughter. They curtailed her social contacts, while reminding her why. The rape was held over her head as a threat to behave in a manner they deemed proper. Even when parents restricted her life because of loving concern, the transition to reestablishing independence was hindered.

Many victims recalled acting more childlike than they had before the attack. They spent increased time with their parents, especially their mothers, feeling more protected when within their sight. They then found these new behavior patterns hard to break.

Ideally, the parents of adolescent rape victims should make their daughters feel protected and supported in the aftermath of the attack, at the same time encouraging them to reestablish their independence and autonomy. In some cases, women stated relations with their parents had improved. This terrorizing occurrence reminded parents of the depth of their love. Their daughters' well-being was too important to be lost in chastising words.

It is essential that victims be treated with kindness and understanding. Parents should be alert to changes in normal routine and bodily functions. If these become radically different, outside help should be sought. Either they or their daughter should contact a rape crisis center, hospital, or clinic for recommendations and/or referrals. If sex education has been lacking, this is the time to discuss the topic. Direct, factual information can alleviate many of the victims' concerns about pregnancy, future sexuality, sexual orientation, marriage, feelings about men, and so forth. Parents must make time to listen to the victims' thoughts regarding the rape. During the period of pseudoadjustment, they should continue to watch for signs of renewed depression, somatic changes, withdrawal, and denial of effects. All these indicate the experience is still retarding the victim's emotional growth.

The universal advice remains best: Do not be judgmental. The victim has already criticized herself enough without others joining in. Be loving and supportive.

In many aspects Sharon's story is representative of adolescent rapes. A recent high school graduate, she was living with her parents but planned to move into an apartment. Although she had had several boyfriends, she was a virgin. She was raped by a friend in what she considered a situation much safer than usual. Sharon knew his name, and where he spent his time. Her parents had met him.

Their evening date began with a barbiturate, a drug she agreed to take for the first time, and ended with rape. In between she received a severe beating, scratches, bruises, and a concussion. She endured feelings of guilt, complicity, fear, and confusion. His parting words were that she should inform her parents she had fallen down a flight of stairs. In this stunned condition, she confronted her mother and father.

"It was almost as if it were a disembodied voice saying those words. I felt he had programmed me. I couldn't shake free from his influence. My mother looked at me, glanced at my father, and repressed any doubts she might have had.

"She took me upstairs for a hot bath and then bed. While I was in the tub, she saw my body was covered with cuts and abrasions. She knew I hadn't fallen down any steps. Even though she realized more than I thought, she didn't say a word.

"As I woke up the next morning she came into my room and asked point-blank if I'd been raped. I nodded yes. After a few comforting comments, she left and contacted the police. The next few days become confused. I had so many things on my mind. What to do about the police, medical treatment, the man, my parents, my sanity.

"Dizzy spells, probably resulting from the concussion, would hit. Both my eyes blackened. I thought I was being completely lucid, but then I'd do or say something that didn't make any sense. I decided I couldn't tell the police the straight story, because I didn't want my parents to know about the drugs. I was feeling guilty for stupidly taking them.

"I created a version of the truth to satisfy the police. When they arrived, I said I didn't remember the guy's name. We'd planned to go to a concert, but then he'd kidnapped and raped me. I didn't want him to be caught. I wanted it to end that day and never bother me again.

"In this state I had to tell my story to several different policemen. One's attitude was that my boyfriend had knocked me around and now I wanted revenge. Then he suggested that when my parents saw me I decided to cry rape.

"Another cop turned on my father and said that if he were my father he'd be out gunning for the guy; he wouldn't be sitting around talking. He tried to make my father feel guilty, when he should have been the very one who didn't want him to be a vigilante. I guess he was saying my father wasn't man enough or didn't love me enough to do anything to help me. It was really bad, because my father was the only one I could depend on and look to for strength. My mother fell apart right after the police were called.

"I knew I had to be strong for her and my little sister. I couldn't let them think the rape was bothering me, so I pretended everything was back to normal. I ended up forcing myself to crack jokes to cheer them up.

"Finally I did tell the police the complete truth. Since I knew so much about the rapist, could identify his mug shot, they were able to find him. It turned out he had a previous record including several rapes where he'd used the same method, giving drugs and then raping.

"He was held for one night, arraigned, and let out on bail. What made the situation intolerable was that he knew where I worked as a waitress. He'd come strutting in, and I'd feel pressured to serve him because the boss was there. I couldn't refuse to give him a cup of coffee since that was my job. I couldn't afford to lose it. It didn't seem as if I had any rights as a victim.

"After I got off work, he'd be hanging around outside. I'd have to walk past him and his friends. As he pointed me out to them, they'd laugh. Every time I left my job I was positive one or two of them would be there to mock me. I crept through my days in fear of him, the preliminary trial, everything.

"Only one person, not my parents, not a doctor, asked if I happened to be using any form of birth control; did I have any reason to believe I might be pregnant. That adult reinforced the idea that I could be active sexually without invalidating the rape.

"Next came the trial, which was hard. It was unnerving to have the guy who raped me sitting so near. I hoped he was squirming a little, too. I wished he was feeling uncomfortable when he was bothering me at work, since he knew this day would eventually come. The judge determined there was sufficient evidence for a pretrial hearing. The rapist was let free until it could be scheduled, but he skipped town and was never heard of again. It's been five years now. I don't know what I'll do if they ever catch him.

"The rape affected me in many ways, although I made a conscious decision after it happened that I couldn't live my life in fear, worry, and restriction. My parents did let me move into an apartment with my girl friend. I think they realized I couldn't be sufficiently protected anyplace. I've gone on trips around the United States and to Europe once.

"Lately I've curtailed my life more in some ways than after the rape. It's coming to grips with the fact that rape is a widespread, constant threat. At the time I was a victim I felt absolutely alone. Another thing is there's not really anything you can do to protect yourself.

"I could live a very safe, protected, cautious life and still would have a chance of being raped. If five years ago I'd done that, I'm sure I would have missed many things. It's a hard decision to make. I chose to seek more freedom and pray that nothing else would happen.

"There are things I don't do. I try to use common sense and good judgment. I'd love to go camping alone, but won't because of that nagging worry of being completely on my own. When I have to take my dog out after dark, I never go more than a block from my house. Those are changes and precautions I might not have used if I hadn't been conscious of rape.

"I've had problems with healthy sexual relations because the rape was my introduction to sex. Many men seem to be very curious about this angle of a rape experience. Some asked, 'Are you sure you really didn't enjoy it?' The other day a male friend and I were talking about rape. He wanted information, I suppose, when he said, 'Don't women who are being raped eventually have to have an orgasm?'

"I told him that was absurd. He must have known women who didn't have orgasms under normal circumstances. He acknowledged that was true. He had this concept that didn't stand up under brief examination.

"If a man is a rapist, he can turn himself in and receive therapy. When a woman develops difficulties after being a victim, there's no treatment readily available. He's the instigator, the one creating the problem, and society rewards him with numerous options for help. The victim is offered little.

"No one seems to understand what happens to us. I've talked to more blank, uncomprehending faces than I'd like to count. Once I even discussed rape with an ex-con. He said prisons didn't do any good. They were a horrible experience, had such a lasting affect that no one should have to go through it. I pointed out that the exact same sentiments could be applied to the situation of the rape victim. While he expected me to relate to his statements, he refused to believe me."

Sharon could be evaluated as having integrated the experience into her life. During the first months she received varying degrees of support. She did not suppress the fact she was assaulted.

Bette, another teenage victim, continues to fight for stability. Six years have passed since the evening she was raped by an acquaintance in his apartment. Throughout the first four years, she confided in no one. This is her story.

"Right after it happened, I was stunned, in shock. Because I couldn't get in touch with the reality of it, I could hardly expect anyone else to. I was scared to mention it to the person who'd introduced us for fear he'd laugh at me. He'd go to the other guy, and he'd answer, 'She's just an easy lay.' Friends are important at that age. None of that should have mattered, but then my values weren't right. I cared about whether or not somebody believed me or that I might lose a friend.

"Even though I was close to my parents then, and still am, I never told them. At one point I wished I could lean on them, but I didn't, and consequently I don't think I ever will. They'd be extremely distressed. That's why I didn't bring it up. If I'd had parents who wouldn't have been as freaked by it themselves, maybe I could have spoken to them about it. I didn't think they could handle it. I don't think I'm handling it either, for that matter.

"Contacting the police came to mind, but I didn't think they'd believe me. I hadn't been beaten up, nothing had been torn.

"To me, one of the most insidious parts of rape is not knowing from one second to the next what the man will do to you. He always seems to be the one in control, which is his psychological advantage. Just thinking about the possibility of rape, how you would react, how to gain control of the situation, is a step toward prevention for yourself.

"The first time I talked about my rape was at a consciousness-raising group. We happened to discuss rape. When they asked if I'd ever been a victim, I saw no point in hiding it any longer. I shared my story and hoped the huge weight would magically evaporate. But it didn't. What I thought might be a cleansing tonic instead was a bitter pill. Once more I withdrew. Now I'd feel silly bringing it up. Even with close friends, what would I say? I don't know how to do it. Consequently the rape remains with me. I'm one of the most paranoid people I know. I'm terrified of being raped again, because I don't know how I'd react even after being through it once. I'm scared of how the man would be, how he'd act. I become infuriated with myself when I'm thankful the rapist didn't have a knife, didn't slice me up or kill me. Why should I have to feel that way?

"Do you know what kind of life I have now because of that one man? I don't go out alone at night ever. That's just standard. If I'm going out with somebody I have them come get me if they have a car. When it's two or more women, I make them pick me up. If it's a man, I insist he walk over here. I can't make myself go alone. Coming back from work after dark, I take a taxi with another woman who's scared, too. And that's a drag, because I'd like to go out. I'd like to walk, instead of having to wait for someone else to accompany me. I'm even frightened walking from the car to the house.

"I don't let anyone in my home I don't know. I don't go to any man's house I don't know well or don't know how to get ahold of again. See these windows? I felt that possibly they could be jimmied open. I nailed them shut. It's a sound idea, but on hot summer days the stifling heat and my mood for having to do it match each other.

"I've considered self-defense classes. I don't know why I haven't taken any. I have a whistle! I used to carry a can of spray deodorant, and still do on nights when I'm afraid for some reason. Some nights are worse than others.

"Lately I've been reminding other women to be careful. I was with a friend who wasn't afraid at all. By the time she left, she was terrified. I felt bad about that, but I believe that's something which must be done. Women have to be warned and made aware. There are many women who won't even take me seriously. When I'm talking about it, they assume I'm a neurotic person. I just don't know that many women who are alert enough about rape.

"I vehemently wish there were some way to let women and men know that a rape experience can stay with a victim her whole life. You can add to my list of reactions a nightmare that would destroy my sleep, frequently in the beginning and lately only about once every few months. In it, apes are coming after me. I'm running. There's a house. If I can only get to the house, I'll be all right. But I never learn the ending, because I wake up while they're still chasing me. My God, it's been six years. Six years, and it won't leave me alone!

"Once you've become a victim, you devote more time than is healthy to analyzing all the details of the crime. What did I do wrong? What could I have done? What if I had screamed longer? Why did I trust him?

"Currently, my lone personal solace is reading stories about women who overcome their attackers. There was a report a couple of years ago about two women in Florida who turned on their rapist and killed him with the knife he'd used on one of them. Another account concerned a woman who was walking her dog in a park. A man tried to rape her. Her dog leapt for his throat and saved her. I'm absolutely delighted when I read these things; women defending themselves to the point of even killing the man.

"I hate the man who raped me with a passion, because he's taken up so much of my time these last six years. Someone I barely knew making me squander this much time. It's an outrage. And he has. He put the fear in me, because it wasn't there before. It's not in women I know who haven't been raped. To say I despise and resent him is too mild. I've given him and that fear so much of my life I'll never be able to forgive or forget him."

Adults

Adult rape victims have received wider attention and study than juveniles. Most women interviewed for this book were eighteen or older when sexually assaulted. Because of this greater amount of data, more is known about their physical, emotional, and psychological reactions. Although general behavior patterns can be observed, many variables must be considered. Each victim is unique. Her responses depend upon her age, prerape mental health, specifics of the attack, and postrape experiences.

Rape is a life crisis so debilitating that it impairs a woman's ability to function or cope. The combination of arbitrary suddenness and unpredictability intensify the crisis. It radically disrupts the victim's normal behavior. The woman is in a state of shock. She may be physically injured, have had her life threatened, be exhausted and emotionally drained, and feel guilt about what she views as her complicity in the crime.

The immediate impact can be manifested in a manner similar to that of adolescents. There is a combination of disbelief, shame, fear, anxiety, embarrassment, and anger. Possible physical symptoms include weak pulse, paleness, chills, slurred or slowed speech, restlessness, lessened alertness, insomnia, loss of appetite, and crying. Some regress to child-like actions. They become helpless and dependent. Others submerge emotions and appear composed and subdued or hide their true feelings behind smiles and laughter.

To compound this harrowing dilemma, at this precise moment of acute shock a victim has countless decisions and concerns that may impede her recovery. What type of medical treatment does she need? Should she contact the police? To whom can she turn—parents, friends, lover, husband? What should she tell them? What will be their reaction? If she has children, should they be told? Is there any possibility of pregnancy or venereal disease? She moves from a situation where control and power were completely withdrawn to one requiring rational thoughts and complex decisions.

Nationwide, adult victims consistently cited the following

reactions in the initial stage, from twenty-four hours to a few weeks after the attack. These were heightened in the beginning and decreased with time.

Fear and anxiety topped the list. Some women referred to a general unsafe feeling. They feared offender retaliation and being raped again. This occurred both in reported and unreported cases. If the attacker were apprehended, any anticipated court appearance exacerbated these emotions.

If victims had been assaulted by a friend, many experienced distrust and/or fear of all men. If the offender were a stranger, this was more likely limited to men they did not previously know. In cases of interracial rape, some women reacted with fear especially toward men of the attacker's ethnic background. Lesbians who were raped had further reinforcement of their negative feelings about men. Any previous attempts at peaceful coexistence with the opposite sex were hampered or halted entirely. Many translated their fears into anger and hatred of men in general.

Victims were fearful when away from their residences. It was too vivid a reminder of their vulnerability. Those raped in their homes found no comfort there. Repeatedly these victims either contemplated moving or did so. Even women raped elsewhere frequently sought a temporary new location or a permanent one.

Women were greatly concerned about others' reactions if they learned of the attack. Possible notoriety and publicity generated by the rape were other anxiety-producing elements. Some had economic worries. This interruption to their lives could mean hospital bills; time lost from work, school, or families; and possible counseling expenses.

Although the aggressive aspect was more terrifying than the sexual, many voiced apprehension about the affect on their sex lives. The reactions went from self-imposed celibacy to dramatically increased sexual activity. Lesbian victims bore a dual violation. They may have had male friends, but sexual relations were reserved for women. Thus they were mandated to endure an act that was against their will on two levels. It was forced sexual activity with a man, a person to whom they would not turn for that purpose. Because of this fact, fewer recorded difficulties in reestablishing prerape sexual behavior. Loving experiences with women were far removed from their rape. They were neither forced, nor with a member of the same sex as the offender.

On occasion, these combined fears multiplied to overwhelm the victims. They suffered nervous breakdowns. Their lives were forever changed.

Even in less radical cases, these anxieties impaired the victims' daily routines. Eating and sleeping patterns altered, with most reporting decreases. Nightmares were not uncommon, beginning immediately and sometimes recurring years later. Decision-making faltered. Simple problems seemed insoluble. Various obsessions or phobias developed following the attack. Most women wanted to bathe and/or douche as soon as possible after the assault. In a few cases, this grew into a strong desire to combat feeling unclean. One victim said she showered three times a day for several weeks.

Guilt and self-blame were other responses. These emotions occurred when victims reflected on their behavior prior to and during the attack. They further victimized themselves by accepting society's rape myths. Whatever the circumstances of the offense, they must be at fault, because they had failed to repel the offender. At times this guilt was externally imposed by the very people whom they sought for help and guidance.

The sum of these reactions added to their general feeling of isolation. While they desperately needed to discuss what they were experiencing, many believed it was their problem alone to bear.

As weeks lengthened to months, victims retreated within. This period of believed adjustment found most women denying or rationalizing their earlier expressed feelings about the rape. Many stopped talking about it completely. They returned to their normal pursuits as if mentally healed. Some became hyperactive at this time, changing jobs, schools, taking on additional responsibilities, and so forth. They suppressed anxiety, fear, and possible anger.

Internalizing these conflicts brought about a gradual deterioration. Depression set in. Seemingly unrelated complaints arose, such as tiredness, sore throats, and gastrointestinal problems. Fears returned once more. Many began scrutinizing the rape and their part in it. Too often, the attacks did not fall into the stereotyped myth. The majority had to decipher their feelings about being victims of "unofficial" unreported rapes. Some were confused to the extent they could not even decide whether they had been raped, because they knew the assailant, they had been drinking, etc.

Ambivalent attitudes regarding men resumed. They perceived them as both protectors and rapists. Whether to draw boundaries between those two categories or consider all men rapists was another issue requiring a resolution.

In some measure, all began limiting their lives more than previously. Additional locations and activities were eliminated because of fear of another attack. Then the anger began to grow. Initially, many turned this inward, where it festered. Ultimately, it had to be directed outward, but the victim's dilemma was magnified because there were minimal outlets for this seething emotion.

The process of assimilating the experience in its totality is a slow and measured one. Each victim's pace is highly individualized. Years after the rape, victims who felt they had successfully integrated the attack found one remaining vestige—the resurgence of fear in situations which would not generate concern or apprehension in women who had never been victims.

In any other life crisis, the death of a loved one or becoming the victim of a serious accident, a person would automatically reach out to others. The individual would receive support, understanding, compassion, and kindness. In the case of rape, too many times this is untrue. And of all the factors which enhance and speed the victim's emotional recovery, the positive encouragement and attitude of others are the deciding elements.

Because victims frequently do not tell many people about the incident, those in whom they do confide play a crucial role. The majority of interviewees withheld the information from their parents. Young adults believed their parents would blame them or become overly protective. Older adults' thoughts centered on embarrassment, shame, or not wanting to upset their family. Almost all informed several close friends. When the attack was reported, the treatment by officials spanned a wide spectrum.

An alarming number of women learned no one really "likes" rape victims. Other women do not like them, because they are vivid reminders of the genesis of their fears. Male friends, lovers, and husbands are insensitive, for different reasons. Their sympathies may rest with the assailant, a man they might perceive as unfairly accused. Others react violently, either blaming or doubting the victim. A few volunteer to kill the attacker. Police are guarded toward victims, because rape charges are hard to prove. They, too, consider victim precipitation. Hospital personnel may be unresponsive, for most victims represent a low medical priority, with emotional injuries rather than physical. Lawyers and judges agree with police, knowing best the difficulty in securing convictions. Thus the victims feel misunderstood, shunned, and unwanted.

Even concerned people with good intentions are ill-prepared on how to proceed when confronted by a rape victim. While no simplistic rules exist, common sense combined with these suggestions becomes a starting point. But they are not absolutes.

Because a victim has just endured a crisis event, others might recall a situation in which they felt tremendously afraid and threatened. They were vulnerable, frightened, and in need of comforting. The victim's emotional state is intensified to the extreme. The basic advice cannot be reiterated too often: supportive understanding with a nonjudgmental approach.

A victim's power and control were erased throughout the rape. Therefore their rapid restoration is vital. To aid this process during the first hours after the attack, victims could be assigned purposeful activities. Completing routine tasks, such as locating the telephone number of a rape crisis center, benefits the victim. Although she may experience a temporary dependency on friends for decisions, her recovery begins with the realization that she can perform these duties competently.

A primary motive for turning to selected friends is the need to express her emotions. When this occurs, the victim should be allowed to pace and direct the conversation. If she is denied the freedom to talk as well as to channel the discussion, she may begin repressing the psychological impact of the crime. Her difficulties increase because of this.

No leading, specific questions should be asked. Many victims view these as callous and probing. They interpret them as stemming from unspoken judgments and evaluations. Any doubts they have as to their involvement accelerate. People should listen sympathetically. Let the victim know they care about her well-being. Friends can share their feelings of love and help. They can reflect what most bothers the victim. The focus should be her concerns and fears. Encourage any release, such as crying. Reassure her that it is a natural response. On occasion, victims want to refrain from mentioning the attack entirely, addressing other matters. If this hesitancy develops, move to practical issues.

Her physical safety and medical care are extremely important. Confidants might recommend she seek medical attention, then decide later whether to report the attack. She should be reminded about the possibility of pregnancy and venereal disease. For these reasons alone, she should be urged to consult health professionals. Does she want to be accompanied? Does she require transportation? Will she tell her parents? Is she going to call the police? If she does wish to notify the police, she should do so as soon as possible. Remind her not to change clothes, bathe, douche, or remove any evidence. Ultimately, these decisions are a victim's to make. Caring people can offer advice, but the final choices should be hers.

After talking with the victim, friends could take notes regarding the rape. The woman might include significant details, which will be quickly forgotten. These notes could be valuable when utilized at a later date to refresh her memory if she contacts the authorities or files a report with a rape crisis center.

A rape affects those in whom the victim confides. Any ambivalence toward her should be clarified. Some blame themselves for failing to protect her from the assault. If this is the case, conversations can be guided along these lines. A victim is less likely to suffer from her own self-recriminations when called upon to placate those of friends. She also regains additional control because of this reminder of her need and importance. When a victim alludes to her personal guilt, it should be countered with reassurance that she was not at fault. A woman should be allowed to live as she sees fit. She did not instigate the attack by any combination of clothes, actions, or misconstrued statements.

Victims recalled friends who projected or explained their negative feelings. They may think she was foolish; she took risks which ended in rape. Perhaps the woman was hitchhiking, a practice they oppose. They might believe no woman should live alone, go out by herself, and so on. These negative emotions will be sensed by the victim. Friends who feel this way should repress these attitudes. These conflicts might be brought up later, but never at the height of the crisis.

As time passes after the rape, a victim continues to need sensitive support. Many progress to a period of withdrawal or introspection. They are no longer interested in discussing the assault. Guilt is less likely to occur if she had been badly hurt physically. That is visible proof of her attempted resistance. Additionally, the injuries serve as a point of emphasis in reorganizing her life. She can concentrate on her external recovery.

When she moves to the stage of integration and resolution, she focuses on the attack once more. Frequently there is a renewed desire to discuss it. If the victim is reminded of this gradual shift from suppression to acceptance, coupled with the reoccurrence of problems, she is more able to cope. This return to thinking about the assault does not indicate she is losing control. She is still directing and charting her own life.

Significant people, such as family members, friends, possible counselors, should remain willing to listen, reflect, and help. The effects of rape are long-lasting. How does she feel? What is she doing with her time? Has she noticed shifts in her life-style? When she mentions fears, let her express and specify them. She might list everything she could do to protect herself. Included in this process could be why some would be acceptable, but others would be unacceptable. While she can be cautious, she cannot stay barricaded at home. Even though a weapon might make her feel more secure, she should know how to use it. Discuss the benefits and disadvantages of these actions. Then let her decide which changes she can tolerate and which she cannot.

If a woman is unclear about her adjustment, suggest she examine her own feelings. She should be aware of postrape changes in her behavior patterns. When they are destructive or detrimental in any way, then they should be confronted, rather than dismissed. Again, she could list those changes, matching them with remedies. If she is fearful where she lives, a relocation could be considered an investment in her mental health. If she questions her physical capabilities, she could attend a self-defense class. This evaluation process can be accomplished on an individual basis, with those close to her, at a rape crisis center discussion group, or, if applicable, with professional counseling help.

Even when counseling is provided, this does not replace warm, long-term communication with loved ones. If a victim reports the rape, each individual she deals with can cause conflicts. At every step, from police to hospital through possible court appearances, anxiety and fears increase. Each person should refrain from judging. All should be supportive. Anyone who doubts the victim will intensify the emotional damage. During each level of the reporting process, feelings heighten. Concerned friends must continually be aware of these stressful events. Their presence and understanding must not waver with time.

Above all, individuals should simply be human, and treat the woman as they would any victim of any traumatic experience, any victim who had no control over the situation in which she found herself.

Those shocks and aftershocks, those ripples of anxiety that victims suffer, do diminish. But periods of fear and depression emerge at intervals. The crests of security are coupled with troughs of despair. All a victim can anticipate is that the amount of time between those blackest moments will become greater as each month and year passes. The total emotional upheaval and turmoil they endure cannot be solely their problem. It must be society's as well. At the least, it is her loved ones' responsibility to help her regain mental stability. At the most, all people could make a commitment to lessening the victim's plight.

Victim's words offer dimensions beyond these previous descriptions. These are their feelings, as the days turned to months and then years after the rape.

Anne's rape by a friend went unreported.

She recounted, "When the rape was taking place, it was the closest I'd come to believing I'd be killed. Seeing that side of a human being—the dark, animal nature—while I was helpless, was terrifying. Afterwards, I felt like such a failure as a person. Why me? I'd always been so careful. I'd followed all the rules."

Barbara reported her rape by a stranger to the police. The man was never apprehended.

"During the attack I felt like a part of me ceased to exist. It was as if adrenalin were surging through me. I couldn't relax. Now I believe I'll never be the same person I was before it happened."

One month after the attack, a victim reported these emotions. "Being alone with my thoughts is the hardest part. Wondering if it is the rape or some other problem which is causing my deterioration. Possibly I'm using the rape as a scapegoat for troubles which were already present but I wasn't willing to acknowledge. The memories of that day hover over me constantly. They are a cloud which won't leave me for more than a few hours. Not a single day has passed that I'm not briefly jarred by reminders."

Pam evaluated her actions, three months after the rape.

"With these passing months has come my effort not to let the rape limit my life. I'm still going out at night, knowing I might feel frightened. Leading a restricted life is something I won't accept. I don't want to fear walking around the city where I live.

"I'm more secure and confident within myself. If a situation came up again, maybe I could deal with it. Not just the emotional elements, but the physical aspects. It was the whole thing of being afraid to knee someone. How could I do that to a man? Instead would I let him rape me? If there's a way I can get out of a bad place that means physically harming a man, I'll try to do it now. That's what *he's* doing —physically harming me. If it happened again, it might put me in a much worse spot than this time. It's not right for me to sit on my frustrations and uneasiness toward men. I think if I were assaulted again, I'd be out to kill. I couldn't go through all that shock, horror, humiliation a second time. I'd rather die.

"In all the examining I've done, I'm still unclear how I

might react a second time. I just said I'd rather die, but then there's a part of me that says no. I'd let him do what he wanted instead of losing my life. If a man came up to me holding a gun and said, 'I'm going to rape you,' I'd probably say, 'you sure are.'

"If there were any chance for escape, I'd take it. I'd run, scream, reason with him, badger him. I've even thought of insulting his masculinity, telling him he couldn't get it up if his life depended on it. That's how I'm trying to cope. I'm attempting to look at it in a realistic manner, from all sides. I can't shy away from the effects it's had on me. I've got to overcome my feelings of guilt. It happened and is over.

"I still feel an unbelievable compulsion to explain to my friends why I'm depressed. 'You see, I was raped,' I say, and hope there'll be understanding. Most often those words do nothing but cause a minor interest. I'm scared in situations others wouldn't consider threatening. I want someone to help share my grief. With all my talking, no one seems capable or willing to provide enduring support."

Three months after the attack, a victim who was raped by a friend described her outlet for anger.

"I have so much wrath inside me. I find myself constantly exploding under circumstances that aren't conducive to such a violent outburst. When I'm walking down the street and a man yells, 'Hey, baby, you've got a nice ass,' I scream. 'What right have you to say that?'

"I've also taken up a new pastime—spitting. When any man causes me to feel uncomfortable, I spit not on him, but at him. This really infuriates him. I smile sweetly as I continue on my way. I've suffered enough at their hands and by their words. I'm not going to take it anymore."

Rape is not forgotten in a day or a week. This victim had these thoughts six months after she was assaulted.

"One change that saddens me is the loss of my carefree, curious, adventurous spirit that had made living fun. I feel I know too much. It's hard for me to trust anyone. Moving around freely is nearly impossible. I want to be secure, but I know I'm not.

"The other day a man pulled up in a car to ask directions. As he got out to clarify a point on the map, it took everything I had to stand there and be reasonable. I had to convince myself he was only asking directions. He wasn't going to hurt me."

Trish was interviewed a year after she was kidnapped and raped by a stranger at gunpoint. Although she reported the crime, the man remained unapprehended.

"Because of my background and psychological makeup, I've always tried to avoid confrontation. No one ever yelled in my family. No one fought. I'd led a passive, tranquil life.

"While I was being raped, I tried to become very childlike and feminine, to appeal to the man's sense of power and masculine pride. Because I prostituted myself in that situation in order to save my life, I gave too much. I don't think I could ever do it again.

"I was raised a Catholic. I remember being told about St. Agnes, who instead of being raped killed herself. Now I understand what the church was teaching. Intellectualizing it and facing the reality are two different things. When that man pulled a gun on me, what did I do? I went to pieces!

"I've tried to summarize my reactions to the sequence of events. Here was this man from nowhere, who I would never have even talked to. He came into my life with a particular game he was playing and forced me to play it with him. There's something about doing that to someone—taking away your complete freedom of individuality, everything you are—which is odious. He had absolute power over me to dictate his rules. After the fear settles down, you're outraged someone can say you're going to do this and that. Remove your sense of self. I wasn't a person anymore. That's where the anger comes in.

"The first day I went out of the house after it took place,

I started crying. All those people were too much for me. I felt assaulted by having to deal with so many threatening individuals simultaneously. I couldn't take being out on the streets for months. I'd find little things would trigger off highly emotional reactions.

"I've come to believe you create everything that happens to you. I truly accept the responsibility for what occurred. Previously I'd refused to accept certain realities, like someone with a gun. Now I know this can be part of my life. I've tried to understand and assess men in this context. But it's hard! Consistently, I feel threatened.

"I'd shied away from many other realities that I now address. A friend lent me a gun, which I've learned to use. This was something alien to me, but I wanted to be 'real.' When I was unaccepting of the ugly side of life, I was raped. Now I'm completely aware and search for peace in my new existence. I'll do as much as I can to balance out my basically passive nature. Try to be aggressive. Try to be cold and distant. But I must look at myself as I am and seek comfort in a guarded survival.

"When I'm driving the car, I watch my rearview mirror to make certain no one is following me. I didn't use to do that. When I turn into my street, I take a good look around to see what cars are pulling in. Do they belong there? If I think anything unusual is happening, now I know where the closest police station is. I'd drive there, and lean on the horn until help arrived. I resent all these precautions greatly, but it's my last attempt to deal with reality.

"I've considered what I thought should happen to men who rape, but punishment isn't part of my vocabulary. Everything one does is equalized. When a man rapes a woman, something must change in him as well. He must pay for his action in some way, possibly through his own guilt, fear, or recriminations.

"My little nephew came to me one day with two puppies. He said sometimes he wanted to pick them up and squeeze them to death. I knew exactly what he meant. When people know they have complete power over something, they want to test it. Most don't, but some do. Then you have rape.

"Lately I've wished I could go back to being a child again. Maybe my parents would no longer say you're going to learn to play the piano. Maybe they'd insist I learn to protect myself and face the world as it is. The anger and frustration I continue to endure is incredible."

A year after Dale was raped, she concentrated on her anger. She had been severely beaten, terrorized, and raped by two men. Because she required medical attention, the hospital personnel reported her assault. The men were never apprehended.

"I've found myself becoming more inward in assimilating my experience. I've funneled my thoughts into two alternating fantasies to lessen my anger. One is how a world without rape would be. Whenever I think about that, it's like having a huge weight lifted off my shoulders. The idea of being able to walk around without cringing, to leave my doors open, not to have to worry every time I go out. It's too bad it's only a dream.

"My other fantasy is no more realistic, but it's my personal revenge. In this one, I've been granted permission to be in a room with the men who raped me. With papier-mâché, I first build breasts on them. Next, with a slightly rusty blade, I castrate them. Although I allow them to be administered anesthetic, they are quite aware of what I'm doing. The final scene varies, but I succeed in simulating the cumulative terror and absolute helplessness I suffered that day."

Two years ago, Lilith was beaten, choked, forced to commit fellatio, and raped. She notified the police, but the man was never found. Her description moves from her thoughts immediately preceding the attack to her present evaluation of emotions.

"Those few instants before he came up and grabbed me seemed like one of those slow motion dreams where you try to move or scream, but can't. You're split, realizing this person's coming after you and praying it isn't going to happen. All kinds of bizarre things rushed through my mind. I had a feeling of total terror. I was going to be his victim. There seemed no way out. He was so close, blocking the way, with no space to run.

"There were unrelated things of which I was aware. The sound of footsteps. The noise of the cars on the freeway. He was wearing a leather jacket, and to this day I remember its smell. As he was moving toward me, I had this horrible, sick feeling.

"After the rapist left, I was in complete shock. My real self had gone into a cocoon. I felt the way seeds must when the weather's too dry. They can't germinate, so they shrivel up, become hard, and wait until it's all right to come out. I'll never forget how that rapist looked walking down the path. I just wanted to kill him, make him disappear. I was so angry that he could merely stride away and there was no way I could stop him. I couldn't yell, 'Hey, you, what're you doing?' Nothing. He did that to me and walked away.

"Six months later, I was living in an attic room in a house I shared with two women. I was beginning to get in touch with the anger. Admitting it was there, but not being ready to handle it. After being in school all week, working hard, having something to occupy my mind, Friday nights would come. I'd be wound up like a spring. Usually the others would go away for the weekends, but I was too paranoid to leave the house. Then the furies would strike. I'd freak out. It got to be a regular occurrence.

"I'd go through the house slamming doors, throwing my shoes at the wall, breaking things. I'd scream and run around. When I survived that stage, when I reached the point where I could do something other than those basic thrashing, violent gestures, like beating my bed, I started writing descriptions of my anger in stories and poems.

"I drew things on the wall, a big abstract of hideousities. It helped me to do that, to draw those strange, grotesque figures with terribly pained faces. They were distorted, sexual sorts of pictures. It was good just to let it out. The walls were covered with those scribblings and drawings. When people would come in, they'd take one look. I could tell they were embarrassed. It was as if they were seeing something they shouldn't see. Dirty underwear or something. They'd look the other way, pretend they didn't notice, or comment on my seashell collection.

"But a few women would see it and say they really liked it. I knew they must have been able to relate to it. They had to be very angry somewhere inside, too, because it was ugly and looked like it was done by someone possessed.

"Now it's two years later. I moved a final time. I'm not quite so afraid to go places alone anymore. I started doing that about a year ago. I'm not terrified of all men. I carry a can of Mace, a birthday present from my sister, in my purse. I would not hesitate to use it if someone threatened me. I think it's important to keep my awareness about rape. I try to talk to other women about it. I don't feel I get hysterical or into too extreme a diatribe. I'm objective. That's the way it happened. It's really horrible, but you survive.

"If it's getting dark and I decide to go out, I'll ride the bus. I tell myself I've overcome most of my fears. But then recently, on a Sunday afternoon, I was walking alone to a friend's house. I started getting my old familiar sick feeling, realizing I was the only person on the street. Around the corner came this little, wrinkled man. He couldn't have been any larger than me, but I became terrified. I thought, 'Wait, don't let it get ahold of you.' I kept walking. But that flash of fear was extremely intense. It hasn't left me.

"I quickened my pace, and reached the end of the street, when several men in a car drove by. I knew they could just stop and cart me away. I'd disappear, and nobody would see me again. I didn't have my Mace can because I didn't want to carry anything. It was awful. It wasn't dark. I wasn't far from home. That same terror."

Four years ago, a man broke into Andrea's apartment, raped her, and robbed her. He was never apprehended.

"Because of my experience, I don't feel I'm worth much as a person. I wish I could be independent once more. Forget that night.

"I've tried to make light of what happened to me. Then I've tried to shut it out. I don't talk about it anymore except on rare occasions. I was sorry I didn't know my physical capabilities. I remember how frustrating that was. I couldn't do anything. I had to let somebody fuck me, of all things, when I didn't want to. It was the most humiliating experience I've ever gone through.

"I still remember for months afterward I'd start to cry for no apparent reason. I was emotionally upset, but didn't want to let the incident rule my life. As time went by, my friends told me being raped was something I'd have to handle myself. They were involved in their own lives and didn't seem to have much support left over for me.

"Like so many women, I've thought about karate or judo lessons, but I haven't done anything. The correlation I see is a woman's refusal to use any form of birth control. Then she's admitting she's having sexual relations when she feels she shouldn't. To me, taking any self-defense class would be admitting I could be raped again. I can't face that. I've convinced myself a woman can only be raped once.

"Even while I'm saying that, I know it's absurd. Of course I worry, get mad, take precautions, get furious. It's been four years, and I remain intimidated by most men. I imagine they're following me all the time. I don't like to overreact. There are certain times when it just happens. I've no control over it. I think the fear is gone, but then, whammy, it's back. Sometimes I wonder if I'll ever be free again.

"My whole perspective on life has changed. There are so many things I just don't think of doing for fear I'll be raped again. It's closed off doors. On the other hand, there are certain things I feel I can't let my fear destroy, or else it will destroy my life.

"I want to say something about what should happen to these rapists. I know many people feel prison isn't the answer. We should pat the men on the head, and insist they're really the victims. I say lock them up and forget about them. Let them come to realize what a half-life women have to lead because of them. They stifle our freedom and joy in every way. Look at the changes all women impose upon themselves, especially former victims, those heeding the advice about avoiding attacks. Let those men find out what that life is like. Let them worry about being victims of a homosexual assault while in jail. Let them suffer the fear we daily go through. What can I do but scream my hate and vindictiveness toward all men who force this existence on all women."

Grace became pregnant as a result of her rape twenty-seven years ago. She was a virgin until that night. She has never completely recovered. At age nineteen, after having a total of five dates, she was raped by a man she met while working at a summer resort. He stopped by one evening and asked if she would like to go for a ride. When they arrived at a secluded location, he assaulted her.

"I never physically fought him off in any way, partly because I was frightened, mostly because in my naiveté I thought a girl has to do what she's told. The prime impression I retain after all these years was that I had to obey him, be submissive. All I did was tell him I didn't want to be with him. It wasn't right. I was overwhelmingly confused and defenseless against the whole suddenness.

"Afterwards, I felt dirty, sordid and embarrassed. I told no one. As the summer ended, I felt I must continue my studies. I returned to the university and remained there for four months of growing bewilderment and terror. I discovered I was pregnant. At Christmas, when I told my parents I couldn't go back to school, they were kind, but very sad. I felt renewed guilt and remorse that I had let them down. The doctor they took me to said that if I had come sooner he would have found a way to send me to Detroit for an abortion. To my father, who wanted to lay charges against the man, the doctor said these things could never be proven.

"Soon after I told my parents, I heard my mother crying as she told Dad, 'It's all my fault. I taught her to turn the other cheek. Never hit back. Perhaps she could never fight back physically after that upbringing.'

"Because I became pregnant, I was sent to 'hide out' at a Salvation Army home. That whole experience increased my stunned confusion. Being asked to describe the episode and being harassed by them to admit to frequent intercourse. I cried, denied everything, but I don't think anyone believed me. During the months at the home, guilt was pounded into all of us in a way I hope wouldn't be tolerated today. The staff assumed we were delinquent girls, despite the fact that about half the thirty girls were pregnant because of rape. One had been raped by three men who offered her a ride home from baby-sitting, another by her stepfather. A third had been gone over by four boys at a teenage beach party where somebody had put a drug in her drink. She passed out and couldn't even name the father.

"An agonizing sequel to this story is that I later pieced together enough information to learn where my son is now. I've considered leaving him a note in my will, but each time I try to write the letter I can't get past the barrier of explaining to him that he was conceived against my will by a drunken man.

"Although many of these details might be irrelevant to the general public, they are still vivid and crucial to me. Mine was the type of rape that probably wouldn't be described as such by anyone other than the girl or people who knew her well. In the twenty-seven years since I was raped, I have analyzed the whole affair almost as an obsession. At least now rape is a topic that is being confronted. If nothing else, it is a great relief to me to have written and shared my story."

4: *Women's Wiles*

The historical legacies of the act of rape hold on through present times. For primitive societies, rape was not even considered a crime. Men were expected to obtain a wife from another clan. Stealing her was to the man's advantage, because it brought him increased prestige and distinction among his male peers. When the procedure for marrying grew in formality, with the two families arranging it, rape became ritualized. Tradition dictated that the groom carry off his resisting bride.

As societies became more "civilized," rape finally was defined as criminal. Changing attitudes proved more difficult, as evidenced by the theory of Herodotus, the fifth-century B.C. historian: "Abducting young women is not, indeed, a lawful act; but it is stupid after the event to make a fuss about it. The only sensible thing is to take no notice; for it is obvious that no young woman allows herself to be abducted if she does not wish to be."

For countless centuries, women had neither the legal rights nor the collective power to "fuss" about the crime of rape. They continued to be considered a man's property, with marriage bringing the transference of ownership from father to husband. Through the ages, the application of the laws for sexual assault still reflects the male attitude toward women. And just as consistently, the requirements for a charge and the sentences in earlier eras codified and solidified the false belief that rape is a sexual act, rather than one of control and violence. It was severely punished when the victim was "chaste" and from a wealthy family, disregarded when the court decided her reputation was questionable or her origins lowly. And these sexist and classist vestiges remain to this day.

In ancient Egypt and Assyria, the offender was either castrated or, in some cases, he and his victim could wed. According to Babylonian law, if the woman were a betrothed virgin, the offender was killed. If she were already married, she and the assailant suffered death by drowning. Both could be spared this fate under special circumstances. A benevolent husband was allowed to pull his wife from the water, and the king might pardon the rapist.

Early Hebrew law took the marital status and the scene of the crime into account. Raping someone else's wife brought death to the perpetrator. But if she were only engaged and the assault took place within the city, both were pelted with stones until dead. Attacking a spinster brought certain options, one of which being that the convicted man could pay fifty shekels to her father and then marry her.

By the Middle Ages, the first "crime compensation" approach for the victim was instituted. Revisions in the law made it possible for the woman to keep the money.

During that era in England, men who raped "highborn" women were sentenced to death when found guilty. By the time of William the Conqueror, the penalty was reduced to castration and the loss of one's eyes. An immediate complaint to an official of the law became a new crucial element. The assailant went unpunished in situations where the victim agreed to marry him or he took religious orders. By the 1400s, wedlock or the church were withdrawn as alternatives.

Sir William Blackstone, an English jurist and legal historian, appeared on the scene in the 1700s. He became one of the first to formally define the crime. Even though he wrote centuries ago, most jurisdictions in the United States still use some variation of his theme. The wording differs in length and explicitness, but more than half essentially read:

Rape is unlawful carnal knowledge of a woman, not one's wife, by force and against her will.

Added to that brief definition is our system's case-by-case decisions as to what constitutes rape. By the 1880s, the concepts stabilized. Rape was classed as a felony, punishable by a maximum of life imprisonment or death. Corroboration or supportive evidence became necessary to bring a charge.

These laws, statutes, and decisions remained intact until recently, but traces of them hold firm, and societal attitudes continue to hamper revisions. The original intent of the law was twofold: to protect women from the loss of virginity or chastity; to save innocent men from the harsh penalties if convicted.

The legal sense of rape is unique in our criminal justice system. From the vocabulary to the special requirements, it is unlike all other criminal codes. Perusing entire sections of the code is like skimming a bad Victorian novel, for the very reason that some were written during that period. They contain numerous emotion-laden terms which should have gone the way of high button shoes.

In an overwhelming majority of states, rape remains a sex-specific crime. Only a woman can be raped by a male assailant. The lack of consent evolved as the essence of the act, for this was what changed it from sexual intercourse to rape. The reasoning continued that force was necessary for lack of consent. How much resistance was needed ranged from "utmost" to a nebulous, individual evaluation. Unless the victim resists, the accused could assume she is agreeing. Therefore, the perception depends on both the woman and the defendant. Because of this rationale, the focus moved from the actions of the accused to those of the victim. In the prosecution of no other crime does this occur.

The snowball of irregularities continues, partially because consent plays such a critical role. This factor allows the victim's sexual history to be introduced in the courtroom. After all, if a woman consented to one man, she will agree to others. Therefore, she should be either a virgin or involved in a monogamous marriage. If she does not fall into either of these categories, she is promiscuous. That type of female cannot be trusted to tell the truth. In case after case, this theory, that "promiscuity imports dishonesty," has been pounded home in the courts.[1]

To ensure this point be clear, judges can turn to two special sets of instructions to tell the jurors. The first, generally known as the "unchaste witness instruction," states: "Evidence was received for the purpose of showing that the female person named in the information was a women of unchaste character. A woman of unchaste character can be the victim of forcible rape, but it may be inferred that a woman who has previously consented to sexual intercourse would be more likely to consent again. Such evidence may be considered by you only for such bearing as it may have on the question of whether or not she gave her consent to the alleged sexual act and in judging her credibility."

Sir Matthew Hale, Lord Chief Justice of the King's Bench from 1671 to 1676, was responsible for creating the second instruction, the "cautionary charge." At the conclusion of a trial, prior to the jury's deliberations, the judge informs them: "A charge [rape] such as that made against the defendant in this case is one which is easily made and, once made, difficult to defend against, even if the person accused is innocent. Therefore, the law requires that you examine the testimony of the female person named in the information with caution." Only in rare occasions, such as the testimony of an accomplice witness, does the judge in other crimes ever advise a jury with such instructions.

Another element which sets this crime apart is the concept of spousal responsibility. Marriage implies lifetime consent to sexual relations. Thus, a husband has continuing sexual rights over his wife. In the eyes of the law, he cannot rape her. When a man beats his wife, the charge is assault or battery. If one illegally signs the other's name on a check, the person can be charged with forgery. Rape is the only criminal act for which marriage is a defense.

Although common law never requires corroborative evidence to support a conviction, this is not true with rape. In all other crimes, our system relies on the jurors to weigh the facts and arrive at a verdict. In rape cases, while the amount and type of corroboration required varies, the implication is that the word of the victim alone is not sufficient proof. In some states, the prosecutor must have supportive data for each aspect of the crime, in others for just a few of them.

Another peculiarity is the almost mandatory requirement to have an immediate police report. This kind of proof is generally inadmissible in other crimes. The prevailing principle cited in various court cases is that because rape is such an outrage, a self-respecting woman would not refrain from reporting so that she can find aid and comfort. When her complaint is not prompt, and she remains silent for some time, the inference is that the attack was not committed.

Other crimes are separated into degrees, depending on various combinations of circumstances. In the majority of states, rape is a single degree offense, ignoring the numerous components within an assault. The penalty structure listed is harsh, making juries reticent to convict. Until the Supreme Court banned capital punishment, this sentence was possible in many states, most below the Mason-Dixon Line. Some still have life imprisonment, or thirty, forty, or fifty years. Several states also include a minimum sentence.

The uniqueness of the rape laws comes from a deep distrust of female accusers. This fear of false charges has molded laws and the courts' response to rape. Since scholars, judges, commentators, and historians began writing on this topic, they have warned others to beware. Dean J. Wigmore, the leading authority and most quoted person on rules of evidence, worried about "the evil of putting an innocent man's liberty at the mercy of an unscrupulous and revengeful mistress. . . ." Judge Morris Ploscowe's concerns rested with "spurned females" seeking revenge and/or blackmail. Others have debated women's supposed fantasies about rape. Another popular theory was that people would believe a woman's tale no matter how implausible. Thus, these elaborate obstacles to conviction developed as safeguards against women's wiles.

The problem was that they worked too well. While the number of reported rapes spiraled upward, the conviction rate remained extremely low. Rape victims became further victimized by the laws which were supposed to offer at least a modicum of protection for them.

In the mid-1970s, a combination of forces began gathering. Women's groups, led by crisis center advocates, stressed that there must be a better deterrent than the current inappropriate legal procedures. Members from the National Organization for Women and the League of Women Voters agreed that changes had to be made. As women's role in society was being more accurately assessed, their legal rights became targeted for revision as well.

Police and prosecutors did not see rape in terms of feminist ideology, but as a law-and-order issue. They added momentum to the movement. The final impetus came from legislators and law reformers. They, too, were considering rape in a broader framework. They felt criminal code revisions in general were long overdue. Rape happened to fall into that category.

This strange blend of interest groups has produced mixed results. Since 1974, there have been changes in the statutes in many states, yet others have considered and rejected them. By the end of that year, eleven jurisdictions had taken a first hesitant step in examining and revamping their rape codes. In 1975, twenty-four more followed suit. While few are major transformations, they are at least a start. Wisconsin and West Virginia made revisions most recently. But Vermont's statute, enacted in 1791, remains relatively intact, with only a single amendment since that time.

It is difficult to find a proper balance between protecting the rights of victims and those of the accused. Women uniformly emphasize that they are not asking for special attention. All they want is equal treatment under the law—the same rights and privileges granted any other crime victim by the legal justice system.

A summary of the revisions reveals that the key issues have been the definition of the crime and the types of proof. For most states, rape is still a sex-specific act, with a female victim and male offender. Some jurisdictions merely replaced certain words, making it a sex-neutral offense. Kentucky and Louisiana went farther, by legally recognizing homosexual as well as heterosexual assault. When it came to redefining the crime itself, Florida, Massachusetts, Michigan, Nebraska, and Wisconsin led the way. Several states define rape as sexual assault, while Florida calls it sexual battery. Most states which have altered the definition are attempting to make it closer to assault and battery.

The "utmost resistance" standard is being examined, lessened and broadened to a more realistic approach toward behavior under the circumstances of the attack. Revision of this element is much needed because of the consent issue. A woman cannot simply testify she did not want to have intercourse with the assailant. The judge and jury must be convinced, not only that agreement was withheld, but that the act was accomplished by the use of violence, force, or believable threat of "great and immediate bodily harm." One person's mental image of those headings may differ tremendously from another's. Some may think a woman could never be raped by a relative, friend, or acquaintance because they "would not do that sort of thing." Words alone may constitute force in others' minds, while still others might accept only actual physical violence if they are to believe the woman did not willingly submit.

Instead of needing personal injury as proof, threat of force or coercion is now the requirement in some states. A few jurisdictions allow the threat to be against a third party. The goal of this kind of revision is to shift the responsibility of proving lack of consent beyond a reasonable doubt to the accused, as it is in other defenses.

This total interwoven concept, of consent, force, resistance, and previous sexual conduct, continues to plague legislators. California, Iowa, Michigan, Minnesota, and Nebraska were among the first to restrict the introduction of the victim's sexual history in some manner. By 1977, twenty-two states had to some extent limited this testimony and questioning. All statutes permit information about the relationship between the accused and the victim, as well as about the situation surrounding the assault.

Sexual history has been allowed as evidence to contradict or impeach the woman's testimony and to take advantage of the evidentiary rule used in many states about the "unchaste female." Ironically, the opposite kind of testimony is not allowed. A "chaste witness" instruction regarding the victim's previous conduct would be inadmissible, because that would violate the defendant's right to a fair trial.

California exemplifies the strict procedure established by some states as necessary before questions about the victim's past sexual activities can be introduced into a trial.

First, the defense lawyer must submit a written motion to the court and the prosecutor, explaining his "offer of proof of the relevancy of evidence of sexual conduct of the complaining witness proposed to be presented and its relevancy in attacking the credibility of the complaining witness.

"The written motion shall be accompanied by an affidavit in which the offer of proof shall be stated.

"If the court finds that the offer of proof is sufficient, the court shall order a hearing out of the presence of the jury, if any, and at such hearing allow the questioning of the complaining witness regarding the offer of proof made by the defendant.

"At the conclusion of the hearing, if the court finds that evidence proposed to be offered by the defendant regarding the sexual conduct of the complaining witness is relevant, . . . the court shall make an order stating what evidence may be introduced by the defendant, and the nature of the questions to be permitted. The defendant may then offer evidence pursuant to the order of the court."

It is still up to the judge to determine whether the information is relevant. If he decides to admit the evidence, the victim then has to go through the whole recitation another time, in the courtroom.

The charges to the jury, the "unchaste witness," and the "cautionary charge," have been either done away with or restricted in many states. Three require them. More leave them to the discretion of the judge. A few have banned them entirely.

For the states continuing to employ them, two members of the American Civil Liberties Union, Anthony Amsterdam and Barbara Babcock, have prepared a possible alternative instruction on the consent issue for judges to use: "There has been testimony about the sexual experience of the complainant in this case. You are to judge this testimony by the same standards of credibility which you apply to all other evidence. Even if you find it credible, you should not infer that, because a woman has consented on prior occasions to sexual intercourse, she necessarily consented with the defendant on the particular occasion at issue in this case."[2] At present no states have adopted this suggested replacement.

The spousal exemption remains a hotly debated facet. Wisconsin and a few other states now include rape as a felony between formerly married individuals. In Michigan, a wife may charge a husband with rape if they are living apart and have filed for separate maintenance or divorce. A handful of other states are trying revisions along these lines.

The corroboration issue is finally being examined. Many states have made this evidence less stringent, but still necessary. The type of evidence allowed in court varies, but the District of Columbia Court of Appeals arrived at these possibilities: "(1) medical evidence and testimony; (2) evidence of breaking and entering the prosecutrix's apartment; (3) condition of clothing; (4) bruises and scratches; (5) emotional condition of the prosecutrix; (6) opportunity of the accused; (7) conduct of the accused at the time of arrest; (8) presence of semen or blood on the clothing of the accused or victim;

(9) promptness of complaints to friends and police; and (10) lack of motive to falsify."

This supportive evidence is demanded by the court to back up three components of the crime: (1) force/resistance/lack of consent; (2) penetration; (3) identity of the rapist. Georgia, Idaho, Nebraska, Washington, D.C., and the Virgin Islands have the strictest such requirements. Many states call for lack of consent and penetration to be documented by proof other than the victim's testimony. Others require some corroboration of any part of the victim's statement.

A corroboration requirement that is only minimal does not mean that there will be a high conviction rate. Cases that do not have this additional evidence simply are not taken to trial. Even when corroboration is not legislated, there are other protections against false accusations. These screening devices include the cautionary charges to the jury, psychiatric examinations for victims, polygraph tests, and so forth.

Several states have recognized the variance within the crime by listing differing degrees, with varying sentences. They are trying to get away from the highly restrictive single degree and the emphasis on vaginal/penile penetration. In these states, rape also includes cunnilingus, fellatio, anal intercourse, or, to quote from the Michigan law, "any other intrusion, however slight, of any part of a person's body or of any object into the genital or anal openings of another person's body, but emission of semen is not required."

Those that have several degrees include such situations as the following:

1. Sexual relations when the assailant is armed or through physical injury or threat of harm.
2. The victim is under a certain age.
3. The accused has a special relationship to the victim (a relative and/or authority figure).
4. The victim is unconscious or a drug was administered without her consent.
5. Sexual relations in the course of a kidnapping or burglary.

6. When it is accomplished under coercive circum stances.

7. There is more than one assailant.

8. Physical injury to the victim.

9. When the perpetrator knows the victim is mentally defective, mentally incapacitated, and/or physically help-less.

10. When it includes felonious entry into a building or vehicle where the victim is situated.

11. The victim is over eleven, and the crime committed without consent and using force not likely to cause serious personal injury.

A rape committed in any of these sets of circumstances would then be classified under the applicable category as a first, second, third, or fourth degree offense, with a more appropriate sentence than under the single degree system. Several states have lowered the penalties, to decrease the jury's fear of bringing a conviction.

Beyond these revisions in the rape codes, several states have turned to other victim-related areas. When a woman looks to the legal justice system for help, she gives up much of her privacy. She might have to testify many times in an open courtroom, tell her name and address, and gain media attention. But whenever legislators have attempted to write statutes protecting her from some of these invasions, they run into constitutional questions. For example, when Georgia passed a law prohibiting the publication of the victim's name, it was overturned by the Supreme Court. The rights of the accused have priority over those of the complaining witness.

Ohio took an unusual approach of allowing a private attorney in addition to the prosecutor to aid the victim in answering questions about her prior sex life. A few states, such as Massachusetts and Minnesota, are trying to provide direct victim services through the criminal justice system. Those two, plus Alaska, California, and Ohio, have recommended more education about the issue and additional seminars for prosecutors.

The lawmakers in Alaska also passed resolutions suggesting that a policewoman respond to rape complaints; that self-defense be taught in schools; and that medical protocol include examinations for both physical and emotional trauma. California, Hawaii, Illinois, Maryland, Massachusetts, Nevada, New York, and Washington developed crime compensation bills, but these are highly restrictive for rape victims.

Changing the law is a beginning, but changing attitudes is the crux of the matter. Each legal revision has been paired with a strident chorus of male legislators dredging up all the centuries-old fears about women accusers and women's proper role. These new codes and statutes will only be as good as those who write them and those who enforce them. Only time will tell if they will follow the spirit of the law, as well as the word.

A brief summary of each state's law and the full text of those for Michigan and Washington can be found in the appendices.

5: *A Crucial Decision*

A rape experience does not end with the departure of the assailant. While in an emotionally volatile state, a woman has to make a crucial decision. She has been the victim of a crime. Should this offense be reported to the police? Any crime victim may hesitate at this point, but one who has been sexually assaulted must weigh, balance, and debate the unique additional requirements placed before her by our justice system. She should be aware of many issues, including the fact that rapists have the lowest conviction rate of the criminal population.

The worse the attack, the more likely the woman will receive sensitive attention and a guilty verdict for the offender. The closer the rape matches the stereotype—random, sudden, violent, and by a stranger—the better her chances for a positive response. It is important that there is no societally defined victim precipitation such as hitchhiking, originally meeting the assailant in a bar, and so forth. Strong evidence of use of force, resistance, and penetration are required. The victim must be able to provide a concise, accurate description of the man, have a clear memory of the details of the event, and be willing to complete all the steps of the reporting procedure. Promptness of report is a further vital factor.

The rapist must be someone other than her husband. If she knows the offender, and especially if she has had previous consental relations with him, the possibility of any legal resolution decreases markedly. She must evaluate any interpersonal consequences between herself and the assailant.

Another element to consider is whether the rapist has a previous record. When this is true, it increases the substantive assistance the victim will receive.

We remain a racist, classist nation with the police reflecting this bias when handling rape cases. Any combination of the following circumstances is disadvantageous for the victim. Third world and poor women receive less responsive treatment. If a white offender attacks a minority victim, her position is weakened. If the offender's income bracket is higher than the victim's, she encounters problems in reporting. Reverse these situations and the woman is more readily granted help. Thus a victim should keep in mind her ethnic and economic background as compared to those of the rapist.

Other economic questions must be addressed. Reporting involves time away from a job, school, family, and friends. In many states, a victim is billed for the required medical verification of intercourse. She must determine whether those factors outweigh her individual benefits in terms of satisfaction, focusing her anger, safety, and so on.

A victim must be willing to have her personal life examined. If she goes to court, this data may be made public. She has to reveal very private information regarding her life-style and sexual history, from the time of the rape back through puberty. She cannot have had intercourse with any other man prior to her medical examination. The investigation often begins with a question of this nature.

Reporting is a long, arduous process that severely challenges a woman's emotional and physical stamina. She should evaluate the availability of support. Is there a rape crisis center in her city? These women will provide knowledgeable input and continuing help. When a victim informs her friends and/or family, she should consider whether their solidarity will be maintained throughout the ordeal. Situations of crisis call for aid and comfort. If this is denied, it is harder on the victim.

What is the woman's estimation of her own frustration level? Even though she was raped, there is always a possibility that her case will be marked unfounded. Her self-esteem will suffer, her guilt be renewed. In cases where the assailant is apprehended, the lawyers generally utilize plea bargaining. The victim is not consulted, because she is merely a witness for the state with no control over the prosecuting attorney. But she must live with the results of the attorneys' decisions. Finally, she must determine her personal benefits versus the disadvantages of reporting.

A victim may report and then change her mind about pressing charges. This is possible at any time until a warrant has been issued for the offender's arrest and he has been apprehended. After that has occurred, reversal is difficult. Because she is a witness for the state, when a trial date arrives she will receive a subpoena. If she fails to appear in court, a "body attachment" may be issued. Then she will be brought in by the police to testify.

There are two alternatives to a complete reporting procedure. Some jurisdictions accept anonymous reports that exclude the victim's name. This may be done by telephone, in person, or with a written statement. This contact includes as much specific information regarding the attack, location, and offender. The report can be included in their files, but it will not be added to the total number of reported rapes. Some victims have returned at a later date to follow through on their reports. Others have agreed to prosecute when they discover they are not alone, but one of many the individual has attacked. Some learn the offender is a repeater, and their report provides additional details about his method of operation. At the very least, with this data police may better patrol the area of the incident. Unanimously, police prefer that victims press charges and be willing to prosecute. Some departments perceive accepting anonymous reports as a waste of time. They do nothing with them. No purpose is served.

A second option is referred to as a third-party report. With the victim's approval, a friend or family member can make the report for her. A more effective method is for the victim to contact an antirape support group. After receiving her permission, this information is relayed to the local authorities. As with anonymous reports, not all jurisdictions accept these. The gain is that the crisis center staff can add the facts to their files, as well as help the victim find different methods of protecting other women from this particular rapist.

Ultimately, individual reasons and personal concerns determine whether a rape is reported. Those who chose not to report provided several explanations. Numerous times, they stated that they did not think the police would do anything. They would be nonresponsive, judgmental, skeptical, and probably not believe their account. They refused to expose themselves to even the hint of poor treatment or harassment by police.

Many cited fear of retaliation as another primary motive. Because they had been threatened by their attackers, they were extremely reticent to test those threats. When the offender was a family member, most decided against reporting.

Others experienced guilt because of confusion as to their complicity. They knew the rapist; they had been drinking, hitchhiking, were alone after dark, and so forth. They realistically appraised that they would have minimal success securing a conviction. Embarrassment, or not wanting others to know, were other reasons. A few women bluntly said that it was nobody's business but their own.

Third world and poor women frequently explained that they would never seek police help in any matter, even as crime victims. They wanted no involvement with the justice system. One said the phrase was a misnomer; she called it the "injustice" system. Many women of such ethnic backgrounds as Asian-American or Latina refused to report for reasons stemming from their cultures. When the family bonds were firm, some felt personal shame and did not want this thrust upon their parents. Others said that the attack was handled as a family matter, with fathers and brothers avenging the assault.

Other nonreporters included those who wanted the rape to

end with the attack. They rebelled at having to describe the circumstances. A few had previous records or personal trouble with police. They knew that because of their histories they would be unlikely to receive support, let alone the attacker's conviction.

Those knowledgeable about the true picture of rape laws stated that they were unwilling to go through so much aggravation and turmoil for nothing. After considering the low conviction rate, the difficulty in proving charges, and the time involved, they decided that it simply was not worthwhile.

Grace was raised to be obedient and submissive.

"It was the key motive in my life, until I was raped. I tried to please my parents, teachers, and to do as I was told or what was expected of me. Reporting to the police was something I didn't consider. Would they believe that it never occurred to me to fight back physically, because I had been taught not to?"

A twenty-year-old New York City woman was having her second date with a man she had met through a mutual friend. As he walked her to the door, he asked if he could come in for a drink of water. When she unlocked her apartment, he pushed her into the room and raped her. Even though she began crying, then yelled, fought, and threw a bottle at him, he did not understand the act as rape.

"There was that feeling of it being my fault. I should expect such treatment from men. I shouldn't report or attempt other forms of retaliation."

Cynthia did not report because she knew her attacker.

"What kind of help would I have gotten from the police? My problem became one shared by most nonreporters. How do you handle your anger? If you do notify the authorities, all your emotions can be diffused with hating the rapist, plus the police, lawyers, and judges. I resent having to expend so much energy dealing with men. I've resolved that anger by becoming a lesbian. The last man who touched me was the rapist. I've been fucked over one time too many. It's changed me dramatically. I think the stereotype rapes, the nonofficial ones such as mine, the probable treatment at the hands of all male-dominated elements along the way to a rape trial, create a lot of hateful women. I know. I'm one of them."

Catherine, a white woman of twenty-seven, was walking along a beach at dusk. She was not alone, for others were enjoying the balmy summer night. A black man armed with a gun approached her. After forcing her to a deserted section, he raped her.

"When I returned home, I didn't tell the two girls I lived with. Somehow I believed that what had taken place was my responsibility, because I was outside by myself near sunset. I must have been asking for it. The police came to mind, but I've been around them enough to know they're already prejudiced against black men. I didn't think it was a serious enough event to call to their attention. It was more personal. I didn't want to get them involved.

"I thought of our prison system. After putting a guy in jail, he ends up ten years later much worse than he was when he went in. He'll be more likely to rape or kill to release his pent-up anger. With the decision made, I understood it became my job to deal with any aftereffects.

"In one sense, a rape can be blown out of proportion. There certainly is an aggressiveness to it. But there's aggression in all crimes. Since rape has a sexual element, I think the media play it up because it will sell more copies. We should be aware of that. We all have bodies with sexual organs. Sometimes they fit together in ways that are peaceful and good. Other times they fit together in ways that are painful and hurt. In my case, I was lucky because he didn't physically injure me. It was a sexual act I didn't want to agree to, but felt if I didn't I would be harmed."

Nadine did not notify the police, because initially she did not believe she had been raped. Her insurance agent stopped by with some wine. The drinking continued for several hours, until she passed out. Intermittently, as Nadine revived, she saw the man had removed her clothes and was forcing her to submit to cunnilingus and intercourse.

"I don't think the word *rape* entered my mind at the time. I was angry with myself for having gotten into a situation like that. In a way it was my fault, for getting drunk with him. I didn't have to do that. My picture of a sexual assault included a lonely road, some guy jumping from the bushes, holding a knife at your throat, beating and raping you. With a definition like that, I could hardly call the police."

Vickie went for a job interview at an underground publishing house and ended up being raped by the president of the organization.

"After an hour of talking, the man suggested we go to his car, where he had a better supply of his publications. For some reason I was wary, but I didn't want to spoil my chances of getting the job. While he was showing me the samples it started to rain, so we got into his car. He raped me, even though I fought until I lost consciousness.

"In the safety of my apartment, I became hysterical. A friend who came over later told me I kept saying I wanted to cut out my genitals. I just didn't want to be a woman anymore, no sexuality whatsoever. I made the deliberate decision not to call the police. From all my experience of having men expose themselves to me, telling my brother and having him say 'what'd you do first,' of being yelled at on the way to work, instinctively I knew the police wasn't the place to go.

"Although it's been several years now, I still feel that not reporting was the correct response. I wasn't clear about my own guilt for having originally entered the car. Instead, I did the typical internalizing. The one regret I have is not doing something to protect other women from that particular man."

A schoolteacher from a northeastern state expressed her feelings.

"I've mixed emotions about reporting. On the one hand, I don't trust the police to help women at all. It seems the rape laws were set up to protect women only when they belong to a specific man. I didn't report my rape because I knew the man. He was very prominent in the community. The truth was that his denials would be more believable than my accusations. What satisfaction would it have brought me, anyway?

"Possibly if the rape penalties weren't as severe, there'd be more convictions. Then women might be willing to report. As things stand, they'll get little understanding and only a slight hope of sending the man to prison. I was raped by a middle-class WASP. Why bother, was my final feeling."

"One clashing confrontation was enough for that day," Maria, another victim, summarized. "A human psyche can only withstand a defined amount of strain during a short period of time. Telling the police, reliving that experience, was too much to ask. My recovery has been eased, because I had time to rid myself of some of the more painful things the attacker made me do. Repeating and repeating all that information would have made the rape stay with me longer."

Sometimes the reporting decision is removed from the victim. Another person summons the police. For juveniles, parents or guardians must sign the complaint. In other situations, friends have placed the call without consultation. Occasionally, neighbors or concerned citizens, hearing or noticing a disturbance, have notified police.

Women who did report listed these reasons: some needed medical treatment or assistance. They either had no private physician or could not contact one. Most hospital personnel must automatically tell the police when informed by a patient of a crime or when a case is evaluated as such.

Others reported because they wanted some kind of comfort, support, or help. The police became a place to turn. Still others desired that the rapist be punished for his illegal behavior. Many elected to report because they wished to protect themselves and other females from future assaults by the same rapist. They would feel more secure if he were apprehended.

Some were extremely angry. It was an outrage against them. The police had to be summoned. If they did not report, no one would ever have a realistic count of rapes committed. Men would continue to abuse women. This procedure was a focused, direct outlet for their anger. In a few cases, the women said that because a crime had occurred, it was their civic duty to inform the police. This reason was given least often.

The involved reporting process often begins with trying to locate the telephone number of the correct police precinct. Most victims are unaware that, unless they were kidnapped, the determining factor is the crime scene. They must contact the police whose jurisdiction includes the location of the rape. When doubt arises, a victim should dial either the operator ("O"), information (411), or any emergency number, such as New York City's 911. Usually, the call is transferred to the right police station, but problems do occur. One woman's assault began in one area and ended in another. She called the station nearest her home. After she provided statements for four separate police departments, they determined which was responsible for her case. More frequently, when this takes place one city force will furnish another with a "courtesy report."

When the decision is made to notify the authorities, a victim should not shower, bathe, douche, or change clothes, until given permission. Any of these actions will result in the destruction of needed evidence. The possibility of medical verification of intercourse will be drastically reduced. If a victim has changed clothes, but they have not been washed, she should place each item in a separate bag and turn them over to the officers. Again, these are legal evidence and will remain in police custody. She should bring other wearing apparel with her to the medical facility. After her hospital visit, she may wash and change.

Whatever the location of the rape, police will secure the area and search for evidence. If it occurred in her home, she should refrain from moving or altering any objects or furniture. She could try remembering anything the offender might have touched, such as a glass, windows, a tabletop. The police will look for evidence of a struggle, fingerprints, and so on.

Pat was raped in her apartment. After placing a call to the police, she spent the next twenty minutes "straightening up," as women are taught to do to receive "company." She righted all turned chairs, straightened the lampshade, and wiped off the bedside table where the assailant had placed his knife. When the police appeared, her residence was in order. She was met by disbelief that a rape could have occurred.

When a victim is unsure as to the locale of the attack, she must recall as many details as possible. The uncertainty will hamper her case, but not damage it entirely.

A victim should attempt to have a supportive person stay with her. Without such comfort, it is a long, lonely process.

A report should be made as soon as possible. Victims often begin blocking details from their minds. The assailant is more easily apprehended when little time has elapsed. Evidence is fresh. If the case goes to trial, a speedy report weighs in the victim's favor. Some women first sought medical attention, then the police. They felt that during this period they steeled themselves for the remainder of the process. A report within forty-eight hours will still receive quick attention. Medical verification is possible. While some states accept rape reports as much as several months later, the conviction chances are slim.

People envision reporting as a short telephone call, the arrival of an officer, a statement, and then the wait for apprehension and trial. This is far removed from the actual procedure. Few victims realize what to expect, nor what they can request. Women do not have to follow the police's lead blindly through the mazelike process. Coping is easier when they know their own rights and responsibilities.

Police response to victims varies depending upon the jurisdiction, but the sequence usually falls into a basic pattern. An operator or dispatcher receives the call and determines the extent of the emergency. He bases this judgment on the immediacy of the rape, whether the victim informs him of serious injuries, and her manner of speech, which indicates trauma or stress. The victim gives her name and location. If she is badly hurt, an ambulance is sent. In an ideal situation, the dispatcher records the location, the identity or description of the offender, and his means of escape. Posting a preliminary radio broadcast for all cars and notifying patrol officers are the next steps. After that, the patrol supervisor and/or rape investigators are contacted.

If a victim is terribly distressed or fearful, she should request the police dispatcher stay on the line until the officers arrive. Sometimes this is impossible, because of the volume of calls. In these cases, victims have had their calls transferred to another person who talked to them while they waited. Others asked for the number of a victim support group.

A minimum of two patrol officers arrive at the victim's location. The questioning begins there, at the local station, or, on occasion, after the hospital examination. She repeats information regarding the site of the incident, the description of the offender, whether she knew or recognized him, what type of force was employed, and so on.

Patrol people do not come in contact with many rape victims. They are often the least prepared and most insensitive toward these women. Before an investigation starts, all they are required to establish is that a rape occurred and that there is reasonable cause to believe this. Instead of utilizing the skills for which they have been trained, too frequently they belabor the sexual aspect.

A victim has to describe the attack countless times. If she wants to offer an in-depth discussion, talk about the rape, wants to cry, yell, or express any emotion, she should be encouraged to do so. But she should not be pushed. She can cooperate within her own limits. All police prefer questioning a victim alone. They say it is less distracting. Others assume that a woman leaves out facts which cast her in a bad light or are embarrassing. If a victim wants a friend or support-person present, she can request this. When officers know they are being monitored by a third party, it prevents irrelevant questions from being asked. When they hesitate to allow this, a victim must decide how important this factor is to her.

While the questioning takes place, others may be sent to the crime scene. Among their duties are photographing the area, searching for evidence, and determining whether there are witnesses to be interviewed. Many victims do not want their neighbors to know they were raped. They can ask that this be handled with discretion. The police can state that a crime has been committed, without revealing the specifics. A victim has every right to demand that her privacy be respected. If she desires complete anonymity, she can provide them with instructions on how to contact her so that even friends and family will not learn of the attack. Most crisis centers allow victims to use the center's address and telephone number on the report form.

During this first questioning session, some victims feel intimidated, embarrassed, or hesitant to discuss details in the presence of men. And the majority of patrol officers are men. If this is true, they can request a female investigator be assigned their case. This cannot always be granted, because some jurisdictions have no females or the few employed are already too burdened.

The most important point is a sympathetic, sensitive person, no matter the sex. Some policewomen have been as hostile to victims as their male counterparts. The victim should think of herself. What is most comfortable for her? Police want a cooperative witness and will try to meet as many requests as possible.

The patrol officers take the victim to a hospital for medical verification of intercourse and the gathering of other medically related evidence. They receive all items of clothing worn at the time of the rape. While they remain at the hospital during the examination, they should not be present in the room. They may be nearby in order to maintain the chain of evidence or answer any questions the staff has. Upon completion of this step, they transport the victim to her home or wherever she requests. Their final contact is providing appointment instructions for an interview with the investigators who will then handle her case.

Whenever a victim feels the patrol person's conversation, questions, attitude, or approach is callous or insensitive, she should tell him. If he seems especially blatant, she should file a complaint with his supervisor.

The next interview takes place at a scheduled time, either immediately after the hospital visit or the following day. Although rapists do not work on a nine-to-five basis, most investigators do. Generally, a victim meets with at least one officer during normal working hours. This portion of the reporting process lasts a minimum of one-and-a-half hours. She is questioned along lines similar to the first interview, but in much greater detail.

Again a woman has to repeat how, where, and when the attack began. She is asked about her conduct. While this is done to guarantee that she has not omitted any important facts, it is traumatic to retell the circumstances to a series of people. Some felt that the police were trying to break them or have them drop charges.

Women have come to decry as irrelevant many of the questions. They assert that these have little bearing on the fact a rape was committed. This sample of questions was compiled after discussions with victims: Did the assailant have abnormal genitals? Was he left- or right-handed? Did he have clean fingernails? Did he rip out or disconnect the telephone? Did he admit to having venereal disease? Did he cover your head with a blanket? Did he blindfold you? Were you menstruating at the time of the alleged rape? Did he steal your clothes? Did he bite you? Did he lick you? Did he use lubricant? Did he fondle or suck your breasts? Did he offer you any kind of reward if you had intercourse with him? Did he insert his fingers in your vagina? Did he have you sit on his lap? Were you gagged? Did he apologize? Was there oral or anal intercourse? Was he armed? What exact words did he use while attacking you? Was there anything unusual about his speech pattern?

A major presumption by investigators is that most rapists are repeaters or recidivist sex offenders. There is a good chance their identity or method of operation is known to the police. These questions, although they may seem offensive to the victim, are used in establishing or developing a pattern for a particular rapist. For the victim, it would require keen observation and presence of mind during the rape to be able to make even an educated guess at some answers. And guesses are not permitted as evidence.

Some police departments have no modus operandi (m.o.) files for rapists. They rely on the investigators' memories rather than on any compilation of data.

A further set of questions covered by many investigators center on the victim's moral character. The justification police provide is that their states allow a woman's sexual history to be introduced in court. If the assailant is apprehended, the prosecutor does not want to be surprised by any damaging facts brought out against the woman. One investigator explained, "It's a matter of being prepared. The district attorney doesn't want to be sitting in court with mud all over his face if the defense springs something about the woman's past on him. We investigators have to get as much information as possible to help the DA."

It is the unknowing, unsettled, upset woman who must reveal these items about her sex life that she might otherwise share with no one else. Aside from the alleged rape, when was the last time you had intercourse? Were you a virgin prior to the attack? How many men have you had intercourse with? Do you frequently allow yourself to be picked up? Do you go to singles bars? Would you classify yourself as heterosexual, bisexual, or lesbian? Are you currently sleeping with more than one person? Are you living with a man? Have you been raped before? Did you report it? Are you married, divorced, widowed, single? Do you have any children? Are they legitimate or illegitimate? Sometimes there are open-ended questions requesting any detrimental information the victim can provide about herself. The police acknowledge that when a woman refuses to answer a question it jeopardizes her case and believability in their eyes.

What rights and requests does the victim have? First, she can ask that this appointment be scheduled at her convenience. She has to rearrange her work, school, or family hours, and these are important to her. But it must be completed soon, before she begins blocking and repressing details. The police must work quickly. The chances of the assailant's apprehension diminish with time.

This interview generally takes place at the police station. If she requires transportation, she should request it. A car can be dispatched. If she does not want to create attention in her neighborhood, she should ask that an unmarked automobile be sent. Police stations are not known for their cheery atmosphere. Some victims prefer to have the interview conducted in another location. Again, she can ask, though this is not often granted.

If the assigned investigator makes a victim feel ill at ease, she may state she wants someone else to take over her case. When she feels in need of support, she should ask for a friend to be present. These requests might not be met, but, even so, many women who made their wishes known felt better. They were regaining control over their lives.

Investigators, similar to patrol officers, believe that having others present during a questioning session impedes the progress. But when a victim is incapable of going through this alone, she should say so. A woman must answer questions honestly and directly. Any time she is confused, or wants an explanation, she should ask for clarification. This information is hers to know. Too often investigators are overworked and brusque. They know their job, but forget this may be the woman's first contact with any criminal procedure.

Identification is a necessary part of our legal system. Even though this step is mind-numbing for the victim, it must be completed. When the assailant is unknown to the woman, police departments have several different methods of attempting identification.

Depending upon the sophistication and size of the police force, most have files of photographs, commonly known as mug shots. Some of these are computerized, but most are not. These photos may be segregated as to type of previous criminal record and race. Some are only Polaroid shots, discolored by age. High school yearbooks dating from the mid-sixties proliferate in other stations. The offender could have grown a mustache, shaved his beard, cut his hair, or taken a bad picture.

Other forces also have identi-kits or photo-kits. These are used to make composite pictures of the assailant. They are transparencies or black-and-white photographs of facial features. An officer works with the victim to come up with as accurate a likeness as possible. Some jurisdictions have artists who aid in this procedure.

Other women are required to attend lineups, or showups, as they are called in a few cities. Lineup identifications are difficult because often the lighting is unnatural and some backgrounds lack height markings. The participants are permitted to alter their appearance, and many do. They change their hair styles, shave, or wear a different type of clothes than usual.

Most departments prefer to have the accused in custody and then hold a lineup. A few, such as Tucson, Arizona, and Washington, D.C., attempt on-street identification wherever possible. The assailant is brought under a street light, or in front of car headlights. He is not able to see the victim.

In station lineups, the victim is out of sight of the men as well. If the victim makes a positive identification or knows the assailant, a warrant will be issued for his arrest.

Some police departments combine the preliminary and supplementary reports prepared by the patrol officers and investigators. Other times, adult victims are required to write a formal statement about the attack. Those employing this victim statement believe it provides information which benefits the investigation and prosecution. It prevents gaps in the investigative process and helps prosecutors decide which questions to ask. Sometimes it is used as a gauge in predicting the victim's conduct in court. Because there are long delays between the time of the rape and the possible trial date, it can be returned to the victim to refresh her memory. Many police feel that in each retelling there may be additional facts which the victim will include that were left out of previous accounts. This is a time-consuming process, but some victims say it organized their thoughts. Others find it cathartic, helping their psychological recovery from the rape.

A polygraph test is another variation. This is most frequently administered to check a victim's credibility. A nationwide survey revealed that in nearly 50 percent of the cases it was employed because of "suspicion of complainant deception." Some other reasons offered were that the demeanor of the victim caused suspicion or the defendant appeared truthful, 6 percent; consent was the issue, 12 percent; evidence of prior victim/defendant relations, 9 percent. Polygraphs are not used automatically, but rather as a discretionary matter. In most small jurisdictions with populations less than 100,-000, polygraph machines are not available.[1]

It is inadmissible in court to state that a victim refused to be administered this test. If she does have one and the results are not completely favorable, the information can be excluded from the courtroom. For no other crime is the victim required to submit to this procedure. Rape victims who have taken a lie detector test have been angered, intimidated, and humiliated to realize that an investigation will not begin without this corroboration of their word.

All jurisdictions take photographs of the victim when there is any visual verification of a beating, external injuries, and so forth. Sometimes this is done immediately, but frequently bruises will not appear until days after the attack. If marks are on parts of the body other than the face, either a female officer, investigator, or civilian personnel should take the pictures. On occasion, a nurse at the hospital to which the victim was brought will do the photographing.

Some victims have to be fingerprinted in order to separate their prints from those possibly belonging to the assailants. If a victim believes this is being done for other reasons, she should ask.

The main investigator assigned to the victim's case should provide her with periodic verbal progress reports. If this is not done, the victim should call. Any time she has questions or remembers new information, the police should be notified. In situations where a victim's case is determined unfounded, she is within her rights to be informed of the reasons behind this action. A victim who believes this has been a capricious or unfair evaluation may complain to the investigator or the supervisor. She could contact a victim support group and help bring a class action suit against the police, joining with victims in this similar position.

Victims do not expect or want to be coddled. They do not desire to be treated as helpless, clinging children. They require a dignified, understanding approach. Each has endured a crisis situation. They need and deserve special help and attention. Law enforcement personnel have the responsibility of protecting the innocent. This is remembered especially in rape cases. But the innocent often means only the accused, not the victim. And too often her innocence is questioned and unprotected.

The women I interviewed came forward with neither blanket condemnation nor universal praise about their treatment by police. It depended on the specific officers and investigators. They, too, are human. They bring with them to their jobs all the same myths and stereotypes regarding rape as all society. Their moods vary according to their personal lives, as well as how they view the victim.

Sensitivity, understanding, consideration are individually defined qualities and value judgments. What offends one person passes unnoticed by others. The words "alleged rape," that continually appear in the reporting procedure, are indicative. When a victim hears and sees this, she perceives it as authorities challenging her believability. Police use it in the legal sense. A crime is "alleged" to have occurred until the jury brings in a verdict and the judge denies any motion for a new trial. But reactions and interactions among a victim and law enforcement officials can spring from an issue this basic.

Because of the widespread negative publicity regarding their handling of victims, police have tried to improve. Yet their progress often falters. New theories and policies must be mirrored by good intentions of the people responsible for their implementation.

Victims have recorded the following accounts of contacts with police departments across the country.

While Jane was waiting for a bus, two men came up, pulled her into their car, and raped her. Her landlady reported the attack without consulting her.

"Two precinct officers came to my home and questioned me briefly in front of my landlady. They said I'd have to be taken to a hospital to be examined for court evidence. After getting in the car, they questioned me further, explaining they didn't like to talk to rape victims in front of anyone else.

"They asked if the first man was black. I told them no. Even though I'd said both were fair and had light hair, they kept saying 'Wasn't either of the men colored?'

"On the way to the hospital they discussed the more gory and violent rape cases they'd been sent out on. These were brought up in the normal topics of conversation and seemed insensitive to me. They reinforced the whole experience I'd been through. As they launched into a speech about all the women who came in to report rapes and later dropped charges, I began to wonder if they thought this was true in my case.

"After the hospital, they took me home, but I had to go to the police station the next morning at nine. There, I had to meet with another man and give a fuller statement. I had to give descriptions again, look at mug shots, and bear up under the strain of questioning. Was I on birth control at the time? Was I a virgin? Finally I asked why these answers were needed. 'For your own protection,' he said, and I wondered what I was being protected against.

"At that point, I wished the police had never been called. Although I wanted to walk out, I found I wasn't through yet. I had to look at cars in the police garage to see if I could identify that of the rapists. Everytime I thought I was finished, they'd construct another obstacle for me to hurdle.

"The police did apprehend one of the men, who confessed and implicated the second guy. This meant I had to attend a lineup and try to identify them. My only previous contact with any form of lineup was what I'd seen on TV, which certainly didn't prepare me for the actual event. A policeman told me I should go into the lineup room, not say anything, but write the number of the person I might identify on a piece of paper.

"When I got inside the room, a man in a business suit came up and told me to turn around. I had no idea who he was or what he wanted. I turned away, but was informed by another inspector that I had to have my picture taken. At the same time, they warned me again that I had to do what they said or the evidence gotten from the lineup would be thrown out of court.

"Afterwards, when I questioned them, they finally explained that they had to have a picture of both me and the lineup to show it'd been impartial. Granted this seems like an insignificant point, but they never seemed to tell me why they were doing anything. Also, by this time I'd given my statement to at least four different men. Those details were becoming cemented in my memory.

"I was fingerprinted, something I thought they reserved just for apprehended criminals. I continually asked why, and then they told me they needed to compare mine to those found in the car they impounded. If they'd let me know beforehand, I'd have done it. But so often I was treated as something a little less than human.

"Going to the police was an educational experience, one I'd rather have done without. I don't think women should report being raped to the police. The only time they thoroughly investigate is when they have a vested interest."

When Lida was in college, she shared a house with several students. During a Christmas break, she remained alone in the residence. A burglar added a bonus for himself and raped her. Once he left, Lida was badly shaken and needed help. She dialed the operator, asked for the police, and fell apart. Her initial contact with the police was extremely good. The dispatcher kept her talking on the telephone until a squad car arrived, but then the situation changed.

"Looking back, I'm still appalled by the police. I was frightened, distraught, and didn't want to be by myself for fear the man would return. I wasn't prepared to have the four or five policemen take over my house and myself the way they did. I expected to be asked to recount the rape, but not have them all listen with obvious delight. They wanted to know everything he did to me. After a while it made me think, so what? What does it matter? Possibly in terms of correlating my rape to another one, but, in terms of me, it just seemed absurd to ask such detailed questions. When they asked, did I have an orgasm, I actually laughed. What in the hell did that have to do with the fact I was raped? Did I ever see him following me? Was there anything unusual about the size of his penis?

"Next, they took me to the hospital and then to their station for more questions. After I wrote a description of the assault, they said someone would call me. Several days later, two cops arrived on my doorstep with mug shots and high school yearbooks. I couldn't identify anyone positively. I was afraid that if I made a tentative one, it might be of some person they wanted to get out of spite. By then, I didn't care if they caught the man. I was concerned about other women, but I was mainly glad I hadn't been killed. It's over now, I guess. The police never came up with anything."

Dale's rape-related injuries were so severe she was taken by friends to a hospital. While the doctors wanted her to remain there, she could not afford the expense. The staff called the police immediately, but they did not arrive at her home until the following day.

"I was in my nightgown when they showed up. Even though I physically ached, they insisted I go with them to the station. When changing clothes took more time than they felt was needed, they became surly. At the police department, I was instructed to write a narrative of the entire event. The length of my statement was about eight or ten pages. The item that aggravated the investigator seemed inconsequential to me. During the course of the rape I'd been forced to submit to cunnilingus. At the time I didn't know this word, so I used the more commonly known expression.

"While the officer was reading my statement he came to that section and asked what I meant by it. Didn't I know the acceptable word? What kind of a girl was I? His last comment was it was certainly a good thing I'd tried to resist, because pictures of a bloodied and bruised victim were effective evidence.

"Another thing I didn't like about being at the station was that I couldn't be me. I had to be more naive, much nicer. I felt that if I didn't dissemble to them, they wouldn't believe me. So I did. I was sweet and childlike, hoping this would help persuade them I deserved their assistance.

"A few weeks later, they called to say they were still working on the case, but then I never heard from them again. Maybe the men were picked up for something else, if not rape. I wonder about them sometimes. And then I try not to think about the whole incident or why men do such things."

Mary was raped by a man who broke into her apartment. After he left, she called a friend, who came over with her manfriend. When the couple arrived, the man asked Mary if she had sent for the police. Although she told him she did not want to, he insisted upon it and dialed the number.

"Two policemen came to my home. The older one looked like he had walked out of some forties movie, complete with potbelly and florid complexion. His sidekick tried dressing to pass in a crowd of young people when he was out of uniform. The first question the officer asked was did I take the pill. When I said yes, his reply was, 'Good, now you won't have to tell your boyfriend.'

"The next question was if the rapist were black. After I told them he was, they began referring to him as the 'nigger.' While searching the house, they entered one room where there were pictures from the *National Geographic* of New Guinea tribes. The older cop punched his buddy in the shoulder and told him to write in their report 'unusual amount of interest in Negroes in this house.'

"By the nuances of their questions and looks, I could tell they were becoming convinced the rapist was really a boyfriend. I was just trying to get back at him. They kept asking me if I were sure I didn't know him.

"Meanwhile, more cops arrived to fingerprint the house. My nightgown and sheets were taken for evidence. Later, they told me it was very important to determine for the courts if he'd ejaculated or not. When I went to the station to retrieve those things, they'd drawn red circles and arrows around all the sperm stains.

"After they'd taken my statement and completed their inspection, I was taken to the hospital. Several hours later, I was home and tried to sleep. A few days passed before I was notified to appear at the station to repeat my story to an inspector. I went because I felt I had to, although I was so angry at the way they'd acted and treated me. My hostility was mounting. I began to feel more sympathy, what a strange word to use, for the rapist and fear of the police.

"This inspector was less brutal. He began by saying he was going to have to ask some questions that would be very painful. He was sorry if he used language that was indelicate. He knew I was a lady. I did my duty and told about it. He would periodically mumble 'oh no' or 'poor girl,' and then ask for more description. I looked at the mug shots he brought out. It was very confusing to page through pictures that might have been taken several years before. I didn't identify anyone.

"After that, the inspector called me once or twice, but I never went back to the station. I just couldn't. I have no idea if I'm one of those cases listed as unfounded or if they did try to find him. Soon the cop stopped phoning. Now I'm the only one who has to deal with the problem."

Alice was a middle-class woman living in the midwest with her husband and child. One evening, she attended a party alone at the home of some friends. When another guest offered her a ride home, she accepted. He detoured to an alleyway and raped her. Finally, she managed to escape.

"When I walked in, my husband was waiting up. He looked at me and asked, 'What's wrong?' All I could manage was 'I've been raped!' While I sat down, he dialed the police. They came shortly and first took me to the hospital for treatment. My next stop was the station, where I was taken into a large room that had several long tables in it. At the beginning of the interview, I was surrounded by several officers, plus my husband. Basic questions were asked, and then the detective in charge said they had a hospital report of alleged intercourse. He needed more details. Glancing around the room, he suggested he should be doing this alone. The others left, and there were only the two of us on opposite sides of the table. I still remember his face. Although he was blond and very Nordic-looking, he had a very cruel appearance.

"Then his interrogation got much rougher. 'Are you in the habit of having extramarital sexual relations? Do you often go to parties by yourself? Do you frequent bars? How have you behaved in the past? What is your sex life like at home?' He continued to press me, insisting I could tell him the truth because my husband, Dave, was no longer in the room. I felt I could be extramaritally seeing ten men and that had nothing to do with my being raped that evening.

"While the questioning progressed, we were suddenly interrupted by two policemen with the rapist between them. I was asked if that were the man. He was only a few feet away. I was petrified. As soon as I nodded yes, he began denying it.

"By this time it was about three or four in the morning. The police had taken my statement and said we could leave. Because I had to appear again that morning at eight, Dave and I stayed up. We talked and tried to put into perspective what had occurred.

"The next morning, I had to retell the story to another policeman. He asked me to recall exactly what the man had said during the evening. When I couldn't or would hesitate, he became livid. He worked and worked on me until scraps and pieces I was already carefully blocking came back. When they did come back, it was even worse. These were things I wouldn't have ever remembered if he hadn't prodded. Maybe he had to know if my life had really been threatened, because no one had heard him. No one saw what he did to me.

"My next stop was an appointment with the city attorney. To make an already emotionally charged situation even more blatant, while waiting for him I was told to sit in the same room occupied by the rapist's friends, his wife, and children.

"Once again, I had to go over the incident with the attorney. He told me I should realize that in this state, this offense puts a man up for life. If I took it to court, I'd embarrass my husband and child. It would be very hard on me. If I thought what I'd been through before had been rough, they'd give me four times more in court. Was I willing to risk that or was it, perhaps, just a little fun?

"I had scratches and scrapes over most of my body. My face had been disfigured. The definite imprint of his hands was on my arms and around my neck. It took nearly two months for my black eye to disappear completely. And I had to convince this man it wasn't 'just a little fun.'

"The police also told me I'd be unwise to press charges. They explained that the man had never been arrested before and was a family man. They joined the city attorney's claim that my name would be dragged through the mud, my husband's career affected. They said it would be in all the papers. I wasn't liable to get a conviction. I'd have to spend a lot of time in court. I'd have to answer questions about my sexual activities since childhood. Was I ready to put this man in prison for life?

"Dave and I considered all those factors. He wanted me to press charges and would protect me if I did it. The reminder that if the man were let free he was likely to repeat his offense with other women made me think twice. My husband said it was my duty. By that time, it was nearly forty hours since I'd slept. I didn't feel I could make a sound decision unaided.

"If Dave and I had wanted to be vigilantes, we'd have done that and not gone to the police. They forced an instant answer, and I gave them what they seemed to want. 'I won't press charges, but I don't know if I'm myself,' I told them. Unfortunately, that wasn't good enough for the rapist and his friends.

"We received a call from a nameless voice that warned, 'Those fellows are looking for you. They know where you live.' The terror that had been trying to subside began to grow again. The police would offer no support or assistance. They were too busy to guard a woman and her home against additional threats of violence. My fears multiplied, and we stayed briefly with friends. My thoughts were 'how stupid of me. If I'd only gotten him behind bars I might have been in better shape.'

"Constantly I felt I'd made the wrong choice in dropping the matter. I hadn't stood up for my convictions. Guilt developed over the feeling it hadn't taken the police long to beat me down mentally until I danced to their tune. I was furious with them for pressuring me as they did. All those elements became too great, and I left the city. Dave was pursued for a long while after my departure and, for his own safety, began carrying a gun.

"I heard lately they're trying to improve their treatment of victims. I think they have hired some women detectives. In my case, it's too late to repair the damage."

Colleen knew hitchhiking could place her in a vulnerable position, but she was late for an appointment. Public transportation was inadequate. The man who gave her a ride turned onto a side road and raped her. After she was freed, she called the police. First, they returned with her to the crime scene to gather evidence, then to the station for a statement. Among other questions, they asked if she enjoyed being raped.

"Their attitude was that because I was hitching, I got what I deserved. If I'd been a good girl, I would have spent three hours on a series of buses and, hopefully, no one would have attacked me while I was waiting for them.

"A policeman accompanied me to the emergency room of a suburban hospital. As time went by, he began getting restless. He told me he didn't feel like hanging around. He had other things to do. His parting words were 'why don't you hitch home?'

"That was the last thing I wanted to do, but I didn't have enough money to get home, and he refused to take me. Days passed. I kept expecting them to call me to report they'd caught the man. I'd furnished them with enough help—his license plate number, a detailed description, even his name and the city where he lived. He'd told me those things while we were driving. I don't think they even looked for him. I'm sure I could have found him if I'd wanted to."

Beth Reynolds, of Fort Worth, Texas, was raped by a man she had seen before, but did not know. Once, prior to the attack, he had tried to break into her apartment, but she was able to summon help before he succeeded. She wrote, "His routine was the same the second time. He began knocking on the front and back doors trying to scare me. Then as he was attempting to get through the locked door, I gathered what I could use as weapons and ran for the phone. I was only able to tell the operator to call the police when the phone went dead."

Her fierce resistance was not enough. She endured the rape, bruised ribs, a broken nose, and threats of death if she called the police. But she did contact them with this result.

"Two patrolmen were the first to come to my apartment. One had been there before when the suspect had been bothering me the first time. They were both kind and seemed to sense my emotions had been drained. While they were questioning me, more police came. A sergeant entered the room, and I felt this man wasn't going to believe me. After asking the other officers some questions, he searched my bedroom, although the attack had been in the kitchen. The rapist had never entered my room.

"This man told me I could prosecute only after I'd had an examination at the county hospital. Simultaneously, as I agreed to submit to any tests, he told me it really wasn't any use. His reasoning, as he explained, was that a rape case was hard to take to court, especially when to him it wasn't a 'good rape.' At some of these remarks, the other officers were visibly offended. Once the sergeant was taken aside and told he was being unduly rough. If these younger officers hadn't been with me, I'd probably have quit right then.

"Because I became adamant about being taken to the hospital, he finally agreed. When we arrived, I became top interest because of the sergeant's announcement of 'another rape' in a voice loud enough to wake a man in the back of the room. While the other officers kept me talking, I watched the sergeant laughing and pointing at me from behind the nurse's desk.

"In Tarrant County it's mandatory that a rape examination be authorized by a district attorney. His decision is based upon the investigating officer's opinion of whether it is a bona fide rape. For many victims this would be the end of the line, because without this exam a case can go no further as rape.

"After I informed the nurse that my father, a prominent attorney, was a good friend of the current district attorney, and I'd gladly call him myself, she looked startled. She left the room and delivered my message to the sergeant. When he came in to confirm what I'd said, he looked upset and very nervous. This knowledge must have changed his mind, because he stomped out, and the exam was authorized in less than ten minutes. I'd now been waiting for two hours.

"During that last discussion with him, I asked why he felt he couldn't authorize my examination. After some obvious stalling, he gave me the excuse about some women claiming rape when it wasn't. I asked the younger officer if I were wrong in assuming the sergeant thought I'd broken down my own door, torn up my apartment, and cracked my own nose simply to cry 'rape.' He looked at me for a moment and said simply, 'Yeah, that's what it sounded like to me.'

"Even as I was x-rayed, I was joined by another detective for more questioning. Finally, I was allowed to go home and managed a few hours of sleep before a new detective arrived to begin the questioning process all over again. My next step was an eight-thirty appointment at the station.

"I arrived several minutes early and located the proper office. I didn't know at the time that this office would become part of my life. During the next few weeks, I was at police headquarters at least once a day and usually several times. Frequently, I would receive phone calls from them in the middle of the night when they wanted to clear up certain points.

"I had to meet with the artist, who complained that he had to be in court in forty-five minutes and composites always took at least an hour. When he calmed down, we were able to get the picture completed in less than fifteen minutes. Both the artist and detective seemed amazed. Neither could grasp the fact that I'd gotten a clear look at my attacker, a face I'll never forget.

"After more questioning, I was called for my first lineup. As I sat in the office, the suspects were marched through right in front of me to the lineup room. As I went to view them, another officer came in with me. I felt he was trying to coach me, but the man that raped me wasn't there. In the weeks that followed, lineups were held at different intervals. Then, as interest faded, so did my hope. I resigned myself to the knowledge that the man might never be caught.

"I'd been raised to respect the police and to trust in them. If they'd really put out an effort to catch this man, I believe they could have. Considering every factor, the general procedures used by the police—before, during, and after the attack—were atrocious and incredible. All I can pray for now is that the rapist never returns and I never have to cope with our local police department again. That frightens me almost more than being attacked another time."

Joyce had a much different experience with the police.

"I walked into the station and told the desk sergeant I wanted to report a rape. He told me to wait for a few minutes and a detective would interview me. He returned quickly, came over to me, and in a quiet voice said to follow him. The questioning took about two hours, and the man was highly understanding. He showed sympathy for me, stating he was extremely sorry about what I'd had to go through. Patiently, he explained what would be expected of me and the entire legal procedure in our state. I was asked to go home, write out a complete statement, and bring it in as soon as possible.

"He told me the reason he was concerned about what the rapist had said to me was because they'd had reports of one man who used similar expressions while raping two other women. He felt it might help if they could tie these separate incidents together. I was asked about speech patterns, and came to see this could be helpful, too. Another man was assigned to the case, but, again, he wasn't offensive. They suggested that, if it weren't too painful, periodically I should close my eyes and go over the sequence of events in my mind. During such times, forgotten details might return that could help them in apprehending the assailant.

"One evening, we had to drive to the location of the crime to see if there might be some evidence that had been missed. We discussed the reputed treatment of victims by police. Obviously, they were aware of the problem. They reminded me that they did have to be wary of false reports, although they concurred that this number was less during the past year than the previous one.

"My case was unusual in that the man was caught and brought to trial. Again, the two policemen stayed with me during the entire ordeal. One of them had even been transferred to another department, but he wanted to see how I was doing. The last kindness they extended was staying with me and my family as we waited in the attorney's office for the verdict. This was a long and trying time, but they remained, with only an occasional phone call to wondering wives to explain why they'd be late for dinner. In my case, the police made the total experience easier."

Jean was raped at gunpoint by a stranger. When she returned home, the man with whom she was living decided to contact the police.

"His first impulse was to call for help. I think it was the most sensible thing to do. At the time, I didn't care who made any choice or what it was. I was thankful he was willing to take over the responsibility. I wasn't in any position to come up with an answer. When the police arrived, they were very kind.

The only issue they raised was their own personal dismay that so many women feel they're safe from rape. They stressed that many women don't observe the dangers around them. It both saddens and sickens them to see what horrors can occur.

"Several times, I had to meet with members of the force, once to give my statement, then to look at mug shots, and so forth. While I was at work, I saw a car similar to the one the man had driven. I called the police and they responded rapidly, but it was too late. Any effort they exerted went unrewarded, because the rapist was never found."

Carolyn was raped by a stranger. Afterwards, she fled to the closest lighted building, which happened to be a hospital. Although they refused her treatment, a staff member did summon the police. The offender was apprehended near the location of the attack.

"My confidence in myself began to be restored when I talked with an officer who stands out in my mind as being a good, compassionate person. He was a reassuring combination of the staid, traditional cop, with a touch of gruffness. But he cared. That's what remains with me to this day. After I'd given him my statement, I told him I was highly skeptical about the ultimate benefits of prosecuting. He swiveled in his chair, looked directly at me, and then, in an almost fatherly manner, pleaded that I must.

"He said these guys keep trying it again and again. I had to help get them off the streets. It was my duty and obligation to help the police, myself, and the rest of society. I agreed with him, but I wasn't firmly convinced.

"I did follow the established procedure—give another statement to another man, stand up, wait, sit down, look at photographs. After seeing about five or six, I identified the man who'd attacked me. The Polaroid shot changed the color of his pigment, but there he was staring back at me. The same detective read me the report the other officer had prepared the previous night. It was completely accurate.

"He'd put everything in, and I was pleased. I felt he did believe me, had been effective in including all my disorganized thoughts.

"Things progressed well until the police couldn't decide if they wanted to try the rapist as a juvenile or an adult. I only heard fragments of this problem, but apparently someone decided he was a juvenile. He'd been in trouble with that department before, and they wanted to keep him there. I still didn't know if I wanted to press charges. I wasn't positive if it were legally possible to change my mind.

"There were several reasons why I wanted out. The jurisdictional dispute was only one of them. I remembered the first officer's words, and stuck with it. I went with them to the scene of the crime, watched them take pictures, helped search for the bottle the guy had used on me.

"I had just about decided I'd had enough, when a man called saying he'd worked with this particular rapist before. He wanted me to stay with it for the guy's own good. He thought he needed help, and this was the only way he could obtain it. I felt that committing him, or even a harsher penalty, wouldn't eradicate what had happened or solve his mental problems, and so would be inadequate. The police kept working, and a subpoena arrived. I didn't want to get into legal trouble, so I gave in and said I'd go through with it. After testifying, all I wanted to do was leave. I did call the police later on and was told they'd find out the result and let me know. They never did. I didn't pursue it after that."

After Lilith was raped, anger was her primary emotion. Without hesitating, she found a telephone booth and called the police.

"I was shaking with rage as I searched for a dime. The first man to answer the phone I tore into. My tone of voice was furious, 'I've just been raped and I'm really pissed off. I think you ought to know that this does go on and you aren't doing any good because no one was around when it happened.'

"He sounded surprised, but said they'd send someone out

immediately. He asked me how far away from my house I was, since I'd explained I was calling from a phone booth. I dished out my sarcasm liberally and told him it was only a block. I was sure I'd be all right. I didn't think anyone was going to attack me in the next ten minutes. At least statistics prove it probably wouldn't happen.

"I didn't want to wait in the booth with more lights on me until the police came. People might see me. I walked home, went inside, and as I sat down suddenly it all went through me like a big rush of water. I realized I could completely break down if I let myself. I was on the verge of tears. I went into the bathroom, looked at myself. There were cuts and scratches all over my face. My lip was cut and bleeding. There was blood dribbling from my nose. Nothing really horrendous, but when you see yourself like that, if you care about yourself at all, it makes you upset.

"One of my earrings had been torn out of my ear. My glasses were gone. The heel was ripped from my shoe. I turned off the light and went outside to meet the police, because I didn't want to wake my roommates. When the officers drove up, I got in their car and was still angry enough to be extremely caustic. Even with my attitude, the two guys were understanding. I believe they were embarrassed it had happened and felt bad about it. They took down some information and drove me back by the spot. I showed them where the attack occurred. We walked the way the rapist had walked. It was like a surrealistic nightmare, because it had only taken place thirty minutes before. There I was back. My fears were ridiculous, but I was terrified the man was going to be around and would attack me again.

"After that, we returned to the car and proceeded to the hospital. They had the light flashing and, again, I was embarrassed, more attention. I didn't want anything to draw attention to me. I wanted to be a transparent chameleon and blend into the back seat.

"The next day, I want to the police station for my appointment. I thought I was going to be talking to a female inspector, but it didn't work out that way. I'm ashamed to admit it now, but I put on this heavy female outfit—no makeup, but a skirt, sweater, boots—this whole creation thinking that it would give me more credence if I looked like what the police thought women should look like. I was afraid to go down there wearing pants, thinking they wouldn't listen to me or believe my story if I didn't appear feminine.

"I met with another inspector. When giving my statement, I talked like I'm speaking into a recorder, but this man had to write everything out by hand on long legal paper. He wanted to make sure everything was inserted in the right point in the text. He covered the ritualistic questions. Was there anal intercourse? Did he threaten my life? Did he have a weapon? I don't remember many of the other ones. I've blocked a whole lot out of my head. The questions continued, and I managed to complete the statement, read it, and sign it. He gave me a card with a number to call if I thought of anything else or saw anyone who looked suspicious.

"I went down a few more times to look at photographs. None looked familiar. After the third visit, while I looked at more pictures of people I'd never seen before, I was told there would be more to check. They never called again."

Beginning in the mid-1970s, many police departments began instigating new programs, personnel changes, and workshops, to upgrade the treatment of victims. While concerted efforts are being made, some of the most appalling attitudes are merely being muffled. Sensitivity and positive responses remain erratic. Policies and theories have improved, but the key rests with those who put them into practice on a daily basis.

Police feel they know best how to perform their job. They react guardedly to any outside suggestions. Some have become more receptive to training from victim support groups, but this has been most evident when this cooperation was mandated. Several of these groups have been recipients of Law Enforcement Assistance Administration grants, and the police must work with them as part of the grant requirements.

Even where police might want to make changes, they come up against problems. There are budget limitations and lack of personnel, especially women and ethnic minorities. Insufficient time is also cited. In some jurisdictions, officials believe the number of reported rapes does not justify any special programs or emphasis.

Two major shifts are the creation of special sex details or squads, and the inclusion of women officers on rape cases. Chicago and Los Angeles, for example, have tried using policewomen for the initial interview. They base this decision on the assumption that it will be less embarrassing and traumatic for the victim. They feel a woman will be able to draw more sensitive information from the victim. Chicago has also developed a procedure utilizing review analysts. They coordinate with sex crimes investigators in each section of the city. Then they examine the data, plot rapes on a pin map, and analyze the rapists' methods of operation, trying to ascertain patterns.

Los Angeles County has created an organization called the Sheriff's Comprehensive Rape Investigation Program. They have specially trained female deputies who investigate all rape cases. The deputies attend lectures, view rape-related videotapes, and are given training manuals. The focus is on the definition and exploration of issues involving rape, evidentiary material, the rapist, and counseling for the victim. The first evaluation revealed that the crime laboratory collected 70 percent more evidence than they had prior to the program's inception. A survey of victims indicated that they found their treatment by deputies helpful. Los Angeles is conducting research on the relative competency and sensitivity of male versus female investigators.

An examination of rape reporting procedures was undertaken by the Detroit police department. They emphasized the relationship of that crime to the need for improvements throughout the whole criminal justice system. First, they studied the currently employed methods dealing with the crime and the victim, the methods of educating the public and police, and the techniques of investigation and prosecution.

Then, they began a new approach. When a rape was reported, they dispatched an investigating team, consisting of one male and one female officer, directly to the rape scene, in addition to the normal marked-car response. Each team was provided with a kit for collecting evidence, both at the location of the crime and at the hospital. In some cases, tracking dogs were brought in. The investigators were coached and trained by senior officers. They tried to coordinate warrant requests with the prosecutor's office so none would be denied because of improper or incomplete police action, as had been prevalent in the past. They attempted to be more sensitive in their attitude not only to the victim but to her family also. They stressed the importance of follow-up on prosecution. The sites of all reported rapes were marked on a city map. When all leads had been exhausted in a case, it was then turned over to a unit which had responsibility for identifying rape patterns.

The Berkeley, California, department developed a unique comprehensive rape investigation policy. The services of a psychiatrist are offered without charge to all rape victims.

Minneapolis, Minnesota, instigated a training program for all patrol officers. They are required to view a videotape portraying the right and wrong method of questioning a victim during the first interview and at the hospital. There is a discussion period following the film. St. Louis, Missouri, and New York City also have videotapes, lectures, and workbooks for their officers. For a test period, New York officials had researchers sit in on interviews with victims to assess the investigators' technique and appropriateness of style. St. Paul, Minnesota, has mandatory seminars with lectures by victims, doctors, and emergency room nurses.

Originally, police were faulted for having few female employees. Victims had to contend with a steady stream of male figures. Often they felt this compounded the problem. As recently as 1972, most police forces had either a handful of female officers or none at all. Those that did employ women did not assign them to rape cases. In that year, Los Angeles had nearly 7,000 men and approximately 175 women officers; Miami, Florida, 700 men, 34 women; Des Moines, Iowa, more than 300 men, 3 women. Bangor, Maine, did not have any policewomen. Meridian, Mississippi, 100 police, all men. Salt Lake City, Utah, over 300 men, 2 women.

Now departments have been trying to remedy this, not only in sex details but also in the ranks of patrol officers. This has come about because of combined pressure from community groups and minority hiring programs. In 1976, Los Angeles had fewer women, but some were transferred to the sex detail. Miami had increased to 51 females. Des Moines had 319 men, 9 women; Bangor, 59 men, one woman. Meridian continued to exclude women from their force. Salt Lake City had 9 female officers.

Sex details which include both male and female investigators stretch across the country, but with large gaps in between. Cities that have made this change include New York City; Buffalo, New York; Baltimore, Maryland; Ft. Lauderdale, Florida; Akron, Ohio; Louisville, Kentucky; Indianapolis, Indiana; St. Paul, Minnesota; Minneapolis, Minnesota; Kansas City, Kansas; Austin, Texas; Tucson, Arizona; Seattle, Washington; Oakland, California; San Diego, California; and others.

Victim support groups were queried as to treatment by the police from 1975 to 1977. The results reveal measured improvement.

Joan Robins, director of education for the Los Angeles Commission on Assaults Against Women, stated that there has been progress, but they deal with so many departments within the county it is difficult to see and evaluate changes. "The officers in the black-and-whites have yet to receive adequate training."

A staff member from the Rape Crisis Center in Kansas City,

Kansas, wrote that their police have always been much better compared to others. Their sensitivity toward victims has increased since they began working together in 1973.

The Rape and Sexual Assault Center in Minneapolis opened in 1972. An advocate said, "Since then, the police department has participated in rape sensitivity training. Until recently we had nothing but positive feedback from victims on treatment by the police. In the fall of 1977, however, we have received many complaints about uninformed police officers and a few detectives in the sex division—judgmental comments, not taking the victim to the hospital for the evidentiary exam, and giving misleading information to victims."

The members of the Boston Area Rape Crisis Center have worked with and trained both the Boston and Cambridge police. They, too, see better conditions in the last few years.

Megan Ellis, from the Vancouver, British Columbia, Rape Relief, stated that their city police are "generally insensitive and quite often bungling." They receive four hours training in sexual assaults at the police college. Presently, they are working on changes in the rape curriculum at the police college. The attitude about rape varies among individuals, and certain officers have been known to refer victims to the Rape Relief. The Royal Canadian Mounted Police, which handles all cases outside the city boundaries, are much better. They are well trained and "seem to be more than thugs in uniform."

From the Lincoln, Nebraska, Rape Crisis Center came this response. The sensitivity of police toward victims has been excellent. They allow center members to prepare and present training for all officers. They have access to records, assist in some investigations, and are referred victims without hesitancy.

The Rape Relief organization in Seattle, Washington, had positive words. Jill Milholland explained that the police have improved with the special training which they provide on request. The police have told them their training sessions are "most informative" and "very good." They have received comments from victims who say the police are understanding or at least not making "gross mistakes."

The Rhode Island Rape Crisis Center covers the state, and each police force differs. Generally they have improved, but, as with other locales, they have their "prize good and bad officers."

Cincinnati, Ohio, Rape Crisis Center project director Suzanne Doerge explained that the sex crimes unit which was established several years ago was abolished in 1977 due to a cut in police spending. Now the homicide squad investigates all rapes. "Some of them are good, but most have a very insensitive shell." The center staff is teaching a class in the police academy and has begun getting referrals from the investigators.

Missoula, Montana, crisis center members view the police in a better light over the last two years. They have at least one advocate in each of the local city and county law enforcement agencies.

Rosalie Taylor, from the Oklahoma City, Oklahoma, Rape Crisis Center, felt somewhat encouraged. Until the summer of 1977, the police had been very unhelpful to victims. In October of that year, a sex crime unit was formed, with the crisis center providing part of their training. She looks for marked improvement because of this development.

An advocate from Chicago Women Against Rape summarized the feelings of many staff members nationwide. The attitude and treatment by police toward victims depended upon the woman's background, the circumstances of the assault, and the individual officers. Most of the men are still racist and sexist.

6: *Medical Mismanagement*

An immediate report of rape calls for the collection of medical and legal evidence. Behind that fact lie levels of personal perspective and conflicting priorities.

From the patrol officers' standpoint, it is their duty to gather all possible corroborative data regarding the crime. They must take the victim to a hospital for documentation of the presence or absence of motile spermatozoa, physical trauma, and information which might help identify the assailant.

But this can not be done at just any medical facility. Because there are legal ramifications and additional procedures for the staff to follow, most are reticent to admit rape victims. Neighborhood and university clinics, health maintenance organizations, and private hospitals state that they are unprepared to deal with these unique requirements. Many turn victims away. To preclude this, law enforcement officials coordinate with specific hospitals to ensure the victims' care.

In most locations, this means the victim is brought by police to the major public hospital. Traditionally, these are underfinanced, understaffed, and overcrowded. Most women are raped in the evening and early morning hours, the peak time for emergency room usage. The victim is simply another patient to be admitted and examined. She wishes she were anywhere but approaching the admissions desk with a uniformed patrol escort. She wants to be in a quiet, comfortable environment. Her needs are changing clothes, bathing, resting, and trying to erase the memories of what has occurred.

She does not want to be an object of curiosity. And she is just that. Heads rotate in her direction, whispered conversations begin among others awaiting treatment. Often she is not outwardly injured. There may be no broken bones, no blood. Thus the hospital staff considers her a low medical priority. If she is given preferential treatment, other patients might protest. She waits her turn.

The victim goes through a normal admissions process. She is asked her name, address, date of birth, whether she has insurance, and other pertinent information. Many cities, such as San Jose, California, have extra forms, "Permission for Medical Examination" and "Collection of Evidence." These are initiated by the police and signed by them and the victim. When she is under age, her parents or guardian must sign. Some hospitals provide police with all data relating to a victim without her signing a release form. After this step, she waits for her examination.

This period might seem longer than it is, because the woman is in shock. Two hospitals conducted surveys to determine the time lapse between the victim's being admitted and being seen by a doctor. Louisville General Hospital compiled statistics from February through October, 1974.[1] Approximately 10 percent had to wait a minimum of three hours, 25 percent two hours, 25 percent one hour. The rest began their examination after an hour or less wait. At Philadelphia General Hospital, 24 percent spent at least two hours prior to treatment, 15 percent were seen within two hours, 22 percent within one-and-a-half hours, 21 percent within an hour and 6 percent within a half hour. No figures were cited for the remaining 12 percent.[2]

The patrol officers must stay as well. If they leave, they will be faulted by their supervisors. Many search for outlets to pass the time. Frequently they know the emergency room personnel. It is easier to converse with them than with the victim. Occasionally, they check on others who come to their attention because of loudness or disorderly conduct.

Eventually, the woman provides either a nurse or doctor

with her basic medical history. Although this is a routine practice for any first visit, many view it as another invasion of privacy. Because she is going to have a pelvic exam, most questions deal with her sexual history. What is her marital status? Was she a virgin or nonvirgin? Is she using any form of birth control? What type? What was the date of her last period? Is her cycle regular? Has she ever been pregnant? What was the result, live birth, miscarriage, abortion? If she has children, what are their ages? When did she last have intercourse prior to the assault? Was the man using a condom? Are there any current problems such as venereal disease, vaginal infection? Her temperature and blood pressure are taken. And, finally, the evidentiary examination begins.

After their waiting a comparatively long period of time, many women said this check took only ten minutes. The length varies, depending on the severity of injuries, hospital protocol, thoroughness of the physician, and the age of the victim. Children may be sedated or administered an anesthetic prior to being examined.

At all designated hospitals the medical treatment includes taking a vaginal swab and briefly checking for external injuries, a sperm analysis, and a written report of the results. Beyond those items, there is a wide assortment of procedures. Some test for acid phosphotase, the semen component identifying blood type. Most turn over the victim's clothing to the police as evidence. These are checked for soil, twigs, leaves, hair, and fibers, which the officers judge as important, but many doctors disregard. Bloodstained items are air dried before being placed in containers and given to the police.

Frequently a victim's pubic hair is combed to collect any loose strands that may be the assailant's. Samples of her hair are obtained. One hospital adds the detail that twelve or more hairs "should be pulled out and packaged separately from any collected by combing. These should include the roots and must not be cut." Fingernail scrappings are taken if the victim scratched her attacker.

In appropriate cases, dry swabs are done of the anal area. Sometimes a blood sample is required. This is used not only to ascertain blood type, but also to determine if the victim were intoxicated. Any obvious external injuries are checked, recorded, and treated. A nurse may photograph her as further evidence of assault.

Some procedures necessitate the physicians making a judgment about the victim's mental and physical appearance. They indicate descriptive characteristics such as "apparently normal, agitated, angry, crying, hysterical, lethargic, unconscious, verbose, other."

The woman is told about follow-up treatment for venereal disease, infection, and pregnancy. Between four and six weeks after the attack, she should be tested for these. Although it would be more beneficial if this information were provided in written form as well, few hospitals do this. If the victim believes pregnancy is possible, she is prescribed the "morning-after pill," diethylstibestrol (DES) 25 mg. twice daily for five days. Most physicians explain the immediate side effects of this potent drug, but rarely mention the possible long-range damage. It is even more unusual when they discuss alternatives to DES.

A few hospital staffs strive to lessen or alleviate some of the psychological trauma. They have social workers and support groups on call, or refer victims to trained individuals to answer their questions and offer extended assistance. While this is often the victims' most pressing requirement, it is the least likely to be provided by hospital personnel.

Nurses surveyed feel that doctors should inform victims about all these follow-up measures, from future tests to available counseling. Doctors state that they are the more overworked, so nurses can perform this job. The line of responsibility wavers back and forth. Victim support groups often claim that both physicians and nurses could improve. They have prepared seminars or workshops based on practical, firsthand experience after dealing with hundreds of victims. The professionals say they do not have the time, inclination, or desire to have lay people inform them how to do their work.

These personal concerns clash together. No one is completely right or wrong. It is a matter of degree. But the process can be smoothed without a tremendous strain. The hospital staff, above all others, should recognize that a victim is in a life crisis. She deserves a simple procedure, tailored to her medical and emotional needs.

When the victim is uninformed about what procedure she will be completing, this hospital visit becomes dismaying. No woman enjoys a pelvic examination, even under normal circumstances. When she is confronted by a series of hurried, uncaring medical people, her mental turmoil heightens. What appear to be nonfrightening events, take on different interpretations to victims.

Meanwhile, the police are required to stay near the examining room to answer any questions the physicians may have and to receive evidence. If they enter the room, they are overstepping bounds. The officers and staff determine the balance, not the victim. She feels stripped of control and privacy once more.

After the evidentiary examination, the victim is taken by officers to her home. Adding a last insult to this procedure, most women are billed for this required medical verification of the rape. Generally, public hospitals charge a minimum of $20. Private hospitals cost the victim as much as $75. If there are rape-related injuries, the price of that treatment is added. Although many hospitals flag these accounts and do not dun the victim if she does not pay, the bill is another reminder of the attack. A few states have crime compensation laws which, under limited situations, partially reimburse victims of reported crimes.

The police and attorneys are not asking doctors to make a legal decision whether rape occurred. Rather, they want a medical expert to aid in gathering evidence and to be available to testify in court. The physicians assert that they have been trained in medicine, not evidence-collecting techniques. They do not want to fulfill this role, let alone have to consider interrupting their schedules with court appearances.

To moderate the debate, some locales have developed protocols on the treatment of rape victims. With the doctors' responsibilities clearly defined, problems would cease. But when the New York Health and Hospital Corporation devised such a procedure, physicians refused to follow it. It took too long. Then the American College of Gynecologists and Obstetricians prepared one for nationwide distribution that was more amenable. Some hospitals are now utilizing those suggestions.

Toronto, Ontario, police provided their designated hospital with "Guidelines to the Collection of Physical Evidence by the Physician." It is typical of protocols found in Canada and the United States. It combines practical information, advice, and justifications for their recommended methods.

Since the rules of evidence require that a "chain of continuity" be proven before an object can be admitted as an exhibit at a trial, the chain should be kept as short as possible. This is best accomplished by having the physician or the nurse who collects the samples, hand them directly to the investigating police officer. He should know the proper methods for preserving, packaging, and properly labelling each item. All that is then required of the physician are his initials on each item or label.

Since any court action may not take place for several months after the examination, careful notes should be made during or immediately following the examination. The rules of evidence, if strictly followed, allow a witness only to refresh his memory by reference to notes made personally at the event.

If, for any reason, the police officer cannot be given the items directly, there are a few points for the physician to keep in mind. All items must be identified in such a way that they can be recognized months later as the specific items concerned and not just as something of a similar type. This is usually accomplished by fixing a tag to the item (or its container where appropriate). The tag should bear the following information: 1. The name of the complainant. 2. A brief description of the item (e.g., "blue shirt taken from Jane Doe"). 3. The time, date, and place where the item was collected. 4. The initials or signature of the physician.

Some care should be taken with the description on the tag to avoid anything that a court might consider improper or inflammatory. For example, "Torn, bloodstained panties from rape victim" on a tag would probably result in the panties not being accepted as an exhibit. An acceptable description would be "Panties taken from Jane Doe at 8:50 P.M., 17th of November, 1972, at the Toronto General Hospital."

The entire sequence the doctor must follow takes five pages to describe. That is a great deal of work, much of which is clerical. But a physician is required to complete it, while wondering whether that is the best use of his time.

Who performs these tests is dictated by the individual hospital. Many locations assign interns or residents. This presents possible difficulties, because they are the least experienced physicians. If a trial does occur, the delay between the attack and a courtroom appearance is long. Many interns and residents have finished their programs, moved, and may be hard to locate.

Some hospitals use a family practice doctor. The rationale is that the person is trained to approach medical problems in light of the impact on an entire family. Others feel emergency room doctors are best, because they have experience in trauma treatment. When the victim is a child, pediatricians are frequently called upon. A few places, such as New Orleans, rely on coroners. Most hospitals assign gynecologists this duty. In several areas, for example Central Emergency Hospital in San Francisco, the physicians are civil servants. They are paid a relatively low hourly wage and rotate among the city's public hospitals.

Although less than 10 percent of reported rapes get to the final trial stage, examining physicians worry about being required to testify. An alarming situation was revealed when the case *United States* v. *Benn* was appealed in 1973 in the District of Columbia circuit court. At the trial, no doctor had been summoned to give corroborative evidence of penetration or assault because a medical report of injuries had been submitted which varied from police photographs of the victim's bruises. During the trial, the prosecutor stated that the doctors at the hospital to which the victim was taken were purposely providing such negative medical reports of rape victims so they would not be subpoenaed. The appellate court requested that the Department of Justice inquire into the matter.

This is not the only example of record falsification. But something that occurs much more widely is incomplete and inaccurate information on the forms. Because these are less help in court, the doctor will be unlikely to be called to appear. This action is not intentional. Rather, not all medical staff members are clear what evidence is needed. They may fill out forms too quickly, but without malice.

To alleviate this, a few courts are experimenting with permitting doctors to testify on closed circuit television from the hospitals. Others have been using certified written reports instead of personal courtroom attendance.

The primary purpose of the medical procedure is to document the presence or absence of motile spermatozoa. That appears uncomplicated, until you consider this information. In 1972, the pathologists at St. Paul-Ramsey Hospital, Minnesota, examined 504 cases of reported rape. Sperm was not found in all cases, but not because an attack had not taken place. They believed this happened because the rapist was sterile or had undergone a vasectomy. They recommended tests for semen as well as for sperm. When used together, the tests would be 95 percent accurate up to twelve hours after the assault.

In 1977, Drs. A. Nicholas Groth and Ann Wolbert Burgess published these findings.[3] They studied 170 men convicted of sexual assault, incarcerated at Massachusetts Center for the Diagnosis and Treatment of Sexually Dangerous Persons. They compared this data with statements and medical reports from ninety-two adult rape victims treated at the Boston City Hospital emergency room. These victims were judged convincing and consistent in their rape reports. The offenders and victims were unrelated.

The results revealed numerous sexual dysfunctions among the rapists. The most common was partial or complete failure to achieve erection. These offenders were described as having "conditional impotence." Many women interviewed for this book noted the same situation, especially when the rape was by a stranger. They had been forced to commit fellatio or masturbation of the assailant during the course of the rape, because he was unable to achieve an erection.

The second problem cited most often was retarded ejaculation. Approximately 15 percent were in this category. This figure is high when compared to the general male population, where it is an infrequent complaint. Premature ejaculation either prior to or immediately upon penetration was another assailant problem, although this occurred least often. So for this sample there was a high rate of erective and ejaculatory dysfunction during the assault.

For the victims participating in the study, even with complete data and other clinical evidence of rape, in only thirty-two of sixty-nine cases was there presence of motile sperm. Twenty-three women were raped by more than one man, yet in half these cases there were negative laboratory tests for sperm. In the thirty-seven cases where no sperm was found, the physician recorded definite physical trauma in twenty-seven patients.

The absence of sperm does not mean a woman has not been raped. This could be traced to sterility, a vasectomy, or sexual dysfunction. But medical verification remains one of the cornerstones of the police and legal procedure. The woman must submit to this test.

A further irony in this area was brought out by a survey completed in 1968.[4] While medical examinations were given to 60 percent of the women in reported rapes, the results were used by the police in only 18 percent of the complaints. And then they were generally used to decide whether the case was unfounded. The catch is that police insist on medical verification if the rape occurred not longer than seventy-two hours before the report. They discredit or do not believe the woman if she refuses. Yet they make little use of the evidence derived from the examination when deciding whether to investigate.

The woman becomes dehumanized. She is not a victim, but a witness of a crime for the state. At the hospital, she is treated as evidence. Finally her selfconcept moves to that of an obstacle course runner. If she fails to vault any barrier, stumbles over an illogically justified step in the entire reporting procedure, she will be barred from the race.

Most interviewees said their examinations were performed very rapidly and with little kindness. Scientific tests which could have been employed to gather more information about the rapist were not completed. Those done seemed meaningless. All these accumulated negative factors contributed to make their rape experience more traumatic and long-lasting. It was not the incident alone, but that coupled first with the police approach and then with the medical profession, those people set up by society to help the victims, not process and judge them. All the questions, the required responses, the retelling of the event, made the women feel as if they would never be left to their solitude and mental recovery.

Ellen was raped by a stranger who broke into her apartment. When the patrol officer said he needed medical verification, she asked to be taken to her private physician.

Ellen recalled, "The policeman told me that was impossible. I could see him at some later date, but first I had to go to the one hospital in town that did 'rape examinations.' I hadn't been beaten up. The man had been armed with a chisel, so I wasn't about to fight.

"Since I was crying so much and wasn't too coherent, they finally bent to my pleas to have my girl friend accompany me. We all drove there, and just the drive seemed endless. The attack had taken place at about four in the morning, and by this time it was nearly six. There was no one else waiting for emergency treatment, so I only had to sit there for about a half hour. There were questions to answer, forms to complete, but in my case it definitely helped to have my friend present. At that point I couldn't even get my phone number straight. Eventually a nurse took me into a small, boxlike examining room and merely said to take off my pants and underpants.

"She was an older woman, maybe at the end of a night shift. She handed out the minimum amount of instructions her position needed and left out the human element. I took off my clothes and sat on the table. Even the table was uncomfortably cold. The nurse hadn't given me a sheet to cover myself the way they usually do, so I sat there while she seated herself at the opposite side of the room.

"I started crying again, or maybe I'd never really stopped, and she frowned. Her next order was to spread my legs, because the doctor was coming into the room. I did what I was told. Five minutes went by, still no doctor, so I removed my legs from the stirrups. Almost simultaneously, I heard this bark from across the room 'open your legs!' It was unbelievable.

"I was determined I wasn't going to let her beat me down. I didn't open my legs, instead I just hunched over, assuming almost a fetal position for subconscious protection against her commands. The crying continued, the fear, anguish, and growing confusion about finding myself in a situation that I seemed totally incapable of altering.

"By the time the physician arrived, I'd lost complete control. I felt there was no place to go for any type of help or comfort. He simply breezed into the room, didn't say a word, ask my name, my problem, nothing. He stuck a speculum up me, got a slidefull of whatever he wanted, and walked out. That was that."

To understand Christine's frame of mind when she arrived at the hospital, additional details are required. She was on her first date with a man she had recently met. He suggested a drive in the country, and what began as a pleasant evening ended in a violent rape. Christine still bears a thin, red scar on the side of her face, a constant reminder of that night. The man was never apprehended.

"During the whole ordeal, I'd never felt such hostility aimed at me," Christine related. "I tried to think while it was happening—the beating, slapping, vile comments—what I had done to that man to make him act that way. I was there. That's all I'd done. I started remembering everything I'd ever read in the papers, seen in the movies, had friends tell me about rape, and I still didn't know what to do to escape him. My mind was really racing. I'm ashamed to say I doubt if it's ever worked as fast in my life. It was like a machine gun firing at full tilt.

"I went through so many mood changes, trying to pick a role I could hold him at. He's saying this. What does it mean? I know he wanted to frighten me. He seemed to enjoy that part the most. He was playing with me, and I tried to think who could have toyed with him like that before to have made him want revenge such as this. I wondered, could I become the person that played with him and show him he didn't have to be that way? I was hoping to analyze and cure him in that moment to save my life.

"I told him I knew he could be gentle. 'You could be kind. I liked you before. I don't want you to be like this.' And he'd listen. It was like I was almost convincing him, and then he'd get really, violently angry.

"After he'd raped me, he let his guard down a bit. I still remember running away from him across a field. There was only one thing on my mind—survival. I thought, 'Is this how it is for animals? Is this how it is during a war? It must be. I'm fighting for my life. What have I done wrong?'

"I found a house, pounded and screamed until a man answered with, 'What the hell's going on?' By this time it must have been one in the morning, and I don't know who was more alarmed, myself or the man who opened the door. I was standing on his steps, using a small rag to try and cover my body, shivering, bleeding, and crying, 'Call the police, call the police!'

"Even as I said that, I knew I wasn't sure what I wanted to do. All I really wanted was to be alone for a while to recover, catch my breath. But I knew I also needed some medical attention. He did call them, and when they arrived they began questioning not me but the man who lived there. Gangrene could have been setting in, and they didn't seem to care. Finally, the policeman turned to me and said they'd take me to a hospital. I was in such a state of panic I thought they could possibly dump me off in the middle of nowhere and no one would ever know who or where I was.

"I realized that if I had a cigarette I'd have a weapon. One of the cops was smoking, so I asked him if I could please have a cigarette. Then I gave them a complete description of the man who'd attacked me, and do you know how they answered me? 'Why should we take your word for it?' I didn't know how to contain my anger.

"By the time we arrived at the hospital, I was openly hostile. It was the only defense I could muster. People were standing around the emergency room, giving me dirty looks as if I'd done something wrong. I don't know why, but I expected someone to come over, pat me on the back, and say, 'You've got guts, you know.' I expected a particle of sympathy, that's all.

"Eventually I was sent into see a gynecologist. Among other things, I'd injured my knee, and it was extremely painful, especially when the nurse was trying to bend my leg to put it in the stirrup on the examining table. After what I'd been through, I just couldn't stand anymore pain. I cried out, 'Please, look at my knee. Can't you see I'm hurt?' They seemed so unaware that I was a human being with feelings. The doctor didn't care, either. The only time he made any comment was when he was listing my injuries and mentioned, 'This wouldn't have happened if you hadn't been such a pretty girl.' I had no idea whether he meant that as a compliment or criticism. After that, he just did what was required, and probably hurried back to bed.

"The room I was in became crowded with specialists, doctors, nurses, police. I should have felt like a guinea pig, only I'm sure they treat them better than they were acting toward me. Someone from the laboratory came and scraped underneath my fingernails to get bits of the rapist's skin. Another person was checking my body to see if they could find any 'foreign' hairs. All this time, God, I was in so much pain I couldn't see.

"It was like a circus, and I was all three acts at once. Then I was wheeled down to be x-rayed, and they told me I'd have to have an operation because my jaw was broken. A nurse came in, and she was somebody to talk to. I don't know, but it was very reassuring to hear the sound of my own voice. I'd been having so many mental conversations that I wasn't even sure if I was capable of communicating with another person. I kept talking and talking. I only wanted someone to be on my side, to agree with me. After a while, she asked, 'Why did you fight so much?'

"What a thing to say. Why didn't someone praise me for resisting so bravely? I can't imagine they would have been more sympathetic if I hadn't been hurt. You can't seem to win any way you act.

"Before I was assigned to a room, another nurse came up to me to record my injuries. She asked if there were any aside from those she could see, so I opened my robe to show her. And the policeman looked and leered, too. He didn't have to do that. The officers had been coldly professional up until then.

"I must have been going into shock, because I was continually shivering. The nurse brought me one extra blanket, and then said that was all I was allocated. I could pay for it, but they said I'd used up my supply.

"Because I had so many injuries, including the broken jaw, I had to stay in the hospital. The next day, several nurses were hovering around, getting me ready for the operation. They'd say things like, 'Gee, she looks like she *used* to be a pretty girl.' 'What nice teeth, it would be a shame if she had to lose some.' Those lovely nurses, those angels of mercy, they would have shown more kindness to a dog.

"They'd strapped me down to the table, and I couldn't move. I was fighting and fighting. All I wanted was someone to say, 'It's okay.' But they didn't. They were too busy jabbing me with needles and tubes. Every time one of the nurses would put a needle in me, my arm would jump. Next, they needed a urine sample. I explained all I had to do was relax for a minute. I was like a big, tense muscle. If they'd only let me do it my way. I'd be able to give them their sample, but they wanted it that minute. A schedule had to be met.

"The next performer was the anesthesiologist. He was so blasé, saying, 'My name is doctor so-and-so. I'm your anesthesiologist. I'll be assisting in the operation.' He was like an actor whom I was watching on TV and he was walking to the edge of the set to chat. There was no interaction between us. When I just looked at him and then turned away, he asked one of the nurses, 'What's her problem?'

"It was getting to be too much. So many things had been done to my body without my approval, and no one could comprehend that. I'd never had an operation before and wasn't even sure what they'd be doing to my jaw. I thought it would probably be wired at the top and bottom so I'd still be able to open my mouth. Once the operation was completed, I discovered they'd wired it shut. I was in such a confused mental state, I actually thought I'd died. I remember shaking my head, trying to get my jaws apart. The nurses were back with me. I became so mad because I could hear them talking about me again, but I couldn't answer them.

"I kept trying to speak, but it was hard because the outside of my mouth was swollen. My jaws were immobile. Whenever I started to say anything, I'd begin choking and crying. I was struggling to maintain control, but it seemed nearly impossible. After I'd get a few words out to the nurses, I'd look at their eyes waiting for the feeling you get when you know you're getting through. I hoped for that moment, but it rarely came. Maybe I was being unfair, but I was seeking some encouragement, some warmth.

"Because I was in the hospital for three days and my condition was improving, some nurses did change their attitude toward me. One came in who was the sweet, motherly, cutie-pie type. She patted my bed and said she wanted to say good-bye. She was going off duty and probably wouldn't see me again. She said, 'You take care now.' 'Take care'—and I cherished those words. That was all I wanted."

Claire was beaten and raped by an acquaintance. She had a more positive experience at the hospital, but wished their treatment had gone farther.

"Time is difficult to estimate, for I was aware of so little. I had to give them my clothes, fill out forms, and then receive treatment. They dealt with me very objectively, not as if I were a poor baby, but they were decent. The doctor who attended me didn't talk much. He took a smear and asked if there were a chance of pregnancy. When I said there was, he told me he was giving me one shot to protect me from conceiving and another against venereal disease. I had to sign a consent form in order to receive that medication.

"I had not looked at myself since the rape occurred and didn't know the extent of injuries until the doctor began asking about the scrapes and scratches on my inner legs. I was not even sure where they had come from. In fact, I didn't know how many bruises I had for twelve hours at least, which was the next time I was home.

"I never came in contact with a nurse except the one who led me into the examination room and stayed during the check. In retrospect, I realized a man had given me the forms to complete. The doctor was a man. The officers were men. But my immediate reaction wasn't that there was no woman to comfort and understand me. At that particular moment, I didn't really want anyone handling my body, male or female. I hadn't stopped to think beyond that point.

"It's hard to evaluate their medical procedure. I would

have liked a tranquilizer, but felt embarrassed to admit I wanted that as an avenue of temporary escape. Looking back, I would have liked to have known just exactly what drug the physician gave me to prevent conception. No one has been able to figure that out because it was a single shot, not a prescription for a drug. I have always been wary of any type of medication and only occasionally take an aspirin. But all these thoughts came to me later. When I was at the hospital, I was simply functioning."

Jackie was raped at night by a stranger. "I called the police because I didn't know what else to do. After the questioning, they took me to a hospital, put me in a room, and disappeared. I was alone, wondering why I was there, having no one around to ask, wishing I could go home. Finally, I pulled myself together to find someone to ask what was happening. It was like notifying each part of my body that it was going to move in a coordinated manner. 'Okay, legs, swing off the table. Arms, help me up.' I felt like an automaton, with the controls buried somewhere inside me.

"The lighting was different in the room where I'd been, and as I walked into the hallway I felt my pupils widening to take in the dimness. I located one of the cops, who was standing around drinking that horrible institution coffee, and asked just what was I waiting for. My clothes had already been confiscated. I wasn't mortally wounded. I wanted a little information.

"A gray-haired nurse, who was behind a large, wooden counter, overheard my question and said I had to have a pelvic exam. Still that didn't help. 'Why did I have to have that done?' was my dumb response. I knew I wasn't bleeding. I knew exactly what he'd done to me, what affect it had had. The policeman told me they had to see if there was any damage. Damage? I couldn't understand that either, because I should know if there were any. Of course, later I learned from my reading on the subject they were checking for sperm, but they didn't even offer me that logical explanation that I could have understood.

"After about an hour where I was told to go back into the room by myself, a doctor wandered in to see me. He gave me a shot of something, I think tetracycline, to prevent VD. When he questioned me about the possibility of pregnancy, I answered honestly, 'No, because I'm taking birth-control pills.' With that, his attitude changed. 'Well, I note on your chart you're single,' he said. And then there was a long pause. My God, I was twenty-three years old. He should have been glad I had the wisdom to use some preventive measure, but his approach was disintegrating from cold formality to outright hostility. Obviously, since I wasn't a virgin, I hadn't been raped. That seemed to be his unspoken thought. If I'd been a virgin, he was probably the kind who would have thought I was suffering from repressed sexual longings and had given in to them with that stranger.

"Suddenly, I realized how tired I was. My foremost idea was getting out of there. The rape had taken place at around one. The police were at my house for another hour. I'd been at the hospital for well over an hour. I was drained by the constant flow of energy and emotion. I wanted out."

Even though Marsha's assault included forced fellatio, not vaginal penetration, the police took her to the hospital for an examination.

"We entered the hospital, and hurry-up-and-wait became the key of the next few hours. I think you should include pictures of some hospital emergency rooms. They're often just incredibly bad. This one was stark white, with cold, cement walls. A strange assortment of magazines was strewn around on a low table between some of the couches. There were several other people sitting there with me. One was a man who was very drunk. I don't know why he was there, except it was obvious he'd been drinking a great deal, because he kept nearly falling out of the wheelchair they had him in. A young girl of about seven was waiting to be seen, too. She'd been raped by her older brother and seemed in fairly good shape, but her mother was hysterical.

"So there we were, all together waiting for some attention. After about one or two hours, I was instructed to go into an adjoining room. I don't know what they might officially call it, but it looked like a small dormitory with about eight beds, each divided from the next by movable partitions on rollers. I sat down on the bed I'd been assigned, which was next to a woman who probably was an alcoholic. She had little coordination left, and I was sure any minute she'd roll off the bed and thud onto the concrete floor. All the activity and immediate treatment was directed toward her. I just thought about what would happen when my turn came.

"Some member of the hospital staff, possibly a nurse out of uniform, passed by my bed, and I asked her what could I expect as an examination. She told me she was busy with the other woman, and a doctor would see me shortly. Another half hour went by. Then some man came up to me, again with no type of uniform, and stated he was required to swab my mouth. While he was doing that, he groused that they usually didn't find anything from this procedure, but he had to do it anyway. After he'd finished, he asked if I'd had anything to drink or expelled anything from my mouth since the incident had occurred. I thought the question was verging on the absurd, because of course I'd 'expelled' the semen from my mouth.

"He didn't mention anything about venereal disease, but he did tell me to lean over so he could give me two penicillin shots in my bottom. I had been hit on the arm, but since there was no bruise the physician said there was no point in examining it. His exam was short and functional, lasting only a few minutes. As it was they didn't discover any traces of sperm or semen. The case was temporarily dropped. The police mentioned to me, and I'm not quite sure why they were so truthful, that unless they pushed the hospital to find evidence

the doctors often didn't come up with any. Also, the laboratory technicians seem to have a local reputation for losing
whatever evidence does come in. After a two-and-a-half-hour
wait for a ten-minute check which revealed nothing, I was
sent away."

Lilith described her experience when the police took her
for medical verification.

"By the time we reached the hospital, it must have been
four in the morning. The place was probably built at the turn
of the century and had an oppressive atmosphere. There was
a gnarled, older man, I'd say in his fifties or sixties, behind
a counter with a large yellow book. It looked like an ancient
hotel register, with countless lines and numbers to fill in.
Apparently this is a log for rape victims, either rape or assault
or possibly both. I had to sign my name, and they put in some
numbers for codes.

"At this point I know, because my memories about it are
more and more grotesque, I was literally in shock, getting
farther and farther away from what was happening. The police had me wait while they went and talked to a doctor, who
then called me into an examining room. It was 'The Examining Room' out of a classic horror movie. There was an incredibly unsympathetic nurse who seemed to pride herself
on being brusque and rude. The doctor I'm sure they'd un-
wrapped from a similar science fiction show.

"She told me to sit down, but there weren't any chairs so
I just sat on the floor. This irritated her, because I was patiently resting there, picking little leaves and things out of my
clothes. Bits of burrs and briars were on my jeans, so I
became very preoccupied with systematically pulling them
out one by one. When it was finally time for the examination,
I don't even remember getting undressed. I've blocked that
out of my mind, but I guess I had to. What I remember are
the cosmetics of the scene. The ceiling with its cracks and
crevices. That crinkly, white, stiff hospital paper. I don't recall more than that, but I know it must have happened. I have

a hard enough time going to a gynecologist for a checkup, and this was like I was completely gone.

"The doctor might as well have been examining someone in the last stages of leprosy. He didn't mind showing his disgust at all. He looked at the cuts on my face and listed everything as required. I knew I wasn't as attractive as I might have been, but I wasn't that repulsive because of blood or dirt or filth. He touched me very carefully, cleaned my face a little. There was a cut inside my mouth which he found exceptionally distasteful. Since he didn't want to deal with it at all, he ignored it.

"When he talked, he sounded like a robot with a mechanical tape recorder going in his mouth. He gave some spiel that went very fast, about VD. 'If you have any signs of this or that come back in the next two weeks. The Department of Public Health blah blah blah.' It came out in rigid, computerized words.

"Neither the doctor nor the nurse offered any advice or suggestions on what psychological problems I might develop as a result of the rape. It seemed completely out of the question for them. They seemed bothered that they even had to treat me in the first place. They did the minimum they had to do and forgot the fact that I was a human being with emotional needs."

Carolyn was raped a short distance from a private hospital. Although they refused her treatment, they did summon the police.

"That visit to the second hospital was probably one of the worst parts of the evening. The emergency room was a poor indicator of what such a place should be. The hallway where I had to stand was cold and poorly lighted. Dull yellow lines that you could follow to lead you to other sections of the hospital had specks of congealed blood on them. There was the odor of vomit from one of the wastepaper baskets. The cops made me stand there, wondering what would happen next, while they hollered at a drunk for a while. All I wanted to do was sit down, but I had to obtain approval for that.

"It's hard to relate the total lack of control over my life and body I withstood from the moment I felt myself followed by the rapist to beyond the police and hospital encounter. Eventually, they unearthed a nurse who took me into an examining room. Unearthed became too true a word. While I began undressing, she started asking all kinds of questions. 'Was he black?' 'Did he hurt you?' 'What did he make you do?' And then ended with the delightful fact that some of the other women who came in there looked so terrible. They were all cut up and disfigured. I don't know what causes people to say such insensitive things. Do they really believe they're comforting you?

"She continued to press me about where it had happened, how long he'd taken, and other details I could dredge up. It was demeaning. She treated me as if I were a best-seller pornography book. When the doctor came in, he heard her last words and reprimanded her because she was supposed to be working and not asking all those questions. Then *he* started doing the same thing. He'd called her down for not being professional and then slipped into it, too. These weren't questions he had to ask for a police report, but ones he'd thought of on his own. I don't know if hospital personnel get detached because they're always working with crisis cases, but they certainly didn't offer me any warmth or understanding when I needed it the most.

"The doctor gave me a very inept pelvic exam, told me I'd have to wait before having a pregnancy test, and sent me down to the VD clinic. Since I wasn't carried in piece by piece to be sewn back together, he didn't seem concerned about any mental injuries."

Betsy hesitated before reporting her rape, because the assailant was an acquaintance. After deliberating for several hours, she placed a call to the police. Her treatment is representative of that by hospital staffs who have instigated new procedures for victims.

"Being raped was the most horrifying, degrading experience I'd ever had. What made it more bearable was my reception at the hospital. When I was brought in, a nurse appeared at my side. She began comforting me and then slowly explaining the steps I'd have to follow. She seemed to anticipate my feelings and thoughts.

"Because it was around three in the morning, I was concerned that my roommates might be worried about me. The nurse said she'd make sure they were called if that's what I wanted. After I'd filled out some forms, she took me to a secluded waiting area. Even though she looked tired, she stayed with me the entire time.

"When the doctor came into the examining room, I felt more able to handle the tests because I'd had some time to talk about my fears with the nurse. She had said he'd have to take a medical history. He wasn't asking these questions because he doubted my word. They needed this so their records would be accurate, and I wouldn't be in any danger. As he went through the process, he told me what he was doing. 'I'm going to comb your pubic hair because frequently that of the assailant is transfered to your body.' 'I'm taking a vaginal washing.' At first when he started asking things like was there anal intercourse, I was embarrassed and confused. Then he told me he didn't want to miss anything, ignore any possible damage.

"As he began looking at the scratches on my body, he asked whether I had scratched the offender. I couldn't remember, so the doctor checked my fingernails. He explained that sometimes they found cell particles which could be useful in identifying the offender. He maintained a detached attitude, but it helped calm me down. Anytime I started to freak out, the nurse was right there to soothe me. I wasn't going to fall apart, but I needed a little extra strength. Mine had been used up.

"The physician told me there was always a chance I'd been exposed to VD. He said I could either wait and be tested, or he'd give me penicillin shots right away. I decided to get it over with then. After he left the room, the nurse took me to a shower area. She said I was welcome to clean up there, or

I could leave immediately. They even had some used clothes for me to put on, because they'd given mine to the police. While I was dressing, she gave me some mimeographed sheets of information. She told me that that was something they'd just started. They included all the things she talked about concerning pregnancy testing, VD, abortions. It had names and phone numbers of people and groups to call for later help.

"The nurse said that sometimes women had delayed reactions to rape. If I felt alone or needed any support or suggestions, be sure and call the numbers on the list. I have only good words for their compassion, efficiency, and treatment. I hope more hospitals follow this lead."

Although a victim might believe she has no rights and requests regarding the hospital protocol, she can exercise some control.

If she is embarrassed to enter an emergency room with uniformed police, she could inquire whether a plainclothes officer can accompany her. When the prospect of waiting in the emergency room receiving area upsets her, she should see what alternatives there might be. Some hospitals have semiprivate areas for rape victims. In other cases, there are sections of the hospital which are less frequently used and quieter, where she could remain until the doctor is ready to see her.

Because the medical procedure is rarely explained, she should ask what is expected of her. Being prepared reduces the strain and confusion. When there are no release forms provided for her signature, she should ask whether her medical history and clinical records will be turned over to the police without her consent. If she does not approve of this, she can discuss the matter with the police and hospital personnel.

Many examinations are so brief that physical damage may be overlooked. A victim does not have to feel self-conscious. If anal or oral sodomy occurred, she should inform the physician. This is not something that is automatically checked. Any unusual crime-related injuries should be mentioned to the doctor.

A victim who believes pregnancy might result from the rape could consider other measures instead of DES. The effectiveness of this drug is not guaranteed, and it rarely works when begun more than seventy-two hours after the attack. Frequently it causes extreme nausea, dizziness, headaches, depression, cramps, allergic reactions, or water and salt retention. A few women have had a copper 7 IUD inserted at the time of the examination. This was then left in place as a contraceptive method or removed after the danger of pregnancy was over.

Menstrual extraction is another possible alternative. Doctors' opinions vary as to what time lapse is best before performing the extraction. Some say four weeks after the woman's last period. Others feel that at least six days after the attack is sufficient. It is similar to a suction abortion, is generally effective, and the risks are low. A victim might wait until the anticipated date of her next menstrual cycle. If she misses a period, she can be tested for pregnancy within a month. A small number of rape victims, 5 to 10 percent, do become pregnant. This devastating outcome can be remedied by an early suction, or vacuum aspiration, abortion. It is a short, relatively inexpensive procedure, that can be performed in a doctor's office.

Only a handful of hospitals provide the victim with written information about possible follow-up tests. She could ask for a contact person and telephone number where she can call to receive complete data.

Any time a victim wants a supportive person present, ask. A friend, family member, or advocate may be allowed to fill this capacity.

While the vast majority of victims do not suffer nervous breakdowns because of the attack, emotional and physiological problems can develop. A woman should consult with the hospital staff about the availability of counselors or advocates to talk to immediately or at a later date.

Even if a victim does not report her rape, it is important that she secure some type of medical attention. There could be damage or trauma to the vaginal/anal area. She might have been exposed to venereal disease. If she believes she could have become impregnated, she should be checked for this. Counseling could be provided. A woman does not have to inform the examining physician about the rape if she wants to maintain her privacy. She can request the tests without explaining the reasons behind her concerns.

Some hospitals will treat a victim without notifying the police, but this is a chance the woman must take. Because small clinics and private physicians do not see a large number of victims, they are concerned about the possible legal results. The interviewees who had sought these services received mixed responses. In several instances, they were pressured to contact a law enforcement agency. Other doctors reacted in the opposite manner, hesitating to test for sperm, because the woman might eventually change her mind and report. Unless a victim goes to a free clinic or has some form of medical coverage, she will be billed. Victims of unreported crimes do not qualify for any possible state compensation funds.

Scattered across the country, there are hospital personnel trying to improve their protocol for rape victims, as well as provide additional services. Rape examination kits are now found in more jurisdictions. These have been developed either individually by police, advocate groups, or hospital staffs, or by their combined efforts. The kits' contents generally include an explanation of the steps for the nurse and physician to follow while checking a victim of sexual assault. There are sterile gloves, plastic swabs, packages, plastic envelopes, slides, labels, syringes, and so on. When the examination is completed, the entire kit with the collected evidence is given to the police.

Other hospitals have also focused on more sensitive treatment toward victims and on long-range assistance. Philadelphia General Hospital was one of the first. They have coordinated programs involving volunteer advocates, psychiatrists, therapists, and social workers. The members of Women Organized Against Rape were the driving force behind the initial changes.

The Seattle Sexual Assault Center at Harborview Hospital has been another leader in this field. Specified doctors and social workers are trained in caring for sexual assault victims. They work closely and well with the Seattle Rape Relief. Other hospitals in that city are not as progressive. They find it easier to refer all victims to Harborview, instead of following the example of good, substantive treatment.

The main public hospital in Tucson, Arizona, and that in Denver, Colorado, have special follow-up clinics. Prior to that, the Denver hospital staff had been cited for their lack of sensitivity, which included listing the woman's name and the word 'rape' on a large bulletin board while she awaited help. St. Luke's in Kansas City, Missouri, one of the few private hospitals to accept rape victims, has developed extended services, including referrals. At Breckenridge Hospital in Austin, Texas, social workers meet the victim and take her through the first portion of the hospital procedure. They then work with the local rape crisis center volunteers for back-up and extended assistance.

Some hospitals, such as St. Paul-Ramsey, Minnesota; Washington, D.C., General; and Billings Hospital, Chicago; have instigated training courses for nurses, social workers, and advocates. Those which have tried to include doctors in this process have found them generally unwilling to participate. Huntington Memorial Hospital, Pasadena, California, uses the videotape technique for their training sessions. Professors' wives and students at Stillwater Municipal Hospital, Oklahoma, provide back-up services for the hospital staff.

All these programs must be ongoing, because of the turnover of volunteers and staff. These improvements should be duplicated by hospitals nationwide.

Many victims have questioned the necessity of emphasizing only the legally defined verification of intercourse. If funds are being allocated to examine other rape-related issues, there should be a study covering these points: What percent of reporting victims were required to have a pelvic examination? How many complied? How many refused? What reasons were offered by those who refused? What were the legal results for those who complied/for those who refused? Were the cases of those who refused marked unfounded? When the tests were completed, how were the results utilized? In what percent was there no motile sperm, even though there was other evidence of rape? In what percent was motile sperm present? What was the frequency with which this information was introduced into the courtroom? After all this data is collected, then states should determine if this step must be included in the reporting procedure.

A rape victim should receive thorough medical treatment, but as a help, not a hindrance to her recovery. When hospital personnel fulfill their duties and minister to victims, it is not so much what they do, as how they do it. In the often rushed, tense atmosphere of the emergency room, they sometimes forget that they are human beings, dealing with other human beings. And with human beings who need help and comfort.

7: *Raped Again*

Dealing with the legal justice system in any matter can be time-consuming, confusing, frustrating, and angering. For the rape victim, it surpasses that. The farther she progresses, the more harrowing it becomes. She is embarrassed, humiliated, demeaned, and mentally abused. The woman is no longer a victim, but a "complaining witness" of a crime committed against society. The case reads "The People of the State of —— versus John Doe." But the individual who has been sexually assaulted finds it impossible to be divorced from the reality and see herself in the abstract concept of a witness.

It is equally hard for her to accept objectively the multiple rights of the accused when weighed against the few she is accorded. In any crime, the accused is guaranteed certain things—counsel, a speedy and fair trial, and confrontation by the complainant. These are necessary elements, but knowing that does not make it less trying. Because the further goal of our justice system is to avoid erroneous convictions, it makes it difficult to convict anyone. The application of sexual assault laws results in most of those accused escaping punitive measures.

Tracing the number of reported rapes to those ending in convictions resembles an inverted pyramid. The original large figure of reported rapes, still only a fraction of those taking place, is reduced, then diminished again by the low rate of apprehensions, dismissals, plea bargaining, suspended sentences, and so on. The national statistics compiled by the FBI for 1976 paint an appalling picture.[1] Of the 56,730 reported rapes, only 52 percent were cleared by arrest. Sixty-nine percent of that number were prosecuted for the offense. Acquittals or dismissals occurred in 49 percent of the cases. Forty-two percent were found guilty of the substantive offense, and nine percent were convicted of lesser charges.

That means that for every hundred reported rapes, the accused is never apprehended in nearly half the cases. Of the fifty-two arrested and charged, only thirty-six are prosecuted. Seventeen are either acquitted or have the case dismissed. Three are found guilty of some other charge, frequently a misdemeanor. And, finally, fifteen men are convicted of forcible rape or attempted rape.

When the flow of rape cases through the criminal justice system was analyzed for King County (Seattle) and Jackson County (Kansas City, Missouri), the results were even more alarming.[2] Out of 635 complaints reported, a total of 167 suspects were arrested and identified. Forty-five were charged with forcible rape or attempted rape. Of that figure, 32 were presented to felony court: 10 were found or pled guilty of rape or attempted rape, 10 for lesser offenses, 10 ended in either acquittals or dismissal of the charges. One was determined not competent to stand trial. The other was judged not guilty because of a mental disorder. From 635 complaints to 10 convictions is a sad commentary.

These kinds of statistics are enough to convince some victims not to pursue their cases through the legal justice system. Those who do discover another barrage of confrontations. If the assailant is apprehended, a member of the prosecutor's office interviews the victim prior to filing charges. During this first crucial meeting, the deputy assesses the strength of the case, examines the evidence, establishes rapport, and attempts to win her confidence and trust.

Although this is the most intensive interview she has, few offices follow specific instructions or protocol. The Battelle Memorial Institute Law and Justice Study Center conducted an extensive national survey of 150 prosecutor's offices.[3] Their findings, published in March 1977, revealed that 95 percent had no specific guidelines for interviewing victims. This is despite the fact that 53 percent required them to submit to three or more sessions. Thirty-six percent held at least two, 11 percent one. Only 7 percent had written materials explaining the system, to help prepare the victims and witnesses for their involvement in the criminal procedures. Just one office had written overviews designed expressly for victims and witnesses of sexual assault. Most relied on a combination of the prosecutor's intuition and past experience.

Seventy percent of the victims were surrounded by observers or participants during these questioning periods. Instead of supportive people, such as friends, family, or advocates, those present were generally other lawyers, investigators, or police officers.

With the completion of the initial interview, the filing deputy from the prosecutor's office studies the complaint. According to the Battelle data, generally this person is not a specialist in rape cases and has had no on-the-job training with this type of offense. He looks for three determining elements: (1) Proof of penetration provided by medical verification. (2) Lack of victim consent. (3) Threat or use of force. If any of these is not present, the agency most likely will not charge the suspect with rape.[4]

When the charges are filed, the accused has a presentment hearing in front of a judge or magistrate. The victim does not attend. At that time bail is set. Then the man is advised of his right to counsel, told the nature of the charges against him, and given the date of the preliminary hearing, which is within the following three to ten days. Once he hires a lawyer or has one appointed by the court, if the case is not dropped entirely, plea bargaining ensues.

The respondents in the Battelle survey stated that this method is used in approximately 50 percent of the rape offenses. More than three-quarters of those polled were satisfied with this part of the criminal justice system and thought it necessary. Nineteen percent thought it could be improved. Four percent said it could be eliminated.[5] Sometimes the charge is reduced from forcible rape to something as minimal as trespassing. One lawyer seriously recommends that an indecent exposure conviction is easier to obtain and therefore a victim should aim at that minor accusation. In the vast majority of cases, the woman has no input in what takes place during this stage. She is uninformed that it is occurring and often as to its outcome.

From this point on, she is discouraged from withdrawing her complaint, although about a quarter do. The smaller the county, the more prevalent this is. Prosecutors believed the reasons for the action were fear of the defendant, publicity, further trauma, parental pressure, or embarrassment.

A defense attorney is working for the accused assailant. Depending upon the lawyer's fee, interest, thoroughness, and creativity, he employs various methods to ensure that his client walks away free. Some focus on uncovering information about the victim's background, to discredit or intimidate her. Occasionally, private detectives are hired to go to the woman's neighborhood and talk to those that live around her. These types of questions were mentioned by interviewees: What kind of woman is she? Does she have a lot of men entering her home? Do any of them spend the night? Could you give me the names of any men in her life? Do you know of any drugs she might use? Does she frequent bars? Does she come in at late hours? Does she play loud music? Is she a member of any gang? Is she frequently truant from school? How does she support herself? Others call the victim's friends and acquaintances, trying to ferret out any information that will make the victim appear promiscuous or immoral.

After following one woman for several days, a private investigator learned that she supplemented her $150 Aid for Dependent Children welfare check with sporadic income from crafts she made and sold. The defense attorney said he would report her to the social service department if she did not drop the charges. When she told him to go ahead, he did notify the authorities.

Another victim was offered $1,800 by the assailant's lawyer if she would withdraw her complaint. She refused, but the case was dismissed on a technicality.

Jean said the defense attorney gave the rapist's mother her telephone number. She would call, crying and begging her to retract her original report. Jean suffered great guilt for having been raped. The mother's words increased that feeling. She agreed to change her testimony between the preliminary hearing and the jury trial.

Pat explained that a man telephoned claiming to be the district attorney. He asked if there were any detrimental information he should know about. After telling him no, she called the attorney. Neither he nor any other deputy from his office had contacted her.

Katy was relaxing in the park across from her residence when a stranger approached her. After an hour's conversation, he suggested they drive to the store for some wine and cheese. Once in his car, he forced her at knifepoint to accompany him to his apartment, where he raped her.

Katy said, "A few weeks after the guy had been apprehended a man, who later identified himself as the defense attorney, greeted me by my door. I'd been systematically pushing all the memories out of my mind and here was this man intruding into my life.

"His whole demeanor made me feel extremely uncomfortable. He opened with the retort, 'Well, lady, you must admit this wasn't your classic rape.' In other words, I'd gotten into the car, so obviously I'd been letting myself in for whatever happened. Very successfully he managed to intimidate me. He demanded to know if I were going to press charges and came back with an explanation that another woman the man had raped was prosecuting. He would get sentenced in that incident. The verbal harassment continued, with his stressing the weakness of my case. He tried and succeeded in making me feel guilty to the extent that I gave in and dropped my complaint. Later on, I realized the police never verified the fact he'd raped someone else or that she was going to prosecute. The entire story could have been made up by the attorney so I'd feel he would go to jail without my having to go through any further humiliation."

These are samples of defense tactics toward a few victims prior to the hearing or jury trial.

Women whose cases progress this far have further impediments to overcome. Before their complaints are given to a trial deputy who tries the case in court, the sexual assault generally parallels, but exceeds in severity, the stereotype offense. The following components are present in the majority of cases that are prosecuted: The victim reported to the police within an hour after the attack. She was raped by a total stranger armed with a weapon, probably a firearm or knife. She was forced to perform other acts in addition to vaginal intercourse. Generally the woman was hurt and, if she resisted, the injuries were more extensive. Injuries were recorded in 61 percent of the cases presented to the prosecutor in large jurisdictions (populations over 1,000,000), 69 percent in medium-sized counties (100,000–1,000,000), and 70 percent in small ones (25,000–100,000).[6]

Although the victim did not know the accused, she was able to identify him again. It is unusual in rape charges to have corroborating witnesses, especially eyewitnesses, but these cases had a fairly high percentage of this type of evidence: in large jurisdictions, 43 percent; in medium jurisdictions, 38 percent; in small jurisdictions, 37 percent.[7] Two or more offenders were involved in 41 percent of the cases in large counties, 27 percent in medium, and 27 percent in small.[8]

The assailant had been arrested and/or convicted of previous crimes or sex offenses, and therefore was known to the police.

Another element that separates the cases turned over to the prosecutor from those reported to the police reflects the suspects' backgrounds. The vast majority of the men who were prosecuted were either unemployed or in blue collar occupations. For large jurisdictions the figure was 85 percent; for medium, 88 percent; and for small, 89 percent.[9] "In rape cases reported to the police a substantially higher percent of offenders were considered either professionals or students. This is an important finding, since it suggests that the more affluent and privileged offender is either less likely to be caught or less likely to be charged with rape."[10]

If the case is presented to the trial deputy, the next step is generally the preliminary or pretrial hearing. This takes place in the presence of a judge or magistrate, prosecuting and defense attorneys, the accused, the victim, the police, and possibly interested spectators. At this time, the woman receives her introductory course on testifying as a complaining witness. Frequently the victim does not meet the deputy until shortly before her courtroom appearance. This is because most prosecutors are assigned on a rotational basis a few days ahead of time to either a specific case or courtroom. Many are overworked, too hurried, and inadequately prepared.

The woman makes a recitation of the event and remains for a cross-examination by the defense. The hearing lasts one or two hours, after which the judge determines if there is probable cause to believe the defendant committed the crime. When there is, the accused is arraigned and enters a plea of guilty or not guilty.

Either as an alternative to the preliminary hearing or after it, there might be a grand jury proceeding. Some areas do not have grand juries hear rape cases. In those that do, the accused is not allowed to have a lawyer present. Generally, the victim does not testify. The prosecuting attorney reads her statement and explains how she identified the defendant. The jurors then decide whether or not to indict, based on the evidence they have heard. Occasionally these closed hearings are used as a dumping ground where prosecutors rid themselves of what they consider weak cases. A few jurisdictions eliminate both the preliminary hearing and grand jury proceeding, going directly to plea bargaining or a jury trial.

By this time, most cases are resolved. The few actually presented to a jury arrive there either because the defense knows the odds are in his client's favor or because the prosecutor believes the case is strong enough for the possibility of a conviction. If either side feels they will lose, the case is probably settled by plea bargaining.

Victims felt that working with the prosecutor's office was an exercise in frustration. Some tired of the constant parade of male authority figures with whom they met. From the police to hospitals to the attorneys, men took the reports, asked the questions, directed the investigation, and prepared the case. The 150 respondents in the Battelle study employ several thousand lawyers, the majority of them men. In large jurisdictions, the hiring practices have changed somewhat in the past few years. Those staffs are now 64 percent male, 36 percent female. For medium-sized jurisdictions, the breakdown is 91 percent male, 9 percent female. In small counties, the victim's chances of having a woman lawyer are minute, because only 3 percent are female.[11]

There is no nationwide coordinated effort to improve the procedures and techniques of the prosecutor's offices. When experiments are tried in one area, they are done independently, with the officials unaware of what might have been attempted elsewhere. A quarter of the offices polled have instituted new practices for handling rape offenses in the last three years. These have included emphasizing better forensic methods, more frequent use of female deputies, and special training for trial deputies.

Another quarter anticipated changes. Most of these future projects centered around special training and the development of rape units within their offices. When asked their opinions of what overall improvements were needed when dealing with rape, they removed the responsibility from themselves. Instead, they listed more public education on the subject, better police investigative techniques, and additional police training. Only 10 percent thought revising prosecution policies was necessary.[12]

The formal trial takes place six months to a year after the attack. And trial is the appropriate word, for the victim as well as the accused. She is not entering a swearing match with the accused as to the facts of the case. Rather, she endures a draining, mortifying two days to two weeks in the courtroom. The few victims reaching a jury trial said that it was second only to the rape in terms of traumatic upheaval. When the date finally arrived, all their fears and anxiety were realized.

Those present include the accused, sitting several feet from the complaining witness, at least two attorneys, a judge, and the twelve-member jury. All police involved with the case must testify. Also in the room are any corroborating witnesses, friends, family, and any spectators who care to attend. If the proceedings are closed, those not directly related to the case are excluded from the courtroom.

Once the jury selection is completed—another lengthy process—the victim is generally the first called to testify. The prosecuting attorney leads her through a description of the events prior to, during, and after the attack. Following that, she is cross-examined by the defense.

The defense attorney wants to prove one of the following: The event did not take place. It might have occurred, but the witness is identifying the wrong man. It did happen, but was consented to. The victim is a liar, with a bad reputation. If the woman offers positive identification of the accused, the consent issue is targeted. From that stem questions about her "chastity." The theory is that if she has agreed to sexual relations with one man, she is more likely to agree to others. Then the door is swung open to inquiries about her prior sexual history. The double-edged purpose of this line of attack is that "loose females" cannot be raped and that they are also dishonest.

Assault or robbery victims do not have to prove they fought back, did not consent to the attack, or did not give

their money away. The law presumes no one would willingly
do that. But rape victims remain in a unique category. If they
did not try to repel the assailant, it is assumed they agreed.
When they are no longer virgins, many believe they willingly
"gave" themselves to the offender. Ninety-two percent of the
prosecutors said the major difficulty in obtaining a jury conviction was the victim's credibility. Although technically she
is not the person on trial, that is what she becomes.

She is badgered and degraded. In 86 percent of the jurisdictions, her prior sexual activity may be introduced into the
courtroom, although recently many states limit this testimony in some ways. No state specifically forbids the use of
the judge's cautionary charge to the jury about believing the
woman; three require it by statute. Over 80 percent of the
prosecutors admitted that it unduly prejudiced the jurors
against the victim and could adversely affect the case.[13]

The length of time the woman spends on the stand differs
greatly. New York Assistant District Attorney Leslie Snyder
cited a case where a judge permitted a victim to be cross-
examined for nine hours, much of it regarding her past. One
interviewee testified for four straight hours.

Defense lawyers have learned techniques to use in criminal
cases. In a rape charge, the complainant is, at a minimum,
drilled about her immediacy of reporting; the examination at
the hospital; her opportunity to observe the accused; the
lighting, location, length of time together; their conversation; the assailant's penis and its placement; her position; and
her reaction.

While each attorney develops his favorite methods for
questioning the witness, the following patterns are well-
known in criminal proceedings.

One technique is repeating the same question over again.
The lawyer's hope is that the woman will vary her answer
somewhat, thus damaging her statement. The response may
change imperceptibly, but the court stenographer records
everything, and the attorney is acutely aware of what he desires to happen. Sometimes he sprinkles the question at ran-

dom. Others prefer to ask it two or three times in a row.

Another approach is the seemingly innocent question, with a sequence unfolding in this manner: Are you engaged? Have you ever been engaged? But you've lived with a man, haven't you? The woman's character may then be evaluated by the jurors as that of a promiscuous person, and her case will be harmed.

Asking questions out of related order is a further tool. He may ask where she works; how long she has been employed in that position; what kind of training she received to qualify for the job. And then—"Are you in the habit of accepting rides from strange men?"

The lawyer's questioning continues. He may even call for the victim to remember minor details. Although he requests information one would not normally recall, the goal is to shake the woman's testimony and the jury's confidence in her memory. An interviewee reported that the defense attorney asked her what color socks the assailant was wearing the day of the offense. Next he challenged her to state the color of his eyes. After a long series of "I don't know," "I don't remember," she feared the jury would doubt her ability to accurately identify the man.

To further demoralize a victim, some attorneys narrow their questions to minutiae about the rape. The excerpt below is from an actual trial, and was reported in a pamphlet distributed by the Santa Clara Valley Rape Crisis Center in California.[14] Those questions with asterisks were objected to by the judge.

Q. *Did he [the rapist] have any trouble inserting his penis?*
Q. *When was his penis erect?*
Q. *Have you [the victim] ever had intercourse before?*
Q. *When was the last time you had intercourse prior to the rape?*
Q. *How far did his penis enter your vagina?**
Q. *Was his penis still hard when he removed it?*
Q. *Did you climax?**
Q. *Did he climax?*

Q. *Did you get a good look at his penis?*
Q. *Was it circumcised?*
Q. *Did it seem large? Larger than average?**

Another technique often used is that of several questions introduced with the phrase, "Isn't it true." This can be followed by such statements as "Isn't it true you were sleeping with two different men during the month prior to your alleged attack?" "Isn't it true your neighbors have complained to your mother about your behavior?" "Isn't it true you smoke marijuana?" "Isn't it true you often attend all night parties?"

A variation of this is the leading question. These are often the ones that can be answered with a yes or no. "You accepted a drink from this man, didn't you?" "You live with a man, don't you?" "You've been married, haven't you?" "You entertain men in your home frequently, don't you?" Although these all may bring negative responses, the victim must contend with the knowledge that the jury may believe the attorney had some basis of fact or he would not have proposed them.

Some lawyers add the no-win question. In this situation there is no "good" answer. Examples are: "When did you quit the local teenage gang?" "When did you stop the practice of hitchhiking?" The woman may never have been a gang member or stuck her thumb out for a ride, but she must simultaneously refute the question and the supposition as well.

Often her emotions race from intimidation to frustration to rage because of the defense attorney's choice of words. The device is simple. He takes her words or phrases and replaces them with others to make them sound compromising. Darleen recounted that she testified she took off her slacks only after the armed rapist told her he would kill her if she refused. The lawyer said, "You assisted this man by removing your clothes." Another recalled she had been required to testify as to any conversation she had had with the assailant. The only words they had spoken were when he asked how old she was, and she responded with her age. The attorney then discussed their pleasant conversation.

The defense's behavior while questioning a victim is his chance to practice his thespian talents. His voice levels may alter radically. For a time he may talk in a normal, low-keyed tone, and then suddenly he will become loud and aggressive. He might smile at the witness, drench his sentences with sarcasm, or do the opposite, come across as an all-around nice guy with an equally charming client who would never dream of doing anything as horrible as rape.

After the victim testifies, all other witnesses are questioned and cross-examined. Any evidence is introduced and explained by the person presenting it to the court. Following the defense and prosecutor's summaries of the case, the jury leaves to determine the verdict. Finally, the proceedings are reconvened to hear their decision.

Throughout the trial, the victim may scan the room for sympathetic, understanding faces. Her gaze could rest on the jurists. She has probably been cautioned about them by the prosecutor. Neither the victim nor the accused is really judged by a jury of her/his peers. In most trials, the jurors will generally be middle-aged, conservative in life-style, and white. The woman is frequently advised to wear a dress, use stilted terminology when describing the "act" such as "private parts" in place of vagina, or clinical words instead of the more commonly used expressions.

She is aware that these people are evaluating her, and strange dynamics surface among them. The men often relate to the dilemma of the accused. The women summoned for duty might be considered sympathetic because they can identify with the plight of the victim, but actually they sometimes become harsher critics. If they think of themselves as morally upstanding, they may feel they would have reacted differently; they would not have allowed themselves to have been raped. If the victim has a questionable reputation, moral evaluations come forth, and they may believe she is not a credit to her sex and should be treated accordingly.

An empirical study was done to examine jury reactions to a rape charge. A target group, all women, were presented with seven hypothetical situations which were rape in the legal sense. The participants had to list those cases in which they thought rape had occurred. The incidents ranged from an attack by a stranger in a parking lot to a date's unwanted sexual advances. Ninety percent stated the attack had been rape in the first situation, but by the time they reached the last description over a quarter were certain the woman in question had not been raped. Twenty percent believed she had. Only in three of the seven cases, all involving strangers, were more than half the respondents certain that what took place really was rape. Of the four cases where there was some previous acquaintance, none received the majority of votes in favor of rape.[15]

Harry Kalven, Jr., and Hans Zeisel, professors from the University of Chicago Law School, conducted a national study of the jury system.[16] The jurors reacted severely toward the victim whenever they considered she in some way brought on the attack. They punished what they viewed as an unchaste woman, even when there was no precipitatory behavior.

Juries generally acquitted when there were no outward indicators of physical force. If she had been drinking or picked up, they saw this as promiscuous behavior. The woman took the risk and was not worthy of a conviction of the accused. All the cases examined involved violence, a stranger, and/or more than one attacker. In one situation, three men kidnapped a woman from the street, took her to an apartment, and raped her. The jury acquitted. The veiled reason was that the unmarried victim had two illegitimate children. Of the forty-two cases Kalven and Zeisel examined, the judges would have convicted in twenty-two of them, but the jury found the accused guilty in only three.

Shirley Feldman-Summers and Karen Lindner investigated the "Perceptions of Victims and Defendants in Criminal Assault Cases." Their findings, published in *Criminal Justice and Behavior*, indicated that as the respectability of the victim decreased the jury's perception of her responsibility for the rape increased. A further injustice was the belief that as the victim's respectability declined the impact of the crime on her lessened.[17]

Another element which often arises among jurors is sympathy for the offender and ambivalence toward the victim. A nineteen-year-old west coast secretary was raped in an outside area during the daylight hours. Because a corroborating witness made a positive identification of the assailant, it was one of those rare times the victim felt confident the man would be found guilty. She was wrong. The defendant's woman friend testified in his behalf. Evidence could not be admitted that he had been acquitted on a charge of assault with intent to rape only nine days earlier. After he was found not guilty, one juror stated that he could not believe a man with an attractive girl friend would have ever wanted to rape a plain-looking female.

Washington, D.C., produced an example, in the case of two George Washington University students who were victims. They both had good reputations in the community, were mentally stable, reported immediately to the police, and had medical verification not only of intercourse but also of bruises. The teenager, a stranger, who raped both of them during the same evening, confessed his guilt to a police officer, but the confession was inadmissible because of a technicality. The case seemed airtight, until the jurors' deliberations. He was set free, because in their estimation the women had not fought hard enough to resist the attack.

In Boston, even Superior Court Judge Walter McLaughlin was enraged by the jury's not guilty decision in one rape offense. The victim had testified that the suspect coerced her into leaving a single's bar with him by refusing to return her purse. He took her to his apartment, forced her into his bedroom, and raped her. Evidence was introduced—bloodstained bedding, a couple who had heard the woman's screams for at least twenty minutes. The nine men and three women agreed with the defendant, already a two-time loser for other crimes, who stated that she had accompanied him by her own choice and denied he had raped her.

After the verdict was handed down, the judge was quoted in a UPI news release as stating, "I have never said a word of criticism or a word of rebuke to a jury. The juries have the power to decide facts, determine guilt or innocence, and that is the law of the country. We should abide by it without criticism. . . .

"When we have a trial, instead of trying the defendant, you make the poor girl the defendant. And I think that philosophy is led by the women, who should be more considerate.

"You had two responsible citizens of this commonwealth, irreproachable of integrity and principles, who testified before you that they heard screaming there for twenty minutes. Can it be, ladies and gentlemen, that you believed the screaming, terrified girl, with bloodcurdling calls, consented to the advances of the defendant?

"Can you disbelieve those people? And can you believe a defendant who stood with two convictions, one that he was a thief and one that he dealt in stolen property? That strikes to the basic fundamentals of honesty. Believe him and disbelieve them? Well, that's what you have done."[18]

Does the judge become the one island of unprejudiced fairness and honesty in a rape trial? Not always. Carol Bohmer interviewed thirty-eight Philadelphia judges in June 1971 and reported the results in an article entitled "Judicial Attitudes Toward Rape Victims" for *Judicature* magazine.[19] She determined that they were far less impartial than frequently supposed. The judges seemed to feel that there were three basic categories of women in rape trials. One was the "genuine" victim, the victim of the stereotype crime with a stranger committing the assault and her attempting to resist. In these situations they were generally sympathetic. But if the woman fell into the classification of vulnerability because she had met the man at a bar, hitchhiked, seen the man before, they termed those "friendly rapes" or "assault with failure to please." Their understanding diminished accordingly. The third heading was the "vindictive" female. This was often the case when victim and assailant were acquainted or when she might have some personal reason for "getting back at him." In these, they assumed either intercourse was agreed to or it did not take place.

The judge is in a powerful position in the courtroom. He controls the amount and kind of testimony regarding the victim's reputation, prior sex life, methods of resistance, hearsay evidence, and so forth. The victim and society should hope for blind justice levied impartially by an unbiased judge, but rather he brings with him his preconceived theories about women, their roles, and their actions.

Some revealing judges' comments in Bohmer's study were made when responding to whether any particular types of victims made better witnesses. There was general agreement that older women were best and children the least easily dealt with. But then racist undertones appeared. Some alluded to the life-styles and attitudes of "ghetto inhabitants" without stating that they meant minorities. Several seemed to correlate this category automatically with "vindictive" females. One mentioned that, "With the Negro community, you really have to redefine the term rape. You never know about them."[20]

Herbert Kritzer, of Rice University, and Thomas Uhlman, from the University of Missouri, St. Louis, examined 23,560 criminal cases in a major American city to determine if there were a relationship between the sex of the judge and the final dispensation. Would female judges hand down harsher penalties to various violators, particularly rapists? Their analysis showed that this was not true. While they were tougher in manslaughter, robbery, and drug trials, the women matched their male counterparts when it came to rape. Kritzer and Uhlman concluded that female judges behaved in a manner similar to the males, perhaps because they had "made it in a man's world."[21]

In the few occasions when the accused is found guilty, sentencing becomes an area of controversy. Prosecutors in the Battelle survey were asked the "average sentence actually imposed" on convicted rapists in their jurisdictions. They answered with a span of years for the minimum and maximum. More than a third of the average minimum sentences required no imprisonment, merely a suspension or probation. Twenty-nine percent received one to five years, and the same number received six to ten. Most served only a fraction of the time before being paroled. The median maximum sentence was twenty years.[22]

In Alaska, renowned for its leniency toward rapists, two men took a woman into their car, beat, threatened, robbed, and raped her. A military spokesperson for the one man who was in the service at the time told the sentencing court the occurrence was very common and took place numerous times each night in Anchorage. "Needless to say, Donald Chaney was the unlucky G.I. that picked a young lady that told." The judge sentenced him to two concurrent one year sentences and urged immediate parole.[23]

Judge Bernard Glickfeld, in San Francisco, gained fame because of his misuse of power and sentencing in a rape trial. The case involved three men who kidnapped, tortured, and raped a young woman. Prior to the trial, Glickfeld reputedly made an agreement to give the accused light sentences if they were found guilty. In court he yelled abusively at the prosecutor, police inspector, and victim, while treating the defense with great civility. When addressing the accused, he generally called them "sir" or "mister," but subjected their victim to "an incomprehensible tirade," to quote the appeals court. Among other things, he called the woman "a horse's ass." After a guilty verdict was received, he gave minimal sentences for all, with one getting fifty-two weekends in jail. This earned Glickfeld the distinction of being the only San Francisco judge to be censured by the State Supreme Court.[24]

In 1971, in Washington, D.C., a man raped and pistol-whipped a woman. He fled to escape trial, but returned three years later only after an arrest warrant had been issued for him. The victim was assaulted in a car near her home, then managed to escape. She was chased by the man, who beat her and threatened to kill her if she did not return to the car. The examining physicians said she had received one of the most severe beatings they had ever treated. Because of the attack and her injuries, she had been forced to take leave without pay for a year from her job. She paid her hospital bills out of her life savings. Timothy Robinson, who covered the trial for the *Washington Post*, reported: When determining the sentence, Judge Charles R. Richey listened to the defense attorney, who stated, "There will be no gain to this community at this time to place Mr. Morgan [the rapist] in a penal institution." He suggested that if Mr. Morgan were given a supervised probation "he would be a walking example to the community" that such activity is being deterred. The prosecutor rebutted that "the city doesn't need a walking example, it needs protection." The sentence—three years. The judge said, "I'm sorry I have to do this. I wish there were some alternatives that were available to you and to this community." He recommended the rapist use that time to "reflect on your life.... I wish you good luck, and I hope you will think about the victim."[25]

A Suffolk, Massachusetts, Superior Court judge took the opposite tack with three men who were found guilty by an all-male jury of forcible rape, armed robbery, armed assault in a dwelling, and assault and battery by means of a dangerous weapon. The men had viciously brutalized a thirty-two-year-old, ninety-pound woman. Additionally, they stole money and valuables totaling $6,810. According to a *Boston Globe* account, in announcing the sentences, Judge James C. Roy explained, "This part of the judicial system—sentencing—is not a pleasant task for me." He continued, "What the defendants did to this victim was horrendous and monstrous. The details of this case are a horror story.... One feels almost ashamed to be a member of the human race when one sees what one human being can do to another. What they did is beyond description." He gave two concurrent life terms for robbery and armed assault, with a third for rape for two of the men. The third, who committed assault and battery with a dangerous weapon and had "threatened the victim with horrifying mutilation," received the same three life sentences with an additional nine- to ten-year term and a concurrent three- to five-year sentence. The sentences were reduced on appeal.[26]

Judge Archie Simonson, in Madison, Wisconsin, caused a furor when he decided on the nonpunitive sentence of probation for a convicted fifteen-year-old rapist who had assaulted a teenage coed in a high school stairwell. His justification, as quoted in a *Time* magazine article, was that "women [should] stop teasing. There should be a restoration of modesty in dress and elimination from the community of sexual gratification businesses. . . . Whether women like it or not they are sex objects. God did that; I didn't. . . . Are we supposed to take an impressionable person fifteen or sixteen years of age and punish that person severely because they react to it normally?"[27]

The women of that community were angered and called for his resignation. They picketed the courthouse and gathered petitions demanding a recall. On election day, he was defeated, and a feminist lawyer replaced him. Simonson did not change his position after he left office. He commented, "I might have said them a little differently. But the context would be the same."[28]

Another case drew nationwide attention in the summer of 1977. A three-judge California Court of Appeal overturned the conviction of a Los Angeles man who raped a female hitchhiker. In explaining the reversal, Justice Lynn Compton wrote that the "lone female hitchhiker, in the absence of an emergency situation as a practical manner, advises all who pass by that she is willing to enter the vehicle with anyone who stops and in so doing advertises she has less concern for the consequences than the average female. Under such circumstances it would not be unreasonable for a man in the position of the defendant here to believe that the female would consent to sexual relations."[29]

The National Organization for Women joined with other groups in asking for disbarment of Compton. Deputy Attorney General William Ponders stated that if the Appellate Court did not reverse the decision he would petition the state Supreme Court to review the case. Finally the conviction was thrown out for other procedural reasons, and the all-male panel revised the wording of its ruling after the public backlash.[30]

The facts of these two cases did receive extensive coverage. The other previous examples occurred before 1975 and went largely unnoticed. A Harris Poll conducted in the fall of 1977 had several questions about these last two judges. By a 51 to 28 percent majority, the respondents felt they should be removed or made to resign from office. A 57 to 27 percent majority thought that the attitude of male judges who released accused assailants "on the grounds that women spur the men to rape them, indicates those judges have a deep bias and prejudice against women." Males polled were less convinced of this than females.[31]

For a victim, there is no easy way to endure the days spent in court. There is never a guarantee the accused will be found guilty. Even if this occurs, the case can be appealed, and reversal is possible. A Michigan defendant twice raped his fifteen-year-old daughter. He explained to the police that he was trying to educate her. Although he was convicted, it was reversed on a technicality.[32]

In 1975, an Illinois conviction for rape and deviant sex acts was overturned. The assailant had threatened force and used a weapon. The court ruled that the victim should have cried out as the accused was forcing her across a busy street in daylight hours.[33]

Even though Patty was only five, she was required to testify in a preliminary hearing in the same manner as an adult. What she experienced in the courtroom is typical of child victims. A neighbor in his sixties was accused of sexually assaulting her. When Patty sat behind the railing to testify, only her head was visible, because she was so small. She was wearing a white dress with an embroidered yellow daisy on the front. Her hair was pulled back with a piece of thick, white yarn tied in a bow. As she spoke, her words could barely be heard, despite the microphone in front of her. She had a childish lisp that made her hard to understand.

After she was sworn in, the prosecuting attorney asked her if she knew what it meant to lie. The little girl nodded, and the judge interrupted, saying she must answer using the word "yes" or "no." Next, she was asked who would know if she told a lie. The answer came, in a solemn, sweet voice, "Jesus would know."

"Are you in school now, Patty?" the prosecutor continued. "What's the name of your teacher?" But the adults did not hear her response clearly enough. She had to repeat the name several times, while she peered around the courtroom for her mother. "What would happen if you lied to your teacher?" "She wouldn't be happy," was her reply.

Just establishing the order of events proves difficult with child victims. In this case, after Patty had finished napping, her mother told her and her younger brother to go outside. They were playing patty-cake when George, who lived across the apartment courtyard, came over and offered her some gum. He took her to the basement of his building and assaulted her. Then she went home, told her mother George had "fooled" with her, and was taken to a doctor. She was bleeding.

The questioning centered on two points: Was George smoking a cigarette? Had he completely removed her jeans?

These are some questions and responses that were heard that day in court.

Q. *What time of day was it?*
A. I don't know.
Q. *Was it light or dark out?*
A. Light.
Q. *What were you wearing?*

A. Jeans and a shirt.

Q. *Where was your brother when George was with you?*

A. In front of where we live.

Q. *Was George smoking a cigarette?*

A. Yes.

Q. *What happened to the cigarette?*

[Her answer was unintelligible and had to be repeated several times. She had knocked it from his hand.]

Q. *What did George do to you first?*

A. He had me sit on his lap.

Q. *Were your jeans pulled down by George?*

A. Yes.

Q. *How did you get down from George's lap?*

A. He put me down.

Q. *Did George touch your pants?*

A. Yes.

Q. *Did George touch your body?*

A. Yes.

Q. *How did you get your zipper down?*

A. He unzipped it.

Q. *What did he do to you then?*

A. He hurt my "Sally."

Q. *Would you point to your "Sally."*

[The child pointed to her vagina, and the prosecuting attorney instructed the court to record that.]

Q. *Were your jeans on or off at this time?*

A. On.

The questions continued for thirty minutes, after which the little girl was cross-examined by the defense and then was dismissed. A neighbor was called to testify. She stated she had seen Patty being led off by George. She was asked if there were any commotion outside. The response was, none that she had heard. "If there had been some would you have heard it?" asked the defense. This question was objected to by the prosecutor.

In summarizing the case, the defense attorney said there

was great confusion about whether Patty had had her jeans removed. At one point, she had said yes, at another no. He disregarded the fact behind her words that her jeans were pulled down, but not completely off. The judge agreed with him, saying the testimony was contradictory. He stated he could not hold the defendant now, but if the district attorney wanted to rebook him, he could.

Liz was seventeen and had her first job. After she left work at the end of the day, she discovered her car had been towed away because of a parking violation. She walked to the nearest bus stop and began waiting for the first of three transfers required to get to her home on the opposite side of town. While she was standing there, a man pulled up and asked where she was going. He said he was driving in that direction and offered her a ride. Instead of taking her home, he drove around, stopped three times, talked to her, and then raped her. The twenty-year-old defendant was in the courtroom with his wife.

The prosecuting attorney led Liz through a recitation of the crime. These are a few of the questions he asked.

Q. *What is your name?*

Q. *Where do you work?*

Q. *How long have you worked there?*

Q. *Did you go to work on July 14th, 197—?*

Q. *What is your normal way of going to work?*

Q. *Why weren't you using the car then?*

Q. *While you were waiting for a bus did anything unusual happen?*

Q. *Can you identify the defendant?*

Q. *Do you know what kind of car he had?*

Q. *Was there anything in particular that you noticed about the car?*

Q. *What kind of seats did it have?*

Q. *What did you talk about while you were riding in the car with him?*

Q. *What direction were you heading?*

Q. *Did he ever stop the car?*

Q. *When and where?*
Q. *What did you talk about each of those times?*
Q. *What did he do?*
Q. *Did he try to kiss you?*
Q. *Where? On the cheek? Lips? Neck?*
Q. *Did you resist?*
Q. *How?*
Q. *How did you finally get away from him?*

Next the defense attorney questioned Liz. He returned to each detail she had included and expanded upon it. This is an abridged sampling of the questions.

Q. *Where did you park your car at work?*
Q. *When did you discover it had been towed away?*
Q. *Could you describe how fast Mr. ——— was driving prior to approaching you at the bus stop?*
Q. *Had you attempted to get rides from other passing automobiles?*
Q. *Was there any conversation between you and the defendant?*
Q. *What did you talk about?*
Q. *When you were in the car was your door locked?*
Q. *Did you or the defendant lock it?*
Q. *Did you attempt to get out of the car the first time you stopped?*
Q. *Was the conversation friendly?*
Q. *Did you accompany the police to try and find the road where you stopped?*
Q. *Did you find it?*
Q. *What was the first aggressive move he made?*
Q. *After he tried to kiss you, was there any more conversation?*
Q. *What did you talk about?*
Q. *What part of your body was he holding?*
Q. *Can you describe your position in the bucket seat when he was pushing you down?*
Q. *Where was your head?*
Q. *Where were your feet?*
Q. *Were you on your side?*
Q. *Were you on your back?*
Q. *Describe how he pushed you down.*
Q. *What exact part of your body was being pushed?*

Q. *Were you struggling?*

Q. *Describe how you were struggling.*

Q. *Did you try to scratch the defendant?*

Q. *When you pulled his hair, were you trying to hurt him?*

Q. *Did he indicate in what manner he would end your life?*

Q. *Were you wearing slacks?*

Q. *To get them off would you describe what the defendant would have to do?*

Q. *Do you still have those slacks?*

Q. *Were they ripped?*

Q. *Did he get them fully off?*

Q. *Were you wearing panties?*

Q. *Were you wearing any other undergarments?*

Q. *Did he ask you to help?*

Q. *Did he do anything to your blouse?*

Q. *Did he take down his pants?*

Q. *Was he wearing underpants?*

Q. *What position were you in then?*

Q. *Was the hand brake up or down?*

Q. *Where were his feet?*

Q. *Where was your head?*

Q. *Where were your arms?*

Q. *Do you know where the defendant's feet were?*

Q. *Afterwards, what did he do?*

Q. *What did you do?*

Q. *Did you try to get out of the car after the intercourse?*

Q. *Did you scream?*

Q. *How often?*

Q. *What did you yell?*

Q. *Do you live alone?*

Q. *Who do you live with?*

Q. *How long have you lived with him?*

Q. *Are you engaged?*

Q. *Have you ever been married?*

Q. *How old are you?*

These are edited examination texts, because the entire proceedings would require hundreds of pages.

Sarah, a teenager, was raped by her date. She attempted to be philosophical about her courtroom appearance.

"I tried to think about it in terms of a learning experience. I've always been interested in seeing things from the inside, how they function, and being on the stand taught me what could occur. This was just a preliminary hearing, so they go a little more lightly than in an actual trial. It's during this time that they establish whether or not there's enough against the man to convince a relatively suspicious person that the victim's story is true. I think I'd say it was radicalizing, even though I didn't know the word then.

"What I quickly discovered was that the hearing was all a game, and the one who could play it better was the 'winner.' I forced myself to remain cool. I never explained or answered a question beyond giving the bare minimum. If I thought the man's lawyer was trying to confuse me or put me in a compromising position, I'd make him rephrase his questions until I could figure out what he was driving at. I refrained from making long, wordy speeches that he might be able to attack. They might have set up the rules, but I tried to bend them to my advantage.

"I was amazed at how little homework the defense had done prior to the trial. He was clumsy in his questioning, I felt, since there were several points I would have brought up if I'd been in his place. Either he didn't think of them or he didn't really care. Also, his presentation of some important evidence was ineffective, and he even lost other pieces.

"The session began by the city attorney putting me on the witness stand and saying 'now I'd like to take you back to the night of July 3, 19——.'

"To start off, I told the basic facts of the case, but it was confusing because I had to remember the exact time sequence. We'd been in and out of the car several times before the actual rape, and I wanted to make sure I included all those details. My lawyer was familiar enough with the case so he'd guide me through his questions back to anything I might have temporarily forgotten. I had to recite which time he'd forced me to go down on him; when I'd lost what article of clothing; estimate where we were then. I had to remember what words he'd used in threatening my life.

"When my initial testimony was over, the defense attorney had his field day. The first thing he started asking about seemed totally irrelevant and bewildered me at the time. He asked about the high school I'd graduated from. I told him the name, and then he questioned, 'Isn't it true you were in special classes there?'

"I said, 'No, just college prep.' He insisted, 'Well, are you sure you weren't in any classes where they took you along a little slower, covered easier material with you?' Again I answered, 'No.' I guess he was trying to establish I was mildly retarded and in my stupidity had agreed to go along with what the guy suggested.

"When that didn't work, he changed pace and tried to say the guy was a long-haired hippy, and I should have known better than to go out with him. That tactic faltered, because he'd cleaned up for the trial and didn't have a beard or long hair anymore.

"He gave up on that and turned to the fact that I'd agreed to go swimming with him. That obviously showed I was going to put myself in a situation which to every male is sexually irresistible. Seeing my body would immediately put his maturity on the level of a three-year-old, so rape wasn't really his fault because he couldn't be expected to keep his emotions chained up or be responsible for his actions.

"There was also great debate and questioning as to the length of time a man can maintain an erection. His lawyer's defense was it would be impossible to have an erection after that much physical exertion.

"After the game was over, the judge determined there was sufficient evidence for a pretrial hearing. The rapist again was let free until it could be scheduled, but he inserted a rule of his own and disappeared. He was never heard of again. I wonder if the police really searched very long and hard to find him. It's been five years now. I don't know what I'll do if they ever catch him."

Marsha was raped by two men, but charges were not filed until they had sexually assaulted two more women. Then the prosecutor's office began working.

"It finally reached the stage of preliminary hearing, and two of the three of us were willing to testify. I met with the district attorney for a grand total of ten minutes prior to the hearing. He was the impressed-with-himself type, young and very confident. He told me we didn't have to discuss anything in great detail, because he'd read the police report and knew what had taken place. I had heard enough about rape trials, so I had requested my sister and several other women to come and act as moral support. All of them knew the basic details of the case. All had agreed to be there.

"While we were waiting in the courtroom for my case, we had to sit through a hearing for a particularly brutal child-beating charge where the baby had died. It was a very emotional scene, because the mother was testifying against the man she'd been living with. They had scores of pictures with circles around the child's bruises. My friends sat and heard all that was said, and waited for my case which had been delayed.

"When that was over, I got ready for my hearing. This one was involving just the man who had actually forced me to commit fellatio, rather than both him and the driver of the car. The judge began by requesting that everybody who was not directly involved leave the courtroom. All but one man remained seated, so he said, 'I see the men are leaving, but the women are staying.' Then he turned to the defense attorney and asked if he wanted to send everyone out of the room.

"That lawyer debated, because in addition to my friends, the assailant had also brought along a group for his rooting section. His family had been calling the police daily, saying what a nice man he was; he couldn't possibly have done anything evil. The defense might have felt it would be beneficial to have solid, physical support for his client. When he hesitated, the judge insisted it was a sensitive issue, so finally the attorney made a motion to have everybody cleared. It had been perfectly in order to have my friends listen to the prior case, but they had to leave when the hearing involved me. They knew what had occurred, wouldn't have fainted, and certainly wouldn't have created any outbursts.

"Obviously, at that point I wasn't supposed to say anything, but I asked the prosecutor if he would do something, overrule the motion. He informed me he didn't want to do that because the judge was a very erratic person and you just didn't want to upset him in a trial. Of course, no one seemed to care whether I would be upset or not. The judge used his power and asked, 'What is this, some kind of a classroom study of a trial?'

"Finally, his wishes became rule. As everyone left, he said to my friends, 'Sorry, girls, you can't stay this time.' The district attorney asked if a friend of his who was studying to be a prosecutor could remain as part of his preparation. That man was allowed to be present. I was the only woman, with the exception of the court stenographer. As the hearing was about to officially begin, one of the marshals went and locked the doors. The judge looked up in surprise and yelled, 'Don't lock those doors.' Then it was the marshal's turn to be somewhat miffed. He said, 'Isn't it a closed hearing?' The judge's answer was a milestone in ambiguities: 'Yes, this is a closed hearing, but it's an open courtroom.' And with that initial brush with the legal system, the hearing got under way.

"While I was on the stand, I felt very isolated in that there was no one to look to for support and insight into my emotions. I hadn't felt any kind of rapport or closeness with the district attorney or the police inspector. They were both there, and they were both men who were primarily concerned that this be a good court hearing. They weren't deeply concerned about my feelings or the case. They weren't taking any measures to overrule any questions.

"I was also very aware of what I looked like and the presentation of my side that I made. I had considered wearing a dress, but decided that none of the courtroom procedures would be improved if I continued doing what I thought would wrongly influence prosecution, what women shouldn't have to do in order to be listened to. I believed I should be able to dress as I wanted.

"They asked me what I was wearing when I was attacked, which I thought was irrelevant, but apparently makes a difference. I had on a T-shirt and jeans, plus underpants, but no bra. I didn't wear a bra to the trial either, even though I'd been told it was a good idea. I wanted to be me and judged on the truth I told, rather than on my appearance.

"There were several questions about my 'condition' the day of the assault. There was a big issue about my hitchhiking, which was the way I'd met the men. Did I normally hitch? How often? Where? When? Why? And I answered them directly. 'No, I don't hitch often, especially in the city. It was an unusual circumstance. Of course, I wished I hadn't gotten a ride with those men, but I had and nothing I could say would change that.'

"Also I was questioned about the word 'french,' which was the expression the men had used for oral intercourse. Had I ever 'frenched' anyone before? 'Yes,' and by then because of the atmosphere of the courtroom I began to wonder if they were going to arrest me for a prior unnatural sex act. I had even considered lying, but decided against it.

"My testifying was eventually over. As I left the room, the judge reminded me that he had hoped I'd learned not to hitchhike anymore. The implication was that I should understand what I could and could not do in American society.

"When I was in the hallway, I passed the second woman who was to testify. She was younger than I, about nineteen, and she said the police had told her to come down to identify mug shots. She had had no idea she was going to be called to testify instead. She hadn't prepared herself psychologically for that. She lived two blocks from the men and hadn't even made the decision whether she was going to prosecute. Her realistic worry was that they might find her. She didn't trust them at all. There were real troubles for her living in the city. She was considering leaving, not hassling through with this case. Still, they made her go on trial, but she refused to identify the man as the rapist.

"Maybe she did this to protect herself from them, or possibly she could have been confused. There had been two men, and the one who wasn't there that day might have been the one who raped her. There wasn't enough evidence on which to prosecute him any further, even though I'd positively identified him. Out he went, home free.

"I wasn't sure if I were finished with everything, but soon I learned there was more to come. Again, I was notified there would be a second preliminary hearing, because the third woman agreed to press charges. More mental preparation, more counseling from friends, more time lost from work. This time, a woman district attorney had been assigned the case. She was a little more compassionate. I'd been informed what a good DA she was, because she'd just put somebody away for forty-five years. I wasn't sure if I thought that was such a marvelous thing to do. This hearing was to involve the second man, the driver of the car. The other woman had gone to visit a friend who lived above the men, when she was brought into their apartment and raped.

"At the hearing, this man admitted involvement, so all my anxiety had been for no purpose, because I didn't have to testify. He was to have a commuted sentence of one year, and three years probation. I left the courtroom and wondered if now it would be over. But it became more complicated. If you think you're having a hard time following all this, you can imagine how I felt.

"The first man, the one who'd actually attacked me, skipped town, and I don't know what's become of him. A judge decided to review the sentence of the second guy to determine whether he was 'criminal-minded.' Since he had the interest and concern of his friends and family, he might have been just a befuddled individual hanging around with bad influences.

"What happened? The obvious—I was called a third time, to testify against him at another preliminary hearing. This time the big issue was whether I could positively identify him. I was asked absurd questions like 'Did he have a full set of teeth?' I answered, 'I didn't know.' I was sure if I'd said yes he would have smiled and revealed an extracted wisdom tooth. If I'd said no, they would have brought dental charts to show every last one of his teeth. Then I had to recall if there were headrests in the car, to establish my field of vision during the attack. Could I actually see him well enough to identify him? Eventually that issue was resolved, and I was told he'd be given some kind of sentence. That was four months ago. I haven't heard a word since then.

"My experience with the legal procedure was bad. Not only because of the time and frustration it involved, but also because there was never anyone who directly related to my feelings as a rape victim. In a courtroom, you're supposed to suppress any kinds of emotions that will damage a case. Generally, you deal only with men. Some are protective in being big brothers to you, but not in viewing you as a human being who should have the same rights as the men who attacked you. Even the woman district attorney was very much wrapped up in the court proceedings, whether the case would go well, rather than in my feelings.

"I personally would have been in worse shape if I hadn't gone to a private lawyer on my own. He told me there are certain things that I could refuse to have admitted as evidence. With that knowledge, I insisted the prosecutors not let my address be known, my last name, or where I worked. Things like that apparently just go right into the text without any concern that most rapists probably won't be convicted. They'll be out on the streets and full of revenge against the woman who tried to put them away for a short period of time.

"The legal system and the punitive measures it hands out

are ridiculous. Incarceration doesn't do anything about curing rapists or any other criminals. I think rape is totally related to our sexist, capitalist society. The only solution is a slow process of replacing those wrong values with human ones.

"I'm confused when trying to evaluate whether it was better to set the wheels in motion by reporting my incident. In some ways, it was more difficult emotionally because through all those sources—police, hospital, courts—I got no personal support. Other than my friends, whom I would have talked with anyway, there was no kind of outside help happening. There was so much frustration and anger in dealing with the authorities that they made my experience worse. I can completely understand why many women don't bother to go through it.

"On the other hand, I believe it was good to report, because those particular men would have raped more women. They seemed to have a whole pattern, had it together in that they never used names or anything like that when talking to one another. I thought they'd done it before and would rape again. I thought my turning to the police might halt them for a while. Psychologically, it was better in thinking I was doing something to get rapists off the street. But now, after watching how the process blunders—watching the police lose evidence, the doctor's lack of insight into my troubles, the continual meanderings of the hearings, which still might not be over—and knowing those men are out here, uncaring, I don't know why I bothered."

Jane, whose case was described in a previous chapter, was forced into a car by two men, taken to a park, and raped. One man involved was a juvenile, the other an adult, so she had two separate divisions of court with which to deal. Jane explained what happened.

"About a month after I was raped, I had to appear in juvenile court. Those cases are closed hearings, so I had to testify before a judge, a defense lawyer, and a probation officer who was acting as the prosecuting attorney. As I recall, the defendant also brought along his parents, a girl friend, and one of her friends. I was alone.

"I was questioned about the incident for about an hour. Then I was instructed to leave the room while the defendant's girl friend and her friend testified on his behalf. I wasn't allowed to hear what anyone else had to say. As I was getting ready to go home, one of the inspectors from the sex squad told me I would be notified once the judge sentenced him. But I was never notified, so I don't know what the outcome was.

"A month later, the second trial was held, involving the adult defendant. Many questions were asked which were designed to reflect on my reputation. Was I on any form of birth control? Was I a virgin? How many men was I dating at the time? How many men had I had intercourse with? Then the approach changed, and confused me tremendously. The defense attorney asked whether I'd ever been in a mental institution. That was overruled, so he asked if I'd ever been under psychiatric care. Even though I said 'no' to both of those questions, he followed them with, 'Are you presently seeing any type of therapist or psychiatrist?'

"I had no idea what he was driving at. Since the prosecuting attorney kept objecting, the defense lawyer began getting very angry. He even got into an argument with the judge over it. Slowly, the problem came out. The defense attorney had received a typed statement stating that this man had been charged with a certain crime, but some numbers of the code had been transposed. He thought he was defending this man on the charge of having sexual relations with an adult mentally incapable of giving consent.

"I felt completely lost and bewildered. Even at that early time in the proceeding, they had me in tears. By the time it was over, I was in worse shape. The attorney told me there was enough evidence for a jury trial, and I would be subpoenaed when the court date was established. I lived at the same address for six months more, but no notification ever came.

After moving to another apartment, I picked up my mail, and there was a letter from the police department. They wanted to know my position on probation for this man. I didn't know why they were asking me or what had been happening during the passing months. I couldn't even tell if that meant I might have to testify at another hearing, but I assumed it did. They couldn't just put somebody on probation without having a trial.

"Since going to the police and through a hearing and a trial had been awful experiences, I wasn't sure what I wanted to do about any of it. Prison wasn't an answer, but being on probation on the streets wasn't either. Nothing seemed to make sense to me at that point. To solve all those problems, I moved away and never responded to their letter."

No victim should feel awed or intimidated by the staff of the prosecutor's office. They are there to help her. The more contact she has with them prior to the hearings and trial, the better prepared everyone will be. If she is uninformed about what is expected of her, she should ask for an overview of the procedures. She is entitled to a realistic appraisal of the strength of her case, the time involved, the types of admissible evidence, the laws in her state, and so forth. When the filing or trial deputy is too busy to provide this service, she should ask for a contact person within the office. This individual could be responsible for explaining the current status of the case.

If a woman is hesitant about pursuing a criminal charge, she could consider a civil suit. (This action will be explained in a later chapter.)

She can also inquire about sentencing options. A victim might be glad to have the complaint bargained to a lesser offense in exchange for a guilty plea. This will relieve her from having to testify. Few interviewees were consulted about plea bargaining, but it is within their rights to offer an opinion.

Postponements of hearings and trials happen with great

frequency. This tactic is used to discourage the victim to the extent that she will change her mind and drop charges. Each time a delay happens, she should demand an explanation. She should inform the prosecutors that she wants minimal delays.

When a courtroom appearance is required, she can ask if there is some place she can wait prior to testifying other than the hallway. Prosecutors should have sufficient sensitivity to realize that it is frightening to sit with the accused, his friends, and family.

If grand juries hear rape cases in the victim's jurisdiction, she could request bypassing the preliminary hearing and going directly to this step. That would mean fewer times to testify.

Another possible option is seeing if someone else can take the witness stand for her. Sometimes the police officer or investigator who recorded her statement can perform this service.

The legal proceedings become less grueling when a victim is surrounded by friends, family, or advocates. Any woman can ask these people to attend the hearings and trial. Ultimately, the judge decides whether the courtroom is open or closed. The wishes of the accused weigh more heavily than a request from the victim. Thus, individuals she wants present for support may be denied entrance. But whether the session is opened or closed, the complaining witness still has to testify. Whether the audience is six or sixty makes little difference.

Occasionally, victims have contacted private attorneys or neighborhood legal aid services as to their rights. They felt the prosecutors were too busy or uncaring to answer their questions. Minor indicators may exemplify this attitude. Some consistently mispronounced the victim's name. Most did not provide any information about the legal process. Many women had no idea of what to expect or even of the penalty for rape in their state. By seeing a lawyer on their own, they hoped their interests would be better served. If they disagreed with the prosecutors, they could consult their attorney for a further opinion or explanation. Recently there have been legislative attempts to provide this type of private counsel, in addition to the prosecuting attorney. Those who could not afford this would have court-appointed legal assistance. Her lawyer could argue against having the victim's name and address revealed, or her sexual history.

Any victim may request limitations on public access to her name and address. Many victims fear offender retaliation or embarrassing notoriety. For these reasons, they do not want the information publicized. Although they must state their name when testifying, they can refuse to give their exact address as a safety measure. Most media try to respect the woman's privacy and delete the information from their accounts.

Although it may be highly damaging to a victim's case, a few have refused to answer questions which they thought were irrelevant. Primarily these had to do with prior sexual activities. There is a tremendous risk in not answering, because it is likely to prejudice the judge and jury against her. The assumption is that if she refuses to provide requested information, she must have something to hide. The decision is the victim's as to what she does and does not reveal. For her own protection, she should narrow her replies to the specific data asked. At all times, she should speak clearly, concisely, and honestly.

For child and juvenile victims, parents must consider the benefits versus the disadvantages for their daughter's mental health. They should work closely with prosecutors in determining whether any special measures can be used. Plea bargaining could be better than a courtroom appearance. Possibly experiments with testimony delivered via closed circuit television could be attempted. Adult victims' requests for such changes are infrequently met.

No improvements alter the fact that the victims must be in

the same room with the accused, recount the details of the case, and live with the verdict. Even when the assailant has been found guilty, his sentence is comparatively short.

And yet, the two major goals of pressing charges cited by interviewees were to seek a legal resolution of the case and to know the man would not be free to rape other women.

8: A Common Goal

Most rapes go unreported. The victims feel isolated after the attack. Even those obtaining legal or medical aid may have their questions and emotional needs disregarded. Where can they look for practical information, assistance, understanding, and support?

Prior to 1972, the answer would have been nowhere. Not a single individual nor organization was specifically geared to help them. Then, several small collectives of feminists began discussing the topic. Women should not be left alone to combat a crime which affects every female. They should turn to each other to provide comfort and strength, while simultaneously working to end the threat of sexual intimidation, harassment, assault, and violence.

Groups in Washington, D.C., Philadelphia, New York City, Chicago, Detroit, and Berkeley began coming together, with limited knowledge of each other's efforts. Some developed because a woman had been raped and discovered she was on her own when dealing with the aftermath. She and her friends decided something must be done. More joined forces because of a political commitment to feminism, and the fervent desire to prevent rape.

The advocates carefully documented the insensitive treatment victims received if they reported the rape. They pointed out that because the justice system was ineffectual in rape prosecution, there had to be other solutions to the dilemma. They listed problems encountered by all victims. The media picked up the issue, not only out of genuine concern, but also

because in their estimation it contained two vital components
—sex and violence.

After operating in a vacuum, the word spread. By 1978,
these community-based centers number over two hundred.
They are known by such names as Women Against Rape,
Anti-Rape Squad, Women Against Sexual Abuse, Rape Re-
lief, Women Organized Against Rape, Women United
Against Rape, Rape Crisis and Sexual Harassment Center,
Rape Distress Center, Sexual Assault Center, Citizens
Against Rape, Anti-Rape and Sexual Assault, and Rape Coa-
lition. What began in the United States is now being dupli-
cated in countries around the world. Rape crisis centers can
be found throughout Canada and in scattered locations in
Europe and Australia.

Some, though not the majority, of the women who staff
these organizations have been raped themselves. Their par-
ticipation serves a dual purpose: they can channel their anger
and firsthand experience, and they can pass on their advice
and knowledge to others. Nonvictims listen and learn about
the situations with which these women contend. Their concern runs as deep. Completion of extensive training courses
is mandatory for all members.

Many groups do not have office space. Instead, they hold
meetings in a women's center, YWCA, church, hospital, or
private home. Their numbers and mailing addresses are in
the telephone directory. If one cannot be found under *R* for
rape crisis center, a person should check the other names given
here. More cities have women's centers, chapters of the National Organization for Women, neighborhood health clinics, teen drop-in centers, and so forth, than have specifically
crisis-oriented ones. These organizations could be contacted, because their staffs should know whether any local
antirape projects exist.

Primarily, these collectives concentrate on victim services.
Although their priorities differ, most begin with a telephone
hot line. The number is often a prefix followed by the too-
easily remembered letters *R-A-P-E.*

While they try to provide twenty-four-hour-a-day assistance, budget and personnel limitations sometimes prevent this. At a minimum, they have an answering service to relay emergency calls, or a recording device on which to leave messages. If this type of organization exists near her, a victim of sexual assault should call. Free, confidential help is guaranteed.

Women have dialed these switchboards minutes, days, months, and years after being raped. The advocate who answers gauges what services might be required. A first step is asking about the immediacy of the attack.

If the attack has just occurred, the lay counselor assesses the woman's emotional state and physical safety. She listens for signs of extreme fear and shock. Reassurances are offered. The advocate reminds her that she is there because she cares. She may request the victim's name, location, and telephone number, in case they are disconnected or for follow-up services. But she will not pressure her for this information. The victim does not have to hide her feelings. She can cry, yell, or talk freely, without embarrassment.

When the woman wants the counselor to come to her address, if possible someone else stays on the line until they meet. She is encouraged to discuss the assault, while the counselor acts both as a sounding board and reflector. In situations where the offender is still nearby or has threatened to return, the advocate asks what course of action is best for the caller—contacting the police, a trusted neighbor, etc. The victim will be questioned about the severity of her injuries. If they are serious enough to require an ambulance, one is summoned. Additional general medical data is provided by the counselor.

The victim often asks about reporting the rape. Because of her previous in-depth research, the advocate can respond with accurate information about the procedures in their jurisdiction. She leaves the final decision on this issue to the victim, but it is demystified and therefore less frightening. The caller is told what to do if she decides to report. The process is arduous. Overlaid with the victim's physical and psychological condition during that time, the impact increases. The advocate will offer to accompany her through any and all stages of notifying the police, seeking medical attention, and prosecuting. In most areas, the victim who wishes to report but cannot prove penetration is advised that she may still go to court. The complaint could be assault with intent to commit rape, a felony; intent to rape, a felony; breaking and entering, a felony; assault and battery, a misdemeanor; or failure of a public official to uphold the law, a charge brought against the police, a misdemeanor.

If the call comes within seventy-two hours of the attack, much the same process is followed by the advocate. She might ask why the victim did not act prior to this. If guilt or shame were the reasons, she is reminded of her blamelessness. The counselor often clarifies information the victim is concerned about, including: the low incidence of pregnancy, venereal disease testing, the fact that rape can happen to any woman, and so on. Throughout these contacts, the counselor works against the victim's becoming overdependent on her. Her position is providing support and information, not being a decision-maker.

When the victim fears the assailant's return, she is told how to obtain an injunction to keep him away from her residence. Medical verification of intercourse might still be possible, and she is advised of this. The legal system is explained, including that any time lapse between the incident and the police report decreases the possibility of successful apprehension and conviction.

If the call comes more than seventy-two hours after the attack, the victim's feelings may be buried under self-recrimination or denial. Once more, she is encouraged to talk about the experience. She is told about the emotions and actions that victims normally reveal. Then she does not perceive herself as being quite so alienated or unusual. Delayed legal restitution is explained. Testing for pregnancy, VD, infection, etc., are advised.

The advocate fills many roles. She is a model, ally, teacher, and possible witness. Her interest makes the victim understand that she has continual caring and support. Her being raped is a potential for any woman. The counselor will be present as an ally throughout the reporting process. If the authorities are not notified, the staff member and the victim will work together to find an appropriate outlet for her emotions. As a teacher, the advocate helps the victim learn a greater sense of self-control over what is happening to her. She might recall others who have undergone traumatic experiences with the end result of increased strength. Because the counselor may be the first to hear about the crime, she could be subpoenaed to testify. For this reason, notes might be taken of the conversation to refresh her memory later. (These are not released without the permission of the victim.)

Friends and relatives often call as well. Their needs and motives are determined. If they ask for ways to help the victim, suggestions are offered. When they are angry with her or feel she was at fault, the counselor listens and then tries to help them understand a rape experience. In cases where the significant other is calling on behalf of the victim, he or she is provided with the requested information to relay.

These groups also have referral lists for a variety of problems confronting victims. They are regularly revised and updated to ensure accuracy. The diverse catagories covered include emergency housing; child care; venereal disease and pregnancy testing programs; where to secure abortions; recommended therapists, doctors, clinics, and lawyers; self-defense classes; and so on.

For example, a victim states that a man broke into her home and raped her. She is afraid to remain there, but does not know where to go. The advocate then provides her with an appropriate name, address, telephone number, and possibly transportation to secure temporary lodging. A woman wishes to report a rape, but does not want to leave her baby unattended. The counselor gives her referrals for short-term childcare. A caller desires anonymity, but requires medical attention. She is advised of doctors or clinics that will not force her to report. As a victim's court date approaches, she has many questions about her rights. If the advocate is unable to answer, she will suggest sympathetic lawyers, who charge fees on a sliding scale. A woman wants to lessen her vulnerability and learn her body's capabilities. After deciding that self-defense is the answer, she is offered information about available courses.

Another vital service these organizations provide is that of catalyst in coordinating rap groups for victims. Talking to a stranger over the telephone is highly beneficial, but other outlets may be required. The staff members either compile names of interested victims or tell them about the regularly scheduled hours for these sessions. When this informal discussion takes place, often for the first time the women meet and talk with others in the same situation. The support and strength they gain in discovering shared feelings of guilt, fear, depression, and fury is tremendous. It is a cathartic experience for all participants. Complete understanding comes through the briefest look, a few poignant words. Sometimes they see one another only once, other times more often. Ventilation of feelings and information about individual methods of coping become the focal points. As each details her emotions stemming from the attack, the rest offer suggestions they have developed to regain control and self-esteem. When the need arises, separate groups are coordinated for significant people in the victim's life.

Eventually, advocates came to realize that their work had to go beyond victim services. Grappling with the problem after the fact would never eradicate the crime or ease the burden for victims. They began numerous programs of community education. They eroded the prevailing myths, discussed preventive measures, and explained the services they offered. Speakers attended club meetings and school classes, where they found receptive audiences.

As their credibility grew, so did their impact. Some police

officers, hospital staffs, and prosecutors attend seminars or workshops conducted by local crisis centers. The emphasis is on better treatment, sensitivity about the issue, changing attitudes, and increased awareness of the victim's point of view.

Revamping the criminal justice system's approach to victims has become another aim. Members and advisors research state laws, draw up suggested revisions, and lobby for their passage. They monitor rape hearings and trials, as well as write letters of criticism and praise to those responsible for handling the cases.

Groups publish and distribute flyers, fact sheets, pamphlets, and brochures tailored to the individual community. They cover such varied subjects as safety and awareness techniques, alternatives to the criminal justice system, reporting procedure, and services provided.

Funding becomes an immediate problem, even if the only resource offered is a telephone crisis line. Sources being used range from private tax-deductible donations, to revenue sharing, grant-giving foundations, YWCA, National Organization for Women, churches, and the Law Enforcement Assistance Administration (LEAA). Other centers resort to month-to-month subsistence by holding benefits, charging for lectures, and so on.

Although the information given here represents the activities and services of less than 10 percent of the antirape organizations, all are linked by moments of triumph and times of despair. Each begins as a small, cohesive unit of women sharing the same philosophy. As their scope broadens, many strive to become more "legitimate" agencies. In order to gain credibility, financing, and improvements in the reporting procedure, they may have to give up some things. They may find they are adopting policies and structures that are uncomfortable. Often, more energy is devoted to filling out forms and meeting grantors' requirements than to aiding victims and stopping rape.

In some areas, debates swell as to who should assume

ultimate responsibility for this work. People become territorial. Some consider rape and victim services a legal "problem." Others say it is a medical emergency, or should be the concern of those in the mental health profession. Because many antirape projects point out deficiencies in the police, hospital, and courts, adverse publicity is generated about these agencies, so they do not want to listen to advocates. Now some groups have gone under the umbrella of existing institutions, or those very institutions have developed task forces of their own. But victims who would refuse to turn to the establishment after being raped would be just as reticent to contact a center that is working hand-in-hand with the legal justice system. Thus, again, there is no place for them to go.

Another controversy springs from the issue of lay versus professional help for victims. Those in authority state that most community-based crisis center members lack professional credentials. They are not doctors, lawyers, therapists, or social workers. By definition, then, they are not qualified to provide aid. But those staffs worked countless hours prior to any professional concern about the short- or long-term difficulties experienced by victims. Their services remain totally free, while most therapists, psychiatrists, etc., charge. They stress self-help, instead of relying on multidegreed people. Their insight is more than proficient enough to know where to guide a woman who requires professional counseling. Victims need most a person who cares, no matter the number of college diplomas.

Both victories and defeats of advocate organizations are listed here in the hope that worthwhile projects can be emulated and problems and failures avoided. Rape is not the problem only of victims or crisis center staffs. It is everyone's. People should be aware of the impediments blocking these groups. They should join with them to solve the dilemmas.

One of the first centers was in Washington, D.C. Originally the members offered only phone counseling, referrals, and speakers. Then they moved into the vital areas of sensitivity training for police and medical personnel, worked to have self-defense taught in schools, and eventually acted as a clearinghouse for other groups around the country. They produce much written material, including a brochure on how to start a rape crisis center. Their address is D.C. Rape Crisis Center, P.O. Box 21005, Washington, D.C. 20009.

After years of aggravation, they finally made a small inroad with D.C. General Hospital, where all city victims are taken. The administrators said that victims would be allowed to wait in the maternity ward instead of the emergency room. The problem is that this hospital lost is accreditation because that ward was so unsanitary. The education programs set up by advocates for junior and senior high age women in public and private schools have been well attended.

Since March 1975 they have received money from the Department of Human Resources, the social welfare branch of the district government. To maintain some autonomy, they sought other sources. In exchange for their partial funding, the city officials wanted an itemized budget, daily schedule of past activities, projected schedule, narrative of all events, and monthly meetings with the contract administrator. The checks reimbursing the center took six to eight weeks to process. Then the government even sent monitors to the speaking engagements.

The staff kept working and providing more services than required by the contract. The money involved was not a staggering amount, approximately $1,800 a month, a minimal item in any city's budget. In the late winter of 1976 it appeared that even this allocation would be denied. The justification was that the numerical decrease in reported rapes could not be linked to the center's work. Finally, they received financial help, but the threat of its elimination remains.

Women Organized Against Rape, 1220 Sansom Street, 11th Floor, Philadelphia, Pennsylvania 19107, suffered growing pains as well. As their membership increased in number and influence in the community, they accepted funding from Philadelphia General Hospital. Conflicts arose with the hospital administration because they did not want the WOAR members to have any control over the program. In the beginning, the women were intimidated, until they realized they could refuse to work with the hospital and function independently. Consequently, they walked out of several meetings and eventually gained more power over the decision-making processes. To ensure their freedom, they secured additional types of funding. The reforms they gained include more immediate attention by the physicians in obtaining the correct evidence from the victim, counselors on call at the hospital if the victim wants to talk, and options other than the morning-after pill. Philadelphia is now one of the nation's leaders in innovative research and programs for victims and their families.

Boston Area Rape Crisis Center, c/o Women's Center, 46 Pleasant Street, Cambridge, Massachusetts 02139, does not seek or accept grants. Since opening in 1972, they have handled over 4,000 calls from women aged six to eighty-four. While one of their major projects is combatting attitudes which victimize women, their primary thrust is service-oriented. They provide the standard operations, including a thorough leaflet for victims.

The Stop Rape Task Force, in Baton Rouge, began organizing in May 1974. By November, they were ready for business. After negotiating for LEAA funding, they succeeded in receiving a grant. In July 1975 they changed their name to Stop Rape Crisis Center (P.O. Box 65037, Baton Rouge, Louisiana 70806). The contractual agreement stated that the center would be separate from the district attorney's office and that victim counseling had priority over convictions. The grant further said, "No one will be denied services if they choose not to report."

During the next year they became embroiled in difficulties. District Attorney Ossie Brown, the project director, notified the center to end services not only to nonreporters, but also those who had reported but whose cases had concluded. When the center's administrator, Virginia Ellis, objected to the new policy, he fired her. Following that, the entire staff, paid and volunteer, resigned. Then the center was operated by employees of the criminal justice system, with a resulting deterioration of victim services.

Instead of being able to devote full time to helping victims, the original members had to counteract the district attorney, gather community support, talk to groups, and publicize the facts of the disagreement. By 1977 things were back on a more even keel, but friction continued.

The Shreveport/Bossier Women Against Rape volunteer crisis line operated for more than a year on community donations. Prior to running out of money, they applied for an LEAA grant. That and other requests for assistance were turned down. They had to close.

The Rape Crisis Center, P.O. Box 843, Tucson, Arizona 85702, has had better luck. In addition to the regular functions, they have a Concentrated Employment Training Administration (CETA) project doing outreach and education in the combined areas of sexual and physical abuse.

The women in Indianapolis also have had good results and less frustration. Organized under the name of Women United Against Rape (Anti-Crime Crusade, 5343 North Arlington Avenue, Indianapolis, Indiana 46226), they have 50,-000 supporters. They adopted a twenty-five-point program, which included having the chamber of commerce send letters to 1,000 industries with the plea to have meetings for women employees on combatting rape. Most industries contacted carried through. After their recommendation, more than 500 meetings of clubs, sororities, auxiliaries, church groups, and other women's organizations devoted discussions and workshops to the topic of rape. A volunteer architect, guided by women, designed a tower for parking lots so twenty-four-hour security could be improved. WUAR was also instrumental in changing the rape laws in their state. These are just a sample of their efforts.

Madison, Wisconsin, residents were concerned about the lack of adequate public transportation and poorly lit streets. After a rape conference was held in the winter of 1973, two projects evolved. One was the Women's Transit Authority (WTA, c/o YMCA, 306 N. Brooks Street, 53706), the other a crisis center (P.O. Box 1312, 53701). They complement each other, but operate independently.

The basic premise of WTA is women joining together to enhance their safety and increase their mobility. It is a non-profit, volunteer, campus-based organization. The members offer free rides for women at night and serve approximately 70 percent students and 30 percent community residents. Their operating hours are between 7:00 P.M. and 2:00 A.M., seven days a week. Each night two cars are used, one a shuttle service stopping hourly at designated points, the other taking passengers to a requested location. The workers at WTA realized they had to establish certain priorities when the volume of calls outstripped the cabs available. The original six-mile radius was narrowed to four. Their emphasis became transporting women alone or in groups of two. When there are more than that, they encourage them to divide a regular taxi fare.

In the beginning, the funding came from the University of Wisconsin, which paid for the office, telephone, gas, insurance, and cars. But the school officials refused to disclose the budget allotment, so the staff had no idea whether they should expand the project or worry about reducing it. Now they have outside financing and rent those items from the college.

WTA was the first of its kind in the country and can serve as a model for others. Although members admit accurate statistics are hard to come by, they believe the number of rapes has declined since the inception of the program.

Other activities in Madison include the Rape Crisis Center and the Dane County Project on Rape, an advocacy organization that grew out of the crisis center. Roberta Stoller, from the center, said, "We do accept donations and encourage groups who invite us to speak to consider making one if they can. A grant has been received from the American Lutheran Church to conduct workshops on rape. In January 1978 we expect to receive county money, which may include Title XX funds. The DCPR was the recipient of CETA funding to organize and conduct a rape prevention program."

One direction of their efforts has been the Whistle Stop project. It is a means both of rape prevention and of bringing aid more quickly to a victim. The DCPR provides legal and medical advocacy, as well as running prevention programs in businesses, schools, and community centers. They encourage victims to form rap groups and take names of interested people. They have more referrals of victims from the police, hospital, and prosecutor's office than of the victim calling them directly. The relationships have smoothed to the extent that the authorities suggest to victims that they contact DCPR.

The group in Cincinnati (Rape Crisis Center, c/o YWCA, 9th and Walnut, Cincinnati, Ohio 45202) has been very active. During the winter of 1977, they began negotiating with police to have advocates accompany them to calls of reported rape. They helped secure the passage of the new Ohio rape legislation that makes it mandatory for all hospitals to provide treatment for rape victims. Most county medical facilities have begun to establish protocols and special assistance for these women.

All groups working with victims have stressed the confidentiality of their support services. If this were not true, some women would never contact them.

The Women Against Rape of Champaign County (112

West Hill Street, Champaign, Illinois 61820) became one of the first test cases. Their policy typifies all organizations on this issue, and reads, "No information regarding a specific case or client is to be released to any person or agency without the client's expressed permission." Two counselors were subpoenaed to answer questions in court about an alleged client. After refusing to respond to the grand jury's questions, they were jailed. Only after the victim granted permission to have this formerly restricted material released were the counselors set free. The woman said that if it had not been such a drastic situation, she would have refused.

A similar situation took place in Pueblo, Colorado (Rape Crisis Center, 509 Colorado Avenue, Suite G, 81004). The records of two victims involved in separate cases were subpoenaed by the local juvenile court. Because the victims could not be reached, the staff members who had originally talked with them, Carole Morgan and Karin Kittrick, went to court without the records. They were then held in contempt and jailed for refusing to hand over the documents. The judge refused to let them exercise their right to counsel. After being held for several days, they were let out of confinement when the victims appeared and granted permission.

The victims were under pressure to sign releases. Had they refused, a writ of prohibition could have been filed which would have appealed the contempt case to the state supreme court. Then Morgan and Kittrick would have been freed pending the decision. They did not know this. The Pueblo center receives LEAA funds. Because of that, there was further pressure not to provide any confidential material. Those records are protected by a federal law making anyone who receives LEAA money and keeps records for the purpose of research immune from any court process regarding the data. If they had released the records without permission, they would have been liable to a jail sentence and/or fine. This procedure is applicable to all centers that are recipients of LEAA grants.

Currently, the only people who do not have to break that confidentiality are lawyers, physicians, and clergy, when acting in their official roles. Some victims cannot afford those private services. Others would not turn to them for help, even if they could provide it. All groups work with victims based on the theory of absolute privacy. If this is broken, victims will both lose faith and refrain from contacting them.

Colorado, as well as California, introduced legislation to grant rape crisis centers the same type of privileges given others in protecting clients. If it passes, it would guarantee confidentiality to victims and eliminate the threat of subpoena to lay counselors. After the publicity generated by the Pueblo case, the crisis center had a tremendous increase in victim calls. Many involved incest, where complete privacy is one of the woman's main concerns.

Kansas City represents another mixture of successes and failures. Their funding is 75 percent LEAA money, with the remainder coming from county revenue sharing, city community development, and student funds from the University of Kansas. During the past two years, they have been instrumental in having more cases prosecuted, devising with the police a consistent record-keeping system, and running good in-service training for the officers and hospital staffs. They count as losses their difficulty in convincing county law enforcement people to take rape cases "seriously," their inability to have reduced the high hospital costs for the victim's mandatory examination, the recurring insensitivity by some of the hospital personnel, and a clerical error by the prosecutor that allowed a reduced plea by an assailant. They keep their presence known by "checking in to see how everything is going" on a regular basis. "We've found this has been the best way to keep gears meshing efficiently."

The Rape and Sexual Assault Center, 2617 Hennepin Avenue, Minneapolis, Minnesota 55408, is one program of a multiservice agency. It opened in 1972 and since that time

206 : Fighting Back

has been financed by six congregations, private donations, and grants. Although more cases are being prosecuted yearly by the county attorney's office, victims still run up against the "good" case versus the "poor." The prosecutors will accept only those they believe they can win. As a result, many women seeking a legal resolution do not get their day in court. They were hitchhiking, drinking, previously acquainted with the accused, and so forth.

Within the county attorney's office is a special program, the Sexual Assault Services (SAS). It was designed to enable a woman to go through the system with as much support and sensitive treatment as possible, and also act as an intermediary among the rape center, police, and courts.

Another innovation to their credit is a new hospital procedure. Now all medical follow-up tests for victims are scheduled for certain days and times at the OB-GYN clinic at the county facility. A counselor from the center is present during those hours and available to speak to victims.

More advocate groups are operating in the midwest. The Coalition Against Rape, 2545 R Street, Lincoln, Nebraska 68503, is assisting in the development of treatment for sex offenders. A few other organizations have similar projects, where they conduct discussion sessions for convicted assailants, sometimes along with victims. These are still in the experimental stage, with no specific conclusions as yet.

The CAR members feel it is important to offer services to significant men in the victims' life. Thus they devised a program of matching up brothers, fathers, and husbands of these women. Unlike many groups, this one strongly encourages women to report rapes and attempted rapes, with the qualifier that they do not have to prosecute. They offer advocacy during and after the legal procedure.

In addition to the standard programs provided by all crisis centers, the group in Missoula, Montana (Women's Place, 1130 West Broadway, 59801), sponsored a violence and women conference. They recommend that all citizens take advantage of a public relations effort run by the police and sheriff's department. People are permitted to ride with these officers while they are on duty, to increase community awareness about the job of law enforcement.

Rape Relief, #4–45 Kingsway, Vancouver, British Columbia V5T 3H7, has been exceptionally effective for the last several years. They have encounter groups at Mountain Prison with convicted sex offenders. Other projects include training sessions for women who are from different ethnic backgrounds. After the completion of the workshops, these people volunteered to be contact and information representatives in their communities. Much of their printed material has been translated into Japanese, Chinese, Greek, Spanish, German, and French. One article they wrote about rape was translated into Punjabi and published in a magazine that was circulated both among local East Indians and in India.

The solicitor-general supplied a grant for them to conduct a series of workshops in cities around the province. These consisted of two weekend training sessions in each of ten small towns. The goal was to instigate the setting up of rape relief-related programs in those areas.

To maintain their own education on the issue, three or four times a year they attend collective seminars. They invite outside guests such as police officers, lawyers, and therapists to speak.

Megan Ellis, an advocate, said, "The constant challenge is to keep clear goals and perspectives, even when all the phones are ringing off their hooks. We realize only too well that if we don't do that, we are in danger of becoming just another social service agency."

The British Columbia police commission and the rape relief members joined together to oversee the production of a film. Bonnie Krepps is the film's producer/director.

The Seattle Rape Relief (University of Washington YWCA, 4224 University Way N.E., 98105), has LEAA funding for a three-part program: rape relief, counseling, and advocacy; work with the medical center, with women social workers on call to aid victims; and training for model police techniques in questioning victims and devising better prosecuting methods.

When asked what successes and failures they had had in the last year, Jill Milholland replied, "It's difficult to answer this in twenty pages or less. We've experienced—both in connection with the police, hospital, and courts—successes, failures, compromises, etc. We've seen more than several cases through to satisfactory outcomes. Others not so satisfactory. Our rape center alone, excluding King County, ten other neighboring ones, and the Seattle sexual assault center, has had 280 separate cases from January to August 1977. In the course of dealing with each individual, we have come up against fair to excellent to totally insensitive treatment by local authorities and hospitals. We have developed comprehensive training programs for our advocates, plus the police and legal personnel. Our advocate training packet is $10. The police sensitivity training manual is $5. We are also working on an outreach program with the aid of a special coordinator and two workers."

When a small group of women decided to open a hot line in Renton, Washington, a Seattle suburb, they received more calls from victims during their first month of existence than the police had gotten in three years. The population is approximately 30,000, and no authorities had considered rape a problem in their jurisdiction. The twelve organizers of the crisis service then began working with NOW to provide for a wider variety of women's needs.

San Francisco has several antirape projects. The Women's Switchboard, 63 Brady Street, 94103, produced plastic-coated cards listing the names and telephone numbers of all California rape crisis centers on one side and emergency information on the other.

Several years ago, San Francisco was one of the first recipients of a $100,000 LEAA grant. The public officials bypassed the extensive experience of the local Women Against Rape, and awarded the money to the Queen's Bench Foundation, an association of lawyers and judges. Rather than direct services to victims, the money went to research. There were high staff salaries, long-distance travel expenses, consultant fees to professionals, and a subgrant to the police department. The officers used it to purchase two squad cars and a pair of binoculars.

The first rape victimization study by Queen's Bench was based on interviews with only fifty-five women. Although the data gathered was supposed to be specifically applicable to San Francisco, only twenty-eight of the respondents were attacked in that city. There was also a lack of racial balance in the participants. The grant was renewed the following year for more research.

Meanwhile the volunteers in WAR continued to provide outreach to hospitals, wrote an excellent handbook, *Not a Fleeting Rage*, and offer the other general services. One unique program they have is coaching for victims prior to their preliminary hearings. In these sessions they use role-playing and take the woman through a mock-up—a rehearsal —of the trial procedure. Participants find this alleviates many of their fears, because they have a realistic picture of what to expect. Funding comes from small grants and private donations. Their address is Women Against Rape, 1800 Market Street, Box 139, San Francisco, California 94102.

Joan Robins, director of education for the Los Angeles Commission on Assaults Against Women, P.O. Box 145, Venice, California 90291, reported they are in the process of developing a community-wide rape prevention program as part of their National Institute of Mental Health grant. The results will be shared at the close of the project. They are also conducting neighborhood organizing, with the emphasis on the Whistle Alert System and self-defense classes. They use two films, *Rape Culture* and *No Lies,* for their programs, instead of *Lady Beware,* which was made by the police department. The commission members find that the last film instills fear in women and keeps up the stereotype of "ladies" by showing women in high heels and skirts.

Statewide coalitions of antirape groups have formed in several areas, including Pennsylvania, Rhode Island, Louisiana, and California. Local, regional, and general meetings are held to exchange ideas and learn from each group's successes.

The goals of the Pennsylvania organization are representative of all. Their work centers around monitoring rape legislation; developing education programs; improving the status of victims in the criminal justice system; promoting victim advocacy; establishing consumer control of mental health services; and improving availability and quality of care from mental health facilities and other community support systems.

Now there is a national network, not only in the United States, but also in Canada and Australia.

The Feminist Alliance Against Rape, P.O. Box 21033, Washington, D.C. 20009, telephone (202) 543-1223, which grew out of the Washington, D.C., rape crisis center, began in the mid-1970s. Their first bimonthly newsletter stated they are "an autonomous organization of community-based and feminist-controlled antirape projects. . . ." Their continuing purpose is to provide a structure that can be used to strengthen the channels of communication and mutual support. FAAR is "dedicated to providing a forum for discussing and developing strategies to end rape." In 1977 they began a gradual merger and consolidation with the National Communications Network to publish a combined newsletter around the issues of rape, woman abuse, and other forms of violence against women.

Portions of the information in this chapter were first reported by FAAR. Their volunteer staff—Deb Friedman, Sue Lenaerts, Nancy McDonald, Loretta Ulmschneider, and Lois Yankowski—deserves much credit for their work. Their affiliate members are Valle Jones, Freada Klein, Jackie MacMillan, and I. Nekenge Toure.

The rape crisis centers in Canada joined together to secure some accountability from a nationally-funded program whose proposed purpose was the "coordination" of these groups. While this was the stated objective, government officials had requested no input from them. After much work, the organization is now headed by a national assistor. It acts as a liaison among centers and a national clearinghouse.

Canadian women fight many of the same battles as their American counterparts. The major difference is that they have a single set of rape laws applicable to the entire country, instead of separate laws for each province. Rape is narrowly defined, with strict corroboration requirements and admissability of prior sexual history. These elements are being challenged. The address is Canadian Rape Crisis Centres, 3710 Jeanne Mance, Montreal, P.Q., Canada H2X 2K5.

In March 1976 a conference was held in Sydney which brought about the formation of Australian Women Against Rape. The purpose was "a national political campaign to fight rape and the laws around rape." AWAR is primarily a coalition of centers, but now they are broadening their work. The Australian rape law is uniform, and its reform is one of the group's goals. The women want legal recognition of rape within marriage; corroboration requirements eliminated; previous sexual history excluded from the courtroom; and the legal definition to include forced anal/oral contact and the use of foreign objects. Their further aim is to change attitudes held by society toward rape.

As both a testament to community women's efforts and a co-opting of the issue, more traditional and conservative groups have now entered the field. In some areas the organizations are under the auspices and control of hospitals, courts, or local governments. If a victim reports a rape, she will be notified by these official channels about the existence of "sanctioned" projects. Their services, such as hot lines, social workers and counselors on call, accompaniment during the reporting procedure, and so on, have been listed in previous chapters.

The response to rape on the federal government level was the establishment of the National Center for the Prevention and Control of Rape (NCPCR, National Institute of Mental Health, 5600 Fishers Lane, Rockville, Maryland 20852). The center's responsibility, as legislated by Congress in 1975, is to "develop, implement, and evaluate promising models of mental health and related services for rape victims, their families, and offenders. The Center encourages research into the legal, social, and medical aspects of rape, and through its research and demonstration program will develop and provide much needed public information and training materials aimed at preventing and treating problems associated with rape."

Their work is concentrated in four areas: (1) funding research; (2) disseminating information; (3) developing and distributing training materials for police, hospital staffs, mental health workers, etc.; and (4) conducting conferences and offering technical assistance.

Research projects that currently are being conducted cover a wide range of issues including, "Rape Reporting: Causes and Consequence," "The Prevalence of Rape and Sexual Assault," "Attitudes Supportive of Rape in American Culture," "Victim Response to Rape: Alternative Outcomes," "The Evaluation and Treatment of Sexual Aggressives," "Marital Counseling for Rape Victims," "Community Action Strategies to Stop Rape," "Consultation in the Area of Sexual Child Abuse," and so on. Even though the center is not permitted, by law, to provide research funds for direct services, the data collected from these projects could aid anti-rape organizations in their work with victims.

The center hopes to compile and disseminate the results of the studies to professionals, as well as the general public. They are developing a directory of nationwide rape-related programs, bibliographies on the topic, and reviews of available material.

Rape is not only a women's problem or issue. An acknowledgment of this fact has been the recent development of men's groups addressing the topic. Although they remain few in number, their presence is being felt across the country. They often organize because a female friend was raped or they know a member of the local women's group. They can be found in telephone directories under the listing of Men Organized Against Rape, Men's Task Force Against Rape and Sexism, Men Against Sexist Violence, Men Against Rape, and others. Groups have sprung up from Boston and Philadelphia to Champaign-Urbana, with the strongest concentration in California in Berkeley, Sunnyvale, and Santa Cruz.

While the major focus has been providing services to husbands, lovers, sons, and male friends of victims, some also counsel victims of homosexual rape. The members try to give the significant men in the victim's life a true perspective on sexual assault. They explain that the rape did not happen to them, it is the woman who was attacked. They discovered that this approach is necessary because many men want to take over the rape as their own problem. The victim must decide what she wants done. The man's role is to offer support and understanding. He should not assume the position of dominant male and take charge.

With the victim's approval, the members of these groups sometimes go and talk with the offender. Frequently the assailant denies the event. They in turn explain that whenever you force sexual advances on an unwilling person, it is rape. The man must stop. He is responsible for his actions, the attack, not the victim. Speakers attend meetings to discuss their goals, objectives, and work. Men who have participated in these programs say it is hard to estimate their success, but they hope they are making some impact.

As the enormity of the problem has been realized, other groups have spun off from the original antirape projects. The issue becomes more than sexual assault. It includes all forms of physical and psychological violence against women.

The Alliance Against Sexual Coercion, P.O. Box 1, Cambridge, Massachusetts 02139, typifies these. Their emphasis is on sexual coercion at the workplace. They list their areas of concern as "verbal harassment, abuse, subtle forms of pressure for sexual activity, as well as rape and attempted rape. Not just employers, but co-workers and clients also. Women suffer this in silence, for fear of losing their jobs. Studies show this silence is emotionally destructive."

They formed with the goal of ending these practices. Their short-term objectives are: documenting and assessing the scope of the problem; acting as a clearinghouse for information related to the issue; developing a more thorough feminist analysis of the topic; educating the community as to the facts of this problem; and creating legal and emotional resources and additional long-range options for women who are subject to this. For those in this situation, they have developed a packet of material available for a $2 donation for the general public, $1 for community-based volunteer groups.

Other specialized organizations are appearing and spreading nationwide. Women have long been angered by the portrayal of females in advertising promotions. In 1976–77 a new twist began. As a selling device, women were depicted as victims of violence. The concern was that people would be lulled into believing these aggressive acts were acceptable. They would become complacent about violence against women.

With this in mind, Women Against Violence Against Women (WAVAW, 1727 N. Spring Street, Los Angeles, California 90012) started working. California NOW joined with them to combat this practice in the record industry. During a matter of months, several companies had produced albums with covers showing women being chained, bound, and mutilated. Elektra/Asylum, Warner, and Atlantic Records (all subsidiaries of Warner Communications, Inc.) were the most blatant offenders. They became the objects of a national boycott which began in December 1976. Although the chairperson of the board for Elektra/Asylum said they would change their company policy, the boycott continues until all three comply and stop using such images in their promotions. WAVAW has a slide show of thirty examples of sexual violence on covers, window displays, and billboards.

The Boston WAVAW geared their campaign against the trend in commercial advertising of having department store windows showing women being murdered, committing suicide, and as victims of mayhem. Bloomingdale's catalog had models in poses suggesting violence, the occult, and lesbianism. WAVAW members demonstrated in front of the stores and launched a letter-writing project. They also recommended boycotting record stores selling the albums mentioned above.

WAVAW is not advocating censorship. The volunteers are committed to first amendment rights, but they firmly believe corporations should have some responsibility and accountability to the welfare of women. The least they can do is withdraw those examples which are highly offensive and show women in degrading, frightening situations.

And the work continues. All these diverse organizations share a common goal. They want to become obsolete.

9: *Alternative Answers*

Rape happens. Minute after minute. Day after day. The only response society prescribes for the victim is a prompt report to a law enforcement agency. During a sexual assault, control and power have been stripped from her. Their quick restoration is imperative. Yet the police, hospital personnel, and prosecutors continue to deny the woman these two elements. She is a witness for the state and remains in a passive role, being told what to do and when to do it.

A report guarantees neither protection from the assailant for the victim nor a warning about him for other women. On the few occasions when the rapist is incarcerated, rehabilitation programs are practically nonexistent. And no authorities supply recommendations for releasing the woman's anger when it begins to boil. Frustration grows to fury with the discovery that these dilemmas have only limited solutions. An action which has changed the victim's life leaves the criminal untouched.

But there are some options. More women are learning that they do not have to be alone or powerless. Many community-based advocate groups have developed procedures to help them. Even if the victim lives in a town that does not have such an organization, certain methods can be used, either on an individual basis or with friends.

The woman must first decide what result she hopes to accomplish. Does she want to concentrate on the specific man who assaulted her or participate in an action directed against all men who threaten and intimidate women? Is em-

barrassment or humiliation of the attacker her aim? Will
monetary restitution help in some way? Does she want to
warn and possibly protect others from the assailant? Would
joining in a unified show of strength aid her? Would learning
self-defense skills help decrease some of her anger, tension,
and fear?

A few women have gained national attention when they
were forced to settle for the ultimate in self-defense. They
killed their attackers. While I am not advocating death for all
rapists, these women vividly document the fact that assailants
can no longer anticipate meager resistance. The original concept that a female should fight to the death to protect her
honor may shift in an ironic fashion. The life that could be
ended might be the rapist's not his victim's.

Confrontations

A man is at his office, surrounded by co-workers. He
has dismissed the fact that he raped his date on Saturday
night. The door opens, and a group of people enter the
room. A woman steps forward and says, "That's the man who
raped me." She is not there to reason with him or accept a
rebuttal. She continues making a statement about his actions,
reflecting on his attitude toward women. He is responsible
for his behavior and must change. His anonymity no longer
prevails. As they leave, a participant places a flyer on his desk
which emphasizes how the man can change. It is not his right
to rape or humiliate women. His actions are being monitored. A few weeks later he receives a follow-up letter reinforcing these same ideas.

This direct confrontation tactic was devised by the members of Santa Cruz (California) Women Against Rape. That
type of scene has been repeated numerous times in their
community. For the victim, it offers the chance to be in a
position of control. She is afforded power over the man who
removed it from her during the attack. If he suffers any embarrassment, it is minimal compared to what she endured.

A confrontation is the decision solely of the victim. If she wants one, and feels safe from offender retaliation, she is encouraged to plan such an event. She decides when and where it will occur. She organizes her thoughts and settles upon what she wants to say. Thus, she can direct her anger and reverse the roles of what took place during the rape. She has the choice of coordinating this activity with a group of her own friends or with WAR members. Occasionally, men accompany them and later attempt to provide informal education on altering the offender's behavior.

The Santa Cruz group has been criticized for disregarding the rights of the accused. People have faulted them for finding men guilty without a trial. To this accusation, they counter with the truth. So few men are ever found guilty of rape, and the rights of victims are so totally ignored, that some things must give. A confrontation is not undertaken in a capricious manner. The woman is trusted and believed. No physical violence has occurred. And if the charge made were ever erroneous, the man can turn to legal channels.

A variation of this practice of direct confrontation is a letterwriting campaign. The victim writes letters about the rape, the man's illegal actions, and her resulting anger, to any person from whom the assailant would conceal this information. This includes such individuals as the man's family, employer, business associates, landlord, neighbors, and women friends. Prior to this kind of action, the victim must evaluate the same variables as in a confrontation. The results are similar, as well.

Civil Suits

Suing an offender in a civil suit is another alternative. In a criminal case, guilt must be proven "beyond a reasonable doubt." For a civil charge, there must be a "preponderance of evidence" that the woman suffered some type of "damage" or injury which was caused by the defendant's wrongful conduct. Instead of being a witness, she hires a lawyer. If she is incapable of paying the fee, she can secure an attorney through legal aid. She works with the lawyer in deciding the best course of action.

The court's function is to "do justice" by making the defendant pay money to the victim for injuries and/or losses directly or indirectly attributable to his behavior. The damages she has suffered can include such things as past and future medical expenses, loss of wages, lessening of potential earning capacity, damage or loss of use of property, damage to her reputation, past or future "pain and suffering," aggravation of a preexisting injury, and so forth. Pleading psychiatric or emotional injury is more difficult for the woman. A state- or defense-appointed psychiatrist will examine the victim and be called to testify. The many steps involved in this process are generally not worth the effort.

Even when those items cannot be proved or did not happen, the court sometimes awards nominal damages, court costs, and, in rare situations, her lawyer fees. At other times, punitive damages may be granted in cases of "fraud, malice or insult, or a wanton and reckless disregard of the injured party's rights and feelings." The court can also order a person to stay away from the victim's residence.

During a civil suit, the man will be publicly charged with his actions. He will not be able to escape anonymously. He will be held accountable for his actions. The woman is much more in control over this kind of proceeding. There is no in-depth questioning about her past sexual conduct, medical documentation of intercourse, and so on. There are psychological benefits to this course of action. She has done something. Her anger has an outlet. She has regained some of the power the man had taken from her. If she wins the case, the court or jury determines the amount of money she will receive from the assailant. When the man does not have a steady income or may not be able to pay the damages, many attorneys are hesitant to handle the case. But a woman has every right to pursue this route. Money aside, the offender has still experienced a degree of public humiliation. The tables are successfully turned.

Another possibility is a civil suit for damages against a public entity, corporation, government, or landlord. This can be done in addition to suing the defendant, because others can be named for negligence of some type. The charge would be maintaining unsafe conditions or conditions where people are unable to move freely without fear. Such things as faulty locks, unlighted stairwells, or lack of security guards could be brought out. For example, the assailant entered an office through a broken window and raped a female employee. Then the entity responsible for the building could be sued. When a rape occurs on school property, the college can be cited for negligence. If a sexual assault is committed by a state or federal government employee during his working hours, even if not on that property, the government can be sued for damages.

Going after large organizations has benefits and disadvantages. They have the finances to spend on high-powered lawyers and are often willing to let the matter drag on in hopes of the woman running out of money, time, and interest. Others fear the negative publicity generated by such cases and want to settle promptly. But this action can serve a greater purpose. It may force them to improve their safety precautions, so other women will be more protected.

It is less difficult to win a civil suit than a criminal one. A woman can also use both legal avenues, but if she has reported the offense to a law enforcement agency it is better to wait until that prosecution is completed before beginning a civil suit.

Some victims have even taken the assailant to small claims court or Justice of the Peace Court as it is called in some jurisdictions. Because there is a limit on how much "damage" can be claimed, with the top monetary award varying from state to state ($150 in Texas to $3,000 in Missouri), the main purpose of this procedure would not be financial gains. The psychological ones are the strong points in this endeavor. Once more, public humiliation and accountability for the perpetrator's actions are the key issues. Appeal is possible in most states under certain circumstances. For futher information, a victim should consult a lawyer to learn the specific process and requirements in her city.

Street Sheeting

Women understand the necessity of protecting each other from the random attacker. Some victims have contacted a rape crisis center for advice on this matter. One means is known as "street sheeting." The victim provides a detailed description of the man, his approach method, and all applicable data. A single-page flyer is then printed and distributed. These are posted on telephone poles, in women's restrooms in bars and restaurants, and on buildings in the locale of the assault. When the man's residence or workplace is known, signs are displayed there as well.

This action occurs only with the victim's approval and when she is free of any fears of possible assailant retaliation. She establishes as much control over the process as she wants.

The sheets often begin with the words "WOMEN. This is a Warning—Rapist at Large in ————," with the name of the town or neighborhood inserted. It goes on to give information about the man and his method of operation. There is a description, height, weight, facts about his manner, clothes style, pattern of attack, whether or not he is armed, and other data about his actions. When the man uses a car, the make, model, and license plate number are included if known. The notice ends with precautions to take and a request to alert other women in the area.

The main concern with such sheets is an injunction against posting, but that problem is minimal. If that happens, it indicates the main purpose has been served. They are being noticed. The injunction can only be against a specific flyer and not any future ones.

Listings

Five women in Dallas, Texas, decided to go beyond
the goal of street sheeting. They wanted to dent the wall of
silence surrounding offenders and to protect all women.
They hoped to make the men think about their actions and
realize they would not go unnoticed. In addition, they wanted
an educational method to raise questions about sexual assault and bring the problem out in the open. After a year's
work in the courthouse, they compiled a list of the men
indicted and the disposition of the cases for sex offenses
against women in Dallas County from 1960 to 1976.

These are not the names of convicted rapists, but rather
ones charged with a sex crime after the district attorney and
grand jury determined there was sufficient evidence against
the assailant to have a trial. These include not only rape, but
also attempted rape, incest, indecency with a child, and so on.

The leaflet contained an alphabetical listing of individuals'
names, the year of indictment, the offense with which
charged, etc. The women acknowledged that their data were
incomplete, because many assaults go unreported. Just because a person was not on the sheet did not mean he had
never attacked a woman. Although 341 multiple offenders
were noted, again caution was advised. They could have committed more crimes and never been accused. The same held
true for men listed a single time. They might have attacked
numerous women and continued their assaults anonymously.

They selected a symbolic title, the Kitty Genovese Wom-
en's Project, in memory of the twenty-eight-year-old New
Yorker who was murdered in 1964 while onlookers failed to
respond to her calls for help or even telephone the police.
Their work is dedicated to women who have lost their lives
"to sexism, a system that grooms women to be victims and
ignores their cries of hurt and anger when they are physically
and psychologically assaulted."

Over 20,000 copies were distributed in beauty parlors,
schools, shopping centers, laundromats, and neighborhood

centers. A local radio station broadcast the names as part of its observance of International Women's Day. Other media picked up the topic as well. When these women were blamed for ignoring the rights of the men, they countered in a similar vein. Few reported cases move as far as the indictment stage; even more never come to the attention of any law enforcment agency. This unofficial channel offered a small release for the anger felt.

The list included disproportionate numbers of minority and low-income men, because those are the ones more likely to be tried. But because they more often attack women from the same background, and those victims less readily turn to the police following an assault, the leaflet can help the women. Since its distribution in March 1977 four other cities in Texas have prepared lists for their jurisdictions.

Women in Pittsburgh, Pennsylvania, started an organization called Pittsburgh Action Against Rape. They publish a monthly *Rape Alert.* This is an easy, inexpensive educational tool which provides specifics about unapprehended rapists. The data are compiled from their telephone hot line and serve as a warning and protection for other women. They also include a "myth of the month" which portrays the crime in realistic terms. Issues began appearing in June 1977, and each is mailed to approximately 3,500 individuals and groups.

The Santa Cruz WAR organization has another innovative program to aid women in their community. For the last several years, they have supplied information for a monthly column in the local feminist journal *Definitely Biased.* The material covers details about men who have either attacked or in some manner sexually intimidated women. They consistently stress that women have more alternatives than turning to the ineffectual criminal justice system. They need not be helpless and powerless in asserting their rights.

Here's an example of their work.

Telephone hassler. Man with fairly high undisguised voice, sort of nervous, no distinguishing accents, 25–30ish sounding, makes obscene phone calls: "Modeling work" job offer, asks measurements and then concentrates on breasts. May work at Leasks or somewhere on Mission Street.

Hassle. Two women in car followed by light green Chevrolet Biscayne PIB 77–from Ocean Street until the women turned off at the Rio Del Mar exit. Men wanted them to pull over to the side of the road and smoke dope. Driver: early 20s, slightly curly blond hair, sideburns, mustache down to mouth, medium build. Passenger: early 20s, mid-shoulder length thin slightly wavy blond hair, clean-shaven, pockmarked, blue eyes, thin build.

Rape. 11-year-old woman raped on cliffs near National Bridges Beach. Man is white, 25–30 years old, 6 feet, 170 lbs., blue eyes, light complexion, medium-brown sandy-colored hair and 3 to 4 days' beard growth, blue Levi jacket and jeans, black gloves tucked under his belt. Motorcycle: red body, chrome fenders, front wheel has semi-extended forks.

There were fifteen items in the issue, ranging from the obscene telephone call to exhibitionists, attempted rapes, and rapes. They did not include the last number of the license plate, as protection against libel suits. They have learned from experience how to take good descriptions, and many women in that area have come to rely on them for warnings about such men.

Midnight Marches

All women know the anger that comes from the fear of rape. When searching for an outlet, some have used demonstrations and marches. In 1976, women in New York joined together for a Walk Against Rape. This unified show of strength and solidarity took place during the evening in Central Park. It was coordinated by a coalition of twenty women's groups, under the auspices of the Rape Prevention Committee of the New York NOW. Nearly a thousand women marched and sang as they paraded through an area usually avoided, especially after dark. Their chants echoed the sentiments of females across the country. "Women United Will Never Be Defeated." "Enter the Park After

Dark." "Rape is Violence, Not Sex." "Fight for the Right to Walk at Night." "Women Fight Back at Men Who Attack."

For a short time the participants were allowed to alter their normal rape-prevention behavior. They had a hint of the total joy and freedom of being able to walk at night in a normally high-risk location without fear.

Self Defense

Ideally, women should learn self-defense skills as a preventive measure against possible attacks. After a rape experience, this type of training remains a realistic response because it can serve several purposes. The victim will learn basic awareness tactics, techniques to surprise an assailant and give her time to escape, how to get out of various holds, her physical capabilities, and so on. With this knowledge she will lessen her chances of becoming a victim again. Her self-confidence and a degree of peace of mind can be restored. Her mental image as a passive individual will be changed to that of one with strength and power.

Not all cities provide self-defense classes. Those programs available are generally sponsored by such organizations as the YWCA, a women's center, an antirape group, NOW, and so forth. Karate and judo are taught in more locations, but serious study of these skills requires great dedication, practice, and time.

These few brief examples of venting anger and attempting to find alternatives to the criminal justice system are overshadowed by the true, bleak picture of the crime. More thought and work is needed to afford page after page of constructive outlets for women.

Death

The few who have resorted to self-defense and killed their attackers have sometimes been swallowed up by the same system which normally saves the rapists from such fate.

Inez Garcia was raped by one man while another held her down. When she returned home, the men called, threatening to murder her if she did not leave town. She took a rifle and walked outside, where she encountered them. When one threw a knife at her, she fatally shot him. Nothing happened to the rapist, but Garcia was tried and found guilty of second degree murder. The prosecution stated that she had not been raped; she was merely upset about an illegal drug deal in which she was involved. During the nineteen months she spent in jail, she became a symbol of women's right to fight back and defend themselves against male offenders. It took three years until she was acquitted of all charges on March 5, 1977.

Joan Little gained national attention when she killed her jailer in self-defense. This black woman was being held on a breaking and entering charge when her white prison guard attempted to rape her. In 1975 she was acquitted for the murder, but still had to serve time for the other sentence. She escaped and fled to New York City, where she was apprehended. On June 9, 1978 she was returned to North Carolina to finish serving her sentence.

Virginia Tierce's case received much less coverage. She had met a man at a bar, and he accompanied her home. Once there, he tried to force her to commit fellatio. She refused, a fight ensued, and she shot and killed him. It took two trials before the matter was finished. In the first one, the prosecutor brought up information about the dress she wore that night, how her home was decorated, and the length of time it was taking her to get through school. He stated that the man, Louis Shark, had been shot in the back while leaving Tierce's home. The coroner's report showed the opposite. Shark was facing her when the trigger was pulled. Even though it was a case of self-defense, she was found guilty of manslaughter. Eventually she was granted a retrial on the grounds of incompetency on the part of her lawyer. During this second trial, her defense attorney introduced evidence about the assailant's background. He had been convicted of rape and burglary in previous cases, in addition to having a history of violence against women. Tierce was finally acquitted.

Although Gloria Timmons' case was largely ignored by the national press, feminist newspapers reported the event. The odds were against her from the beginning because she was young, black, and poor. In 1972 her husband first attacked and raped her. When the police arrived, she was afraid to tell them what had occurred. Of course, she could not report a rape, but she could have charged him with assault.

Her husband's aggressions continued. When she had to be hospitalized because he poured scalding water in her face, she told the staff the truth of what had happened. Another time, he threw her down a flight of stairs. Then, he assaulted her in front of two witnesses when he discovered she had reported the earlier offense. She pressed charges. He was apprehended, but then was released pending the trial. Shortly afterwards, in 1973, she shot him in a bar as he was coming at her with a screwdriver.

She was taken into custody and informed by a lawyer that she had the choice of pleading guilty to manslaughter or having a trial for first degree murder. She took the first option. Her sentence was an indeterminate number of years, with no minimum, but a maximum of twenty. When her parole date came up, it was denied. Not until August 1977 was she granted parole, with a three year probation period. Her supporters are asking for an unconditional parole on the basis of self-defense.

In 1975, in Georgia, two black women, Dessie Woods and Cheryl Todd, were hitchhiking. They accepted a ride from a white insurance salesperson, Ronnie Horne. After he threatened to rape them, they turned on him and killed him with his own gun. The trial took place the next year, and they were found guilty. Todd received a sentence of five years, one-and-a-half of imprisonment and three-and-a-half of probation. Woods' penalty was twenty-two years, with a denial of an appeal bond. According to information provided by the

National Committee to Defend Dessie Woods, when she requested time to return home to make arrangements for her two children, this was refused. The committee further stated she was continually victimized by prison officials, who stripped her, put her into an isolation cell without a bed, and administered drugs to her against her will. Todd and Woods' appeals are still pending.[1]

Rape is a horrifying, humiliating, degrading, brutalizing, angering, demeaning, dehumanizing experience. Far from being sexual, it is a violent assault on the body, the mind, and the spirit. The event itself is hideous enough, but why is it women still have to suffer after the rape? Why does society shame so many victims into maintaining silence about the attack? Why does society point the finger of blame at the victims, not the assailants? Why are the victims evaluated, judged, and too frequently condemned?

Why are those very people set up by society to aid victims —the police, medical staffs, the prosecuting attorneys—so reticent to help? Why do legislators have to be dragged screaming, before they make much-needed revisions in the laws? Why do public officials place so many impediments in the way of community victim advocate groups whose main goals are to ease the victims' plight and to put an end to this crime's occurrence? Why are all women—the potential victims—told *they* must limit their freedom, while men—the potential rapists—may live without restrictions?

How many more women must be raped before our nation will rise up in outrage? How many lives must be irrevocably altered before all people say, "No more." The attitudes that permit the atrocity of rape to continue *must* be changed. And that change must start now.

Rape happens. Minute after minute. Day after day. What do you do with your anger?

10: "...Except Rape...."

WASHINGTON (UPI) DECEMBER 1977. *FBI quarterly crime statistics disclosed a decline in the nation's crime rate for a fourth straight time, dropping 6 percent in the first nine months of this year compared to the same period last year.*

The new FBI report yesterday showed the crime rate tumbled more in big cities than in smaller cities and more in urban areas than in rural areas.

All types of serious crimes reported by police agencies across the country to the FBI decreased, except rape, up 8 percent. . . .

Appendix A

State Rape Laws

Because of space limitations, the following information is only a brief summary of each state's rape laws. Legislative activity is an ongoing process, so some of this data will become outdated. The original language of the laws, codes, and statutes is retained whenever possible. The areas highlighted here include the definition of the crime, corroboration requirements, admissibility of the introduction of the victim's prior sexual conduct, any special measures pertaining to victims, and the sentence structure.

Before the jurors retire to deliberate the verdict of the case, the judge generally instructs them as to what the sentences could be. Then once the jury makes a factual determination of the outcome, they return with a decision of guilty or not guilty. In most states, the judge recommends the sentence unless otherwise noted.

Although examples of the possible sentences imposed in each state are given, few convicted offenders serve the total amount of time to which they are sentenced. Most cases are reviewed after approximately one-third of the original time has passed. Then an Adult Authority, Parole Board, or its equivalent, examines the offender's conduct, movement toward rehabilitation, his attitude, cooperation, and so forth, and decides whether he should be released on parole.

It is recommended that interested readers consult their local law libraries to study their own state rape legislation in its entirety.

ALABAMA

Alabama does not formally define rape in the statute, but rather follows the common-law definition of the crime. Rape is unlawful carnal knowledge of a woman, not one's wife, forcibly and against her will. Rape also includes various circumstances such as when carnal knowledge of a woman or girl is accomplished after the assailant administers her drugs; when the woman is married and the assailant falsely impersonates her husband. Proof of penetration is required, as is actual or constructive (declared such by judicial interpretation) force. Resistance is necessary. Corroboration is not needed, except in the case of a man impersonating the victim's husband. There are no restrictions on the admissibility of evidence regarding the victim's prior sexual conduct. Promptness of complaint is admissible evidence. The sentences range from a minimum of two years to a maximum of death, with the jury determining the penalty.

ALASKA

The Alaska statutes, revised in 1976, make the common-law definition sex-neutral. Rape is unlawful carnal knowledge of another person, not one's spouse, forcibly and against the will of the other person. Carnal knowledge now includes sexual, oral, and anal intercourse. There are limitations on the admissibility of the sexual history of the complaining witness. Corroboration is not mandatory. The statutes combine incest and statutory rape. In 1977 the entire Alaska criminal code was under review, so possibly there will be more changes in the rape laws. The sentence is any term of years, from parole and a suspended sentence to a maximum of twenty years.

ARIZONA

Arizona divides the crime of rape into degrees. First degree is an act of sexual intercourse accomplished with a female, not the wife of the perpetrator, where the female is incapable through unsoundness of mind of giving legal consent; where the female's resistance is overcome by force or violence; or where she is prevented from resisting by threats of force. Second degree is any other circumstance, and where the female is less than eighteen years of age. Corroboration is not necessary, unless there is a conflict in the evidence about the victim's intimidation. The cautionary instruction to the jury is allowed. The essence of the crime is penetration and outrage to the person and the feelings of the female. There are no restrictions on the admissibility of information about the victim's prior sexual activities. The sentence varies according to any previous rape convictions, whether the offender was armed with a dangerous weapon, and the degree of the crime. The minimum penalty is any term; the maximum is life.

ARKANSAS

The Arkansas law was revised in 1975 retaining the word *rape* but expanding the definition. Rape is sexual intercourse or deviant sexual activity accomplished by forcible compulsion, or when the person is incapable of giving consent. Deviant sexual activity is an act of sexual gratification involving penetration of the anus or mouth by the penis or of the vagina and anus by any body member or foreign instrument. Forcible compulsion is defined as physical force, or the threat, expressed or implied, of death or physical injury or kidnapping. No corroboration is required. The rape charge has three degrees. The sexual history of the victim is strictly limited in some cases, widely explored in others. The penalty ranges from a minimum of a fine and/or imprisonment of ninety days, to a maximum of fifty years or life.

CALIFORNIA

In California, rape is defined as sexual intercourse with a female, not one's wife, when her resistance is overcome or prevented through force or threats, drugs or unconsciousness; when she is deceived into thinking the offender is her husband; or when she is legally incapable of giving consent, due to her mental condition. The jury instruction regarding the consent issue and the term "unchaste character" were banned. The cautionary charge, which was mandatory until 1975, is now eliminated. The law restricts and regulates the admissibility of the victim's sexual history in order to impeach her testimony. The defense can request a psychiatric examination of the victim if there is no corroborative evidence. All county hospitals must provide free pregnancy and venereal disease testing for victims. Medical professionals trained in examining rape victims must be on call at county hospitals where the population is over 500,000. The sentences span from a minimum of probation to three to fifteen years to life if there is great bodily injury to the victim of forcible rape. The jury recommends the punishment in a jury trial. There is no probation if the assailant is convicted of rape with force and violence and it is a second offense.

COLORADO

Colorado replaced its rape statute in 1975 with a sexual assault one. It has four degrees, and uses the terms *actor* and *victim*. Sexual assault in the first degree: sexual penetration —sexual intercourse, cunnilingus, fellatio, analingus, or anal intercourse—accomplished by force or threats. Second degree: sexual intrusion—any intrusion by an object or any part of the body except the mouth, tongue, or penis into the genital or anal opening. Third degree: sexual contact—intentional touching for the purposes of sexual arousal, gratification, or abuse without consent. The classification for all degrees is raised if the actor is armed, aided, and abetted, or if the victim suffers serious personal injury. Resistance is not required. There is a spousal exception including couples involved in common-law marriages. No corroboration is necessary. The cautionary instruction to the jury was banned in 1975. There are restrictions on the introduction of the victim's past or subsequent sexual conduct. The sentences are according to the degree of the crime, from a misdemeanor with a fine, to a felony with a maximum of fifty years.

CONNECTICUT

In 1975 the Connecticut statute was rewritten, redefining and expanding the nature of the crime. It is called a sexual assault between an actor and a person and is broken down into four degrees. Sexual intercourse now includes vaginal or anal intercourse, fellatio, and cunnilingus between persons, regardless of sex. Penetration may be by any object. Sexual contact for the purpose of the actor's sexual gratification is illegal. The use of force is defined as the use of a dangerous instrument, actual physical force or violence, or superior physical strength. The corroboration and prompt complaint requirements were repealed in 1975. A bill restricting information about the past sexual history of the victim was introduced in 1976, but failed to pass. The penalties range from fines to imprisonment for an unstated amount of time.

DELAWARE

In Delaware, rape is defined as sexual intercourse with a female, not his wife, without consent, or with a male. First degree includes serious physical, mental, or emotional injury, or when the victim is not the voluntary social companion. The second degree includes all other sexual intercourse and any act of coitus, including with the mouth or anus. The corroboration requirement was repealed in 1974. There are some limitations on the victim's prior sexual activities being allowed as evidence. Delaware has a Crime Compensation Board that can award money to victims of all crimes. In 1975 a bill was introduced, but failed to pass, which would have made a woman who gave false testimony leading to a man's arrest and/or trial on a rape charge liable to be tried for contempt and sentenced to not less than one year imprisonment. The sentences span from a misdemeanor to a felony, a fine to life imprisonment. The jury may bring a verdict of assault in a rape trial.

DISTRICT OF COLUMBIA

In the District of Columbia, rape is defined as unlawful carnal knowledge of a female, forcibly and against her will. For adult victims, corroboration is necessary, but not for every element—medical proof of penetration, lack of consent, threat or use of force—of the charge. More supportive evidence is called for with juvenile victims. The sexual history may be introduced at the discretion of the judge. The sentence is life or any term of years.

FLORIDA

Florida redefined the crime as sexual battery, which includes oral, anal, or vaginal penetration by, or union with, the sexual organ of another, or by any other object without consent. Consent is defined as an intelligent, knowing, and voluntary consent, and shall not be construed to include coerced submission. The language used is offender/victim. Although corroboration is not necessary, the jury may be instructed about the quality of evidence. The sexual history is restricted. In 1974 a law was passed making it a misdemeanor to publish or broadcast information identifying sexual battery victims, but it was then judged unconstitutional. If the victim is fourteen years old or younger, the defense can request a psychiatric examination. The penalty is from a suspended sentence to life.

GEORGIA

Georgia follows the common-law definition of unlawful carnal knowledge of a female, not one's wife, forcibly and against her will. Corroboration is required for the facts of the case, but not identification. A bill limiting the admissibility of sexual history was passed in 1976. The sentences are from one year to life imprisonment, or death.

HAWAII

In Hawaii, rape is separated by degrees, depending upon the circumstances of the attack. First degree rape is sexual intercourse when accomplished by forcible compulsion and the female is not the voluntary social companion, or when bodily injury is inflicted. Second degree is sexual intercourse by forcible compulsion. Third degree is sexual intercourse with a female who is mentally defective, incapacitated, or physically helpless. Corroboration is not necessary, but the complaint must be made within one month of the offense or no prosecution is possible. There are limitations on the introduction of sexual history. Funds have been appropriated to provide comprehensive social and medical services to victims of sexual assault. No minimum sentence is recommended, with a maximum penalty of life.

IDAHO

Idaho's law dates back to 1864 and defines rape as sexual intercourse with a female, not the wife, when the female is underage; when the female is incapable of consent on account of unsoundness of mind; when the female's resistance is overcome or prevented by threats of harm; when the female is unconscious or deceived. Penetration is required, and the prosecution must prove force or violence. Corroboration is necessary when the victim's testimony is contradictory, her credibility impeached, or her unchastity shown. Prior sexual conduct is admissible as evidence. The sentence is at the discretion of the judge, from one year to life.

ILLINOIS

Although the Illinois rape laws were revised in 1973, the statute remains unfavorable to victims. Rape is defined as sexual intercourse with a female, not one's wife, by force and against her will, or where the female is unconscious or so mentally deranged or deficient that she cannot consent. Corroboration and a prompt complaint are required. The woman's reputation for chastity is admissible to impeach her credibility. A bill which would have restricted this, introduced in 1975, was defeated. Medical testimony is not necessary. A Rape Victim's Emergency Treatment Act of 1976 requires that a variety of medical services be made available to victims. The penalty for rape ranges from a fine, to a minimum of four years, to life imprisonment or death.

INDIANA

The Indiana statute defines rape as unlawful carnal knowledge with a female, not one's wife, forcibly and against her will; or if the woman is insane, idiotic, or feebleminded. Penetration is necessary. No corroboration is required. The evidence rules restrict the admissibility of the victim's sexual history. The sentence structure includes a determinate period with a minimum of two years and a maximum penalty of twenty-one years. When the female is less than twelve and the offender is eighteen or older, it is a mandatory life sentence. In 1974 an amendment passed prohibiting suspended sentences for rape convictions.

IOWA

In 1978, Iowa began prosecuting rape under a new sexual abuse section of its revised criminal code. Prior to that, the code, originally enacted in 1851, had been one of the most archaic. Sexual abuse is defined as any sex act between persons when the act is accomplished by force, threats, or against the will of the other person; or when the other person suffers from a mental defect or an incapacity which precludes offering consent. *Sex act* includes vaginal, oral, or anal intercourse. No corroboration is necessary. The cautionary charge is forbidden. Any sexual conduct occurring more than a year before the attack must be proved relevant, away from the jury. Proof of physical resistance is no longer mandatory. The cost of the evidentiary medical examination and any treatment for venereal disease resulting from the assault is paid by the State Department of Health. The penalty is a minimum of five years to a maximum of life.

KANSAS

Rape was formerly a common-law offense in Kansas. It now reads penetration of a female sex organ by a male sex organ committed by a man with a woman, not his wife, without consent; or when resistance is overcome; or when the female is incapable of consenting or resistance is prevented. No corroboration is required. There are limitations placed on the introduction of the victim's prior sexual conduct. Previous rape convictions of the accused are admissible. The sentence is an indeterminate term. The length of time served depends upon the offender's conduct while incarcerated, his rehabilitation, the parole board's evaluation, etc.

KENTUCKY

Kentucky revised the rape statutes in 1974 and 1976. While the crime is between two persons, gender unstated, sexual intercourse retains its ordinary meaning. Rape in the first degree is sexual intercourse by forcible compulsion; or when the person is incapable of consent; or when the person is under sixteen; or is mentally defective, incapacitated, or physically helpless. Sexual abuse is sexual contact without consent. Forcible compulsion is defined as physical force or threat that overcomes resistance by placing the person in fear of immediate death, injury, or kidnapping. Lack of consent

238 : Fighting Back

is an element of each offense. No corroboration is needed. The sexual history may be introduced after the relevancy is determined at an in camera hearing. Impotence of the accused is a defense, as well as proving ignorance or mistake of fact of the victim's incapacity to consent. There is a crime compensation statute for victims. The sentences range from one year to twenty.

LOUISIANA

Louisiana recognizes heterosexual, homosexual, and aggravated rape where resistance is overcome or prevented by force or threat of force. Simple rape is intercourse without consent. Forcible rape is sexual intercourse without consent where the female is prevented from resisting. Aggravated and simple rape apply to both homo- and heterosexual offenses, forcible rape only to heterosexual. No corroboration is necessary. Although the victim's past sexual conduct except with the defendant is generally inadmissible, Louisiana has not established any procedure to determine admissibility. The penalty for aggravated rape is death; for simple and forcible rape, one to twenty years at hard labor.

MAINE

Maine retained the common-law definition until 1976. It is now defined as compelling a person, other than one's spouse, to submit to sexual intercourse by force and against the person's will, or by threats of immediate death, serious bodily injury, or kidnapping of the victim or a third person. Sexual misconduct, abuse, and conduct by force, threat, and unconsented is defined sex-neutrally. Resistance is not necessary. Marriage is a defense, but *spouse* excludes those living apart. Corroboration is required unless the victim's testimony is clear and convincing. Promptness of complaint has decreased in importance. Only maximum penalties are listed, ranging from one to ten years.

MARYLAND

As of 1976, in Maryland, rape is defined as vaginal intercourse with another person by force or threat of force against the will and without consent. Penetration, force, and resistance are required elements. The Maryland code also includes unlawful carnal knowledge of a male under fourteen years of age by a female over eighteen. No corroboration is necessary. The introduction of the sexual history is limited for a forcible rape charge, but victims of other sexual offenses are not protected. There is a crime compensation statute.

The penalties span from a minimum of eighteen months to a maximum of life.

MASSACHUSETTS

Rape followed the common-law definition in Massachusetts until 1974. Now, it is unlawful sexual intercourse or unnatural sexual intercourse, oral or anal, accomplished by force or threat; or by administering a drug to a person in order to enable intercourse; or sexual intercourse other than rape with an idiot. The law is sex-neutral. Corroboration is required in some cases, and the victim's sexual history is admissible in the courtroom. Attempts to change this latter situation have failed to pass. The sentence depends upon the number of previous convictions and the age of the offender. No minimum sentence is stated, with the maximum being life, with no probation upon a second conviction.

MICHIGAN

In 1974, Michigan totally revised its entire legal concept of rape. Its approach has been used as a model for other jurisdictions. The original laws were replaced with ones defining criminal sexual conduct in sex-neutral terms, broken down into four degrees. Sexual penetration is sexual intercourse, cunnilingus, fellatio, anal intercourse, or any other intrusion of an object into the genital or anal openings of another's body. Sexual contact is intentional touching for the purpose of the actor's sexual gratification. First degree: sexual penetration under specific circumstances, i.e., the actor is aided and abetted; is armed; or causes personal injury; etc. Second degree: criminal sexual contact under certain specific circumstances as listed for first degree. Third degree: criminal sexual penetration under specific circumstances. Resistance by the victim is not required. The spousal exception does not include those living apart. Penetration is not required for any offense. Michigan has the strongest evidence provision in effect regarding the admissibility of the victim's sexual history. It is highly restrictive. Corroboration is not required. Each degree is matched with a minimum and maximum sentence, from a fine to life imprisonment.

MINNESOTA

In 1975, Minnesota passed one of the most comprehensive rape reform bills in the country. It is sex-neutral, with four degrees. Criminal sexual conduct is forced sexual penetration—sexual intercourse, cunnilingus, fellatio, or any intrusion of any object where the act is committed without consent. Sexual contact is defined as the intentional touching or coerced touching of another person or their clothing without consent. Consent is voluntary uncoerced manifestation of the present agreement. The degrees of the crime vary according to the age of the victim, the amount of force used, and the harm inflicted or threatened. Resistance is not required, nor is corroboration. The cautionary instruction to the jury is prohibited. Evidence of the victim's prior sexual activities is inadmissible, except in certain circumstances. The consent defense is banned when the complainant is between the ages of thirteen and sixteen. Costs of the medical examination are paid by the county, as are any legal fees the victim might incur. Each degree is listed with an accompanying maximum penalty, ranging from five to twenty years.

MISSISSIPPI

Mississippi uses the common-law definition that rape is unlawful carnal knowledge or ravishing of a female, not one's wife, by force and against her will. Penetration and force are required elements. Corroboration is necessary if the evidence is contradictory. There are no limitations on the admissibility of information about the victim's sexual history. No minimum penalty is stated, while death remains on the books as a maximum sentence.

MISSOURI

In Missouri, rape is unlawful carnal knowledge of a female, not one's wife, by force and against her will. Corroboration is required only when the victim's testimony is contradictory or unbelievable. Specific acts of unchastity are inadmissible, but a reputation for chastity is. The jury determines the sentence. The penalty is a minimum of two years, unless the victim was drugged, then the minimum is five years. The only maximum sentence listed is for assault with intent to rape, five years.

MONTANA

Montana made minor revisions in its code in 1973 and more inclusive ones in 1975. The words *sexual intercourse without consent* were substituted for *rape*. The law is sex-neutral. Sexual assault is defined as when one person knowingly subjects another, not one's spouse, to any sexual contact without consent. Sexual intercourse without consent is where a person knowingly has sexual intercourse without consent by force or threat of force, or if the victim is incapable of consent. There is a spousal exception, but not for deviant sexual conduct. Limitations are placed on the admissibility of the victim's prior sexual activities. Only maximum penalties are stated, ranging up to forty years.

NEBRASKA

The Nebraska rape statute was extensively revised in 1975. The law is now sex-neutral with two degrees, sexual penetration and sexual contact. Sexual penetration is sexual intercourse, cunnilingus, fellatio, anal intercourse, or any intrusion of any object by force; or when the victim is incapable of consent or resistance. Sexual contact is the intentional touching of the victim's or actor's intimate parts or clothing for the purpose of sexual arousal or gratification, by force; or when the victim is incapable of consent or resistance. There is no spousal exception for rape. Relevance of prior sexual activities of the victim as well as the defendant may be determined at an in camera hearing. There is an explicit legislative intent to protect the dignity of the victim. The sentences vary according to degree and to the severity of the victim's injuries. The minimum penalty is one year, with a maximum of twenty-five.

NEVADA

In Nevada, rape is unlawful carnal knowledge of a female, by force and against her will. Corroboration is not required. The *chaste character* terminology is forbidden. The introduction of the victim's prior sexual conduct is limited. As of 1975 the spousal exception excludes couples who have separated. The state pays the cost of the evidentiary medical examination. If the complaint is filed within three days of the rape, the state will also pay up to $1,000 for physical and emotional trauma treatment. The penalty for forcible rape is a minimum of five years with no earlier parole and a maximum of life.

NEW HAMPSHIRE

Prior to major revisions in 1975, the New Hampshire statutes had remained relatively unchanged since the late 1880s. Now they are sex-neutral, with two categories: sexual penetration and sexual contact. Sexual penetration has been broadened to include sexual intercourse, cunnilingus, fellatio, anal intercourse, or any intrusion of any object by force, threat, coercion, and without consent. Sexual contact is the intentional touching of the victim's sexual parts or clothing for the purpose of sexual gratification by force, threat, coer-

242 : Fighting Back

cion, and without consent. The spousal exception excludes
couples who have filed for separate maintenance or divorce
and those living apart. Corroboration is not necessary. New
Hampshire has one of the strictest limitations on the introduction of the victim's sexual history. Only prior consentual
relations with the accused are admissible evidence. The
offense must be reported to law enforcement authorities
within six months or there can be no prosecution. The
penalty structure lists only maximum sentences of up to
fifteen years.

NEW JERSEY

New Jersey defines rape as unlawful carnal knowledge of
a woman, not one's wife, by force and against her will. Force,
resistance, and nonconsent are required. A related offense
covers unlawful carnal knowledge of inmates or residents of
institutions for the feebleminded or mentally ill. Corroboration is no longer necessary. There are restrictions on evidence regarding the victim's sexual history, especially those
more than one year prior to the rape. The sentence structure
includes no minimum, but a maximum of thirty years or a
$5,000 fine.

NEW MEXICO

The New Mexico statute was revised in 1975. It is sex-
neutral, with degrees depending on whether there was penetration or contact, the victim's age, the amount of force used,
and injuries to the victim. Criminal sexual penetration includes sexual intercourse, cunnilingus, fellatio, anal intercourse, or penetration with any object. Criminal sexual
contact is the intentional touching or applying of force without consent to the unclothed intimate parts of another, or
intentionally causing another to touch one's intimate parts by
force without consent. The spousal exception excludes couples living apart and those who have filed for divorce or
separate maintenance. No corroboration is required. Evidence of the victim's previous sexual activities must be
proved relevant before a judge. The sentences depend upon
the age of the victim and whether the crime was sexual penetration or contact. They include imprisonment and/or a fine.

NEW YORK

New York's rape penal law was a disgrace until revisions
were made in 1974 and 1975. Improvements are still needed.
The crime is broken down by degree and is defined as sexual
intercourse by a male with a female, not his wife, by forcible

compulsion; or when the victim is incapable of consent; or when she is physically helpless to resist; or legally incapable of consent by reason of mental defect. Deviate sexual intercourse is contact between the penis and anus, the mouth and penis, or mouth and vulva, by force and without consent. Sexual contact includes any touching of the sexual parts for the purpose of gratifying sexual desire of either party without consent. Corroboration is required for statutory rape and determining the capacity to consent. Evidence of the victim's prior sexual conduct is inadmissible except to prove specific instances of conduct with the accused; the victim's conviction record for prostitution or soliciting; in rebuttal; to explain the origin or source of semen, pregnancy, disease; and then only after a hearing away from the jury. The sentences are indeterminate, with a minimum and maximum listed for each degree. They range from a one year minimum to a twenty-five year maximum.

NORTH CAROLINA

North Carolina defines rape as unlawful ravishing or carnal knowledge of a female, not one's wife, by force and against her will; or when a male unlawfully carnally knows and abuses a female by force and against her will. Rape has two degrees. The first is by resistance overcome, or the use of a deadly weapon, or infliction of serious bodily injury. Second degree is a lesser offense. Proof of penetration is necessary. Corroboration is no longer required. The victim's sexual history to prove unchastity is admissible regarding consent and credibility. The trial judge may order the courtroom closed to nonparticipants. The sentences include a minimum of one year to a maximum penalty, with death remaining as an option.

NORTH DAKOTA

The North Dakota rape code was revised and expanded in 1975. It is sex-neutral, with degrees. The term *gross sexual imposition* was substituted for *rape*. The definition was widened to include a sexual act with another where the victim submits by force, threat of force, or where the victim's capacity to appraise or control her conduct has been substantially impaired. A sexual act is defined as sexual contact between the penis and vulva, penis and anus, penis and mouth, or vulva and mouth. Sexual contact is any touching of the sexual or other intimate parts for gratifying sexual desire by force, or without knowledge or consent. These legislators also outlawed any form of sexual contact with an animal, bird, or dead person, as well as fornication in a public place. For all types of gross sexual imposition, penetration is not required. The spousal exception excludes those living apart under judicial decree. The offenses are upgraded if there is serious bodily injury or if the victim is not the voluntary social companion of the accused. A complaint must be filed within three months of the attack. Opinions, reputation, and evidence of the victim's prior sexual conduct is inadmissible except regarding consent, conduct with the defendant, and in rebuttal. Evidence may be presented to impeach her credibility if first proved relevant away from the jury. The sentences vary according to degree and severity of injuries. No minimum is stated. The highest maximum sentence is twenty years plus a $10,000 fine.

OHIO

Ohio's rape code is sex-neutral and graded by degrees. Rape is sexual conduct (vaginal and anal intercourse, fellatio, and cunnilingus) when the victim is compelled to submit by force or threat of force. Sexual battery is sexual conduct when the offender knowingly coerces the other, or in other circumstances of control or domination. Gross sexual imposition is sexual contact (any touching of any erogenous zone for sexual arousing) when the offender purposely compels or substantially impairs the other's judgment or control. Felonious sexual penetration is the insertion of an object into the anal or vaginal cavity by force or threat. Sexual imposition is sexual contact offensive to the other or when control is impaired. Resistance is not required. Corroboration is necessary for a complaint of sexual imposition. Evidence relating to the victim's prior sexual conduct is admissible to impeach, or to prove the source of semen and previous activities with the defendant. The victim may be represented by private counsel. Her name and the details of the attack are suppressed until a preliminary hearing is held. The accused must be tested for venereal disease. The cost for the mandatory evidentiary medical examination is paid by the city or county. Minors can obtain medical treatment after a rape without their parent's consent. The sentences range up to life imprisonment.

OKLAHOMA

In Oklahoma, rape is defined as unlawful sexual intercourse with a female, not one's wife, where she is incapable of giving legal consent through lunacy or unsoundness of mind; where her resistance is overcome or prevented by force or threats; or the victim is unconscious or defrauded; or she is prevented from resisting by a narcotic or anesthetic agent. Slight penetration is required to complete the crime. There are two degrees. Corroboration is necessary when the victim is less than fourteen or the complainant's testimony is inherently improbable. The victim's previous sexual conduct is inadmissible to prove consent, but admissible in rebuttal. Males less than fourteen are presumed incapable of rape. Rape in the first degree has a minimum penalty of five years, a maximum of life imprisonment or death.

OREGON

The revised Oregon rape statute divides the crime into three degrees. Rape in the first degree is sexual intercourse (the ordinary meaning; occurs upon any penetration, however slight) if the female is subjected to forcible compulsion (physical force that overcomes resistance, or a threat) or is of a certain class of victim. Second degree rape is sexual intercourse with a female incapable of consent or less than fourteen years of age. Third degree rape is sexual intercourse with a female less than sixteen. The spousal exception includes couples cohabitating consentually. No corroboration is necessary. There are limitations on the introduction as evidence of the victim's prior sexual conduct. The penalties range to a maximum of twenty years, with no minimum listed.

PENNSYLVANIA

According to the Pennsylvania rape statute, the crime is defined as sexual intercourse (both the ordinary meaning and intercourse per os or per anus) with another person, not one's spouse, by force or by threat of forcible compulsion that would prevent resistance by a person of reasonable resolution, or when the other is unconscious, or so mentally deficient as to be incapable of consent. Some penetration is required. The cautionary instruction enacted in 1972 was repealed in 1976. The prompt complaint requirement was also repealed that year, although the defendant may introduce evidence about the victim's lack of an immediate charge. There are restrictions on evidence regarding the victim's previous sexual activities. No corroboration is necessary. The penalties include a maximum of twenty years.

RHODE ISLAND

Rhode Island uses the common-law definition of unlawful carnal knowledge of a female, not one's wife, by force and against her will. Corroboration is necessary for a seduction charge (an unlawful carnal connection), but not for rape. Since 1975, limitations have been placed on the introduction of information about the victim's past sexual conduct. Forcible rape is punishable by a minimum of ten years, a maximum of life imprisonment.

SOUTH CAROLINA

South Carolina's rape code was enacted in 1869 and defines the crime as: "Whosoever shall ravish a woman, married, maid or other, when she did not consent, either before or after, or ravisheth a woman with force, although she consent after, shall be deemed guilty of rape." A prompt complaint to the police is sufficient corroboration. Bills have been introduced to limit testimony regarding the victim's prior sexual activities, but have not passed at present. This state has a complex procedure, enacted in 1909, which allows a rape victim to submit her testimony by deposition. The deposition is destroyed following the trial if there is no appeal of the decision. It is a misdemeanor to publish the name of a rape victim. The sentence for a rape conviction is at the judge's discretion, from a minimum of five years to a maximum of forty. There is an additional penalty for being armed while committing a crime.

SOUTH DAKOTA

The South Dakota rape laws, originally enacted in 1877, underwent major revisions in 1975. They are sex-neutral. Rape is defined as an act of sexual penetration (an act, however slight, of sexual intercourse, cunnilingus, fellatio, anal intercourse, or any intrusion, however slight, of a genital area or of any object into the genital or anal opening) by force, threats, or where the victim is incapable of consenting because of mental or physical incapacity. The spousal exception was eliminated. No corroboration is necessary, and the sexual history of the victim is limited. A convicted offender must receive an initial psychiatric evaluation to determine if counseling would be beneficial. The names of victims and the details of the rape may be withheld until the case has concluded. The sentences include only a maximum of twenty years.

TENNESSEE

In Tennessee, rape is defined as unlawful carnal knowledge of a female, not one's wife, by force and against her will. No corroboration is needed. Limitations are placed on the introduction of evidence regarding the victim's sexual past.

The sentence varies according to the age of the woman, death if less than twelve; if twelve or older, minimum ten years and a maximum of life.

TEXAS

In Texas, rape is sexual intercourse (any penetration of the female sex organ by the male sex organ) with a woman, not one's wife, without consent and by force that would prevent resistance by a woman of ordinary resolution under the same or similar circumstances because of reasonable fear of harm. Aggravated rape is that which causes death or serious bodily injury or threat of death. Resistance is required. No corroboration is necessary if the victim told any person about the offense within six months. Relevancy of the victim's prior sexual conduct may be determined at an in camera hearing. As of 1974 the state pays the cost of the evidentiary medical examination. Sentences span from a minumum of two years to a maximum of ninety-nine for aggravated rape.

UTAH

For Utah, the definition of rape is sexual intercourse with a female without her consent; or when force overcomes resistance; or threats prevent resistance by a person of ordinary resolution; or when the victim is unconscious. No corroboration is necessary. A complaint must be filed within three months, unless the victim is less than eighteen or is incompetent. As of this writing, a bill had been introduced to restrict the admissibility of information regarding the victim's sexual history; at present there are no limitations. Rape is a second degree felony, punishable by a maximum of fifteen years. Aggravated sexual assault is a first degree felony, with a minimum sentence of five years and a maximum of life.

VERMONT

Vermont's statute, enacted in 1791, uses the common-law definition of unlawfully ravishes, or carnally knows a female person, not one's wife, by force and against her will. Although there are proposed revisions, presently a prompt complaint or other circumstantial evidence is required to corroborate the charge. The proposed legislation would restrict questioning about the victim's prior sexual activities. When the victim and offender are under sixteen years of age, even though there may be consent, both can be found guilty of a misdemeanor. The maximum sentence for forcible rape is twenty years or $2,000, with no minimum sentence listed.

VIRGINIA

In Virginia, rape occurs when a male unlawfully carnally knows a female, not his wife, against her will, by force adequate to overcome resistance. It is also illegal to have carnal knowledge of female patients or pupils of certain institutions, or to seduce females of previously chaste character. Victims and other witnesses are allowed to give testimony by deposition. The legislators have passed a resolution calling for a study of criminal sexual assault, possible changes in the laws and the court process, and so forth, so there may be many revisions in these laws. The sentence for rape is a minimum of five years to a maximum of life.

WASHINGTON

The Washington state rape code had major revisions enacted in 1975. It is now a sex-neutral offense, with three degrees. Rape is sexual intercourse (the ordinary meaning as well as any penetration by any object and any part of sexual contact involving the sex organs of one person and the mouth or anus of another) with another person by forcible compulsion; or when armed with a deadly weapon; or when the victim is incapable of giving consent; or by threats. Consent is defined as actual words or conduct indicating freely given agreement to have sexual intercourse. First degree rape includes that which is accomplished by forcible compulsion, with a deadly weapon, kidnapping, serious personal injury, or felonious entry into a building or vehicle. Second degree is by force or if the victim is incapable of consent. Third degree is by threat and in all other circumstances. No corroboration is needed. The victim's previous sexual conduct, including divorce history, is inadmissible to impeach her credibility, but admissible on the consent issue after a motion and closed hearing as to relevance. The state pays for the medical examination if the victim reports within seventy-two hours. The penalty for each degree varies, with one unique addition: For first degree and statutory rape there may be no deferred or suspended sentence, no work release or furlough program, and a minimum sentence of three years.

WEST VIRGINIA

In West Virginia, rape is committed when a person has sexual intercourse with another, not one's spouse, by forcible compulsion; or sexual intercourse when the other person is incapable of consent because mentally defective, incapacitated, or under sixteen years of age. No corroboration is required. Evidence about the victim's prior sexual history is restricted. The sentence is life with no parole unless there is a guilty plea or the jury recommends mercy. Then it is a minimum of ten years, a maximum of twenty.

WISCONSIN

In March 1976, Wisconsin's revised rape statute went into effect. It is sex-neutral and separated into degrees. The term *rape* was replaced by *sexual assault.* First degree sexual assault: sexual contact or intercourse (including cunnilingus, fellatio, anal intercourse, or any intrusion by a person's body or an object) causing pregnancy or great bodily harm; or with a weapon; or aided and abetted. Second degree sexual assault: sexual contact or intercourse by threat, or causing injury. Third degree sexual assault: sexual intercourse without consent. Fourth degree sexual assault: sexual contact without consent. They retained the spousal exception, but it does not include those living apart and when one spouse has filed for annulment, separation, or divorce. Corroboration is not necessary. There are strict procedures to follow before any information regarding the victim's sexual conduct may be introduced. The judge may exclude nonparticipants from the courtroom. The penalty structure lists a maximum sentence and/or fine, from first degree, fifteen years and/or $15,000, to fourth degree, maximum of one year in the county jail and/or a $500 fine.

WYOMING

In 1976 a general revision of Wyoming's statute, enacted in 1890, was defeated. Currently the crime has three degrees. The definition is based on the common-law concept of rape occurring when a man unlawfully has carnal knowledge of a woman or female child forcibly and against her will. Penetration is required. No corroboration is needed. There are no limitations on the admissibility of evidence regarding the victim's prior sexual conduct. First degree rape is punishable by a minimum of one year, a maximum of life; second degree by a minimum of one year, a maximum of fifty years; third degree has no minimum, but a maximum of one year in the county jail.

Appendix B

Two State Statutes

The Michigan Sexual Assault Statute and the Washington Rape Law typify the most comprehensive ones now in effect in the United States. They serve as indicators of the direction of legislative reform regarding this crime. They should be examined for such changes as the updated, specific language; the sex-neutral wording; the degree structure; the wider variety of conduct now judged as criminal; the limitations placed on the admissibility of the victim's prior sexual activities; and so on.

MICHIGAN SEXUAL ASSAULT STATUTE

The People of the State of Michigan enact:
Section 1. Act No. 328 of the Public Acts of 1931, as amended, being sections 750.1 to 750.568 of the Compiled Laws of 1970, is amended by adding sections 520a, 520b, 520c, 520d, 520e, 520f, 520g, 520h, 520i, 520j, 520k, and 520l to read as follows:

Sec. 520a. As used in sections 520a to 520l:
(a) "Actor" means a person accused of criminal sexual conduct.
(b) "Intimate parts" includes the primary genital area, groin, inner thigh, buttock, or breast of a human being.
(c) "Mentally defective" means that a person suffers from a mental disease or defect which renders that person temporarily or permanently incapable of appraising the nature of his or her conduct.
(d) "Mentally incapacitated" means that a person is rendered temporarily incapable of appraising or controlling his or her conduct due to the influence of a narcotic, anesthetic, or other substance administered to that person without his or her consent, or due to any other act committed upon that person without his or her consent.

252 : Fighting Back

(e) "Physically helpless" means that a person is unconscious, asleep, or for any other reason is physically unable to communicate unwillingness to an act.

(f) "Personal injury" means bodily injury, disfigurement, mental anguish, chronic pain, pregnancy, disease, or loss or impairment of a sexual or reproductive organ.

(g) "Sexual contact" includes the intentional touching of the victim's or actor's intimate parts or the intentional touching of the clothing covering the immediate area of the victim's or actor's intimate parts, if that intentional touching can reasonably be construed as being for the purpose of sexual arousal or gratification.

(h) "Sexual penetration" means sexual intercourse, cunnilingus, fellatio, anal intercourse, or any other intrusion, however slight, of any part of a person's body or of any object into the genital or anal openings of another person's body, but emission of semen is not required.

(i) "Victim" means the person alleging to have been subjected to criminal sexual conduct.

Sec. 520b. (1) *A person is guilty of criminal sexual conduct in the first degree if he or she engages in sexual penetration with another person and if any of the following circumstances exists:*

(a) That other person is under 13 years of age.

(b) The other person is at least 13 but less than 16 years of age and the actor is a member of the same household as the victim, the actor is related to the victim by blood or affinity to the fourth degree to the victim, or the actor is in a position of authority over the victim and used this authority to coerce the victim to submit.

(c) Sexual penetration occurs under circumstances involving the commission of any other felony.

(d) The actor is aided or abetted by 1 or more other persons and either of the following circumstances exists:

(i) The actor knows or has reason to know that the victim is mentally defective, mentally incapacitated, or physically helpless.

(ii) The actor uses force or coercion to accomplish the sexual penetration. Force or coercion includes but is not limited to any of the circumstances listed in subdivision (f) (i) to (v).

(e) The actor is armed with a weapon or any other article used or fashioned in a manner to lead the victim to reasonably believe it to be a weapon.

(f) The actor causes personal injury to the victim and force or coercion is used to accomplish sexual penetration. Force or coercion includes but is not limited to any of the following circumstances:

(i) When the actor overcomes the victim through the actual application of physical force or physical violence.

(ii) When the actor coerces the victim to submit by threatening to use force or violence on the victim, and the victim believes that the actor has the present ability to execute these threats.

(iii) When the actor coerces the victim to submit by threatening to retaliate in the future against the victim, or any other person, and the victim believes that the actor has the ability to execute this threat. As used in this subdivision, "to retaliate" includes threats of physical punishment, kidnapping, or extortion.

(iv) When the actor engages in the medical treatment or examination of the victim in a manner or for purposes which are medically recognized as unethical or unacceptable.

(v) When the actor, through concealment or by the element of surprise, is able to overcome the victim.

(g) The actor causes personal injury to the victim, and the actor knows or has reason to know that the victim is mentally defective, mentally incapacitated, or physically helpless.

(2) *Criminal sexual conduct in the first degree is a felony punishable by imprisonment in the state prison for life or for any term of years.*

Sec. 520c. (1) *A person is guilty of criminal sexual conduct in the second degree if the person engages in sexual contact with another person and if any of the following circumstances exists:*

(a) That other person is under 13 years of age.

(b) The other person is at least 13 but less than 16 years of age and the actor is a member of the same household as the victim, the actor is related to the victim by blood or affinity to the fourth degree to the victim, or the actor is in a position of authority over the victim and used this authority to coerce the victim to submit.

(c) Sexual contact occurs under circumstances involving the commission of any other felony.

(d) The actor is aided or abetted by 1 or more other persons and either of the following circumstances exists:

(i) The actor knows or has reason to know that the victim is mentally defective, mentally incapacitated, or physically helpless.

(ii) The actor uses force or coercion to accomplish the sexual contact. Force or coercion includes but is not limited to any of the circumstances listed in sections 520b(1) (f)(i) to (v).

(e) The actor is armed with a weapon or any other article used or fashioned in a manner to lead a person to reasonably believe it to be a weapon.

(f) The actor causes personal injury to the victim and force or coercion is used to accomplish the sexual contact. Force or coercion includes but is not limited to any of the circumstances listed in section 520b(1)(f)(i) to (v).

(g) The actor causes personal injury to the victim and the actor knows or has reason to know that the victim is mentally defective, mentally incapacitated, or physically helpless.

(2) *Criminal sexual conduct in the second degree is a felony punishable by imprisonment for not more than 15 years.*

Sec. 520d. (1) *A person is guilty of criminal sexual conduct in the third degree if the person engages in sexual penetration with another person and if any of the following circumstances exists:*
(a) That other person is at least 13 years of age and under 16 years of age.
(b) Force or coercion is used to accomplish the sexual penetration. Force or coercion includes but is not limited to any of the circumstances listed in section 520b(1) (f) (i) to (v).
(c) The actor knows or has reason to know that the victim is mentally defective, mentally incapacitated, or physically helpless.
(2) *Criminal sexual conduct in the third degree is a felony punishable by imprisonment for not more than 15 years.*

Sec. 520e. (1) *A person is guilty of criminal sexual conduct in the fourth degree if he or she engages in sexual contact with another person and if either of the following circumstances exists:*
(a) Force or coercion is used to accomplish the sexual contact. Force or coercion includes but is not limited to any of the circumstances listed in section 520b(1) (f)(i) to (v).
(b) The actor knows or has reason to know that the victim is mentally incapacitated, or physically helpless.
(2) *Criminal sexual conduct in the fourth degree is a misdemeanor punishable by imprisonment for not more than 2 years, or by a fine of not more than $500.00, or both.*

Sec. 520f. (1) *If a person is convicted of a second or subsequent offense under section 520b, 520c, or 520d, the sentence imposed under those sections for the second or subsequent offense shall provide for a mandatory minimum sentence of at least 5 years.*
(2) *For purposes of this section, an offense is considered a second or subsequent offense if, prior to conviction of the second or subsequent offense, the actor has at any time been convicted under section 520b, 520c, or 520d or under any similar statute of the United States or any state for a criminal sexual offense including rape, carnal knowledge, indecent liberties, gross indecency, or an attempt to commit such an offense.*

Sec. 520g. (1) *Assault with intent to commit criminal sexual conduct involving sexual penetration shall be a felony punishable by imprisonment for not more than 10 years.*
(2) *Assault with intent to commit criminal sexual conduct in the second degree is a felony punishable by imprisonment for not more than 5 years.*

Sec. 520h. The testimony of a victim need not be corroborated in prosecutions under sections 520b to 520g.

Sec. 520i. A victim need not resist the actor in prosecution under sections 520b to 520g.

Sec. 520j. (1) *Evidence of specific instances of the victim's sexual conduct, opinion evidence of the victim's sexual conduct, and reputation evidence of the victim's sexual conduct shall not be admitted under sections 520b to 520g unless and only to the extent that the judge finds that the following proposed evidence is material to a fact at issue in the case and that its inflammatory or prejudicial nature does not outweigh its probative value:*

(a) Evidence of the victim's past sexual conduct with the actor.

(b) Evidence of specific instances of sexual activity showing the source or origin of semen, pregnancy, or disease.

(2) *If the defendant proposes to offer evidence described in subsection (1)(a) or (b), the defendant within 10 days after the arraignment on the information shall file a written motion and offer of proof. The court may order an in camera hearing to determine whether the proposed evidence is admissible under subsection (1). If new information is discovered during the course of the trial that may make the evidence described in subsection (1)(a) or (b) admissible, the judge may order an in camera hearing to determine whether the proposed evidence is admissible under subsection (1).*

Sec. 520k. Upon the request of the counsel or the victim or actor in a prosecution under sections 520b to 520g the magistrate before whom any person is brought on a charge of having committed an offense under sections 520b to 520g shall order that the names of the victim and actor and details of the alleged offense be suppressed until such time as the actor is arraigned on the information, the charge is dismissed, or the case is otherwise concluded, whichever occurs first.

Sec. 520l. A person does not commit sexual assault under this act if the victim is his or her legal spouse, unless the couple are living apart and one of them has filed for separate maintenance or divorce.

Section 2. All proceedings pending and all rights and liabilities existing, acquired, or incurred at the time this amendatory act takes effect are saved and may be consummated according to the law in force when they are commenced. This amendatory act shall not be construed to affect any prosecution pending or begun before the effective date of this amendatory act.

Section 3. Sections 85, 333, 336, 339, 340, 341, 342, and 520 of Act No. 328 of the Public Acts of 1931, being sections 750.85, 750.333, 750.336, 750.339, 750.340, 750.341, 750.342, and 750.520 of the Compiled Laws of 1970, and section 82 of chapter 7 of Act No. 175 of the Public Acts of 1927, being section 767.82 of the Compiled Laws of 1970, are repealed.

Section 4. This amendatory act shall take effect November 1, 1974.

WASHINGTON RAPE LAW

9.79.140 Definitions. As used in this chapter:
(1) *"Sexual intercourse" (a) has its ordinary meaning and occurs upon any penetration, however slight, and*
(b) Also means any penetration of the vagina or anus however slight, by an object, when committed on one person by another, whether such persons are of the same or opposite sex, except when such penetration is accomplished for medically recognized treatment or diagnostic purposes, and
(c) Also means any act of sexual contact between persons involving the sex organs of one person and the mouth or anus of another whether such persons are of the same or opposite sex.
(2) *"Married" means one who is legally married to another.*
(3) *"Mental incapacity" is that condition existing at the time of the offense which prevents a person from understanding the nature or consequences of the act of sexual intercourse whether that condition is produced by illness, defect, the influence of a substance or from some other cause.*
(4) *"Physically helpless" means a person who is unconscious or for any other reason is physically unable to communicate unwillingness to an act.*
(5) *"Forcible compulsion" means physical force which overcomes resistance, or a threat, express or implied, that places a person in fear of death or physical injury to herself or himself or another person, or in fear that she or he or another person will be kidnapped.*
(6) *"Consent" means that at the time of the act of sexual intercourse there are actual words or conduct indicating freely given agreement to have sexual intercourse. [1975 1st ex.s. c 14 § 1.]*

9.79.150 Testimony—Evidence—Written motion—Admissibility.
(1) In order to convict a person of any crime defined in this chapter it shall not be necessary that the testimony of the alleged victim be corroborated.
(2) Evidence of the victim's past sexual behavior including but not limited to the victim's marital history, divorce history, or general reputation for promiscuity, nonchastity, or sexual mores contrary to commu-

nity standards is inadmissible on the issue of credibility and is inadmissible to prove the victim's consent except as provided in subsection (3) of this section, but when the perpetrator and the victim have engaged in sexual intercourse with each other in the past, and when the past behavior is material to the issue of consent, evidence concerning the past behavior between the perpetrator and the victim may be admissible on the issue of consent to the offense.

(3) *In any prosecution for the crime of rape or for an attempt to commit, or an assault with an intent to commit any such crime evidence of the victim's past sexual behavior including but not limited to the victim's marital behavior, divorce history, or general reputation for promiscuity, nonchastity, or sexual mores contrary to community standards is not admissible if offered to attack the credibility of the victim and is admissible on the issue of consent only pursuant to the following procedure:*

(a) A written pretrial motion shall be made by the defendant to the court and prosecutor stating that the defense has an offer of proof of the relevancy of evidence of the past sexual behavior of the victim proposed to be presented and its relevancy on the issue of the consent of the victim.

(b) The written motion shall be accompanied by an affidavit or affidavits in which the offer of proof shall be stated.

(c) If the court finds that the offer of proof is sufficient, the court shall order a hearing out of the presence of the jury, if any, and the hearing shall be closed except to the necessary witnesses, the defendant, counsel, and those who have a direct interest in the case or in the work of the court.

(d) At the conclusion of the hearing, if the court finds that the evidence proposed to be offered by the defendant regarding the past sexual behavior of the victim is relevant to the issue of the victim's consent; is not inadmissible because its probative value is substantially outweighed by the probability that its admission will create a substantial danger of undue prejudice; and that its exclusion would result in denial of substantial justice to the defendant; the court shall make an order stating what evidence may be introduced by the defendant, which order may include the nature of the questions to be permitted. The defendant may then offer evidence pursuant to the order of the court.

(4) *Nothing in this section shall be construed to prohibit cross-examination of the victim on the issue of past sexual behavior when the prosecution presents evidence in its case in chief tending to prove the nature of the victim's past sexual behavior, but the court may require a hearing pursuant to subsection (3) of this section concerning such evidence. [1975 1st ex.s. c 14 § 2.]*

9.79.160 Defenses to prosecution under this chapter.
(1) *In any prosecution under this chapter in which lack of consent is based solely upon the victim's mental incapacity or upon the victim's*

being physically helpless, it is a defense which the defendant must prove by a preponderance of the evidence that at the time of the offense the defendant reasonably believed that the victim was not mentally incapacitated and/or physically helpless.

(2) In any prosecution under this chapter in which the offense or degree of the offense depends on the victim's age, it is no defense that the perpetrator did not know the victim's age, or that the perpetrator believed the victim to be older, as the case may be: Provided, *That it is a defense which the defendant must prove by a preponderance of the evidence that at the time of the offense the defendant reasonably believed the alleged victim to be older based upon the declarations as to age by the alleged victim. [1975 1st ex.s. c 14 § 3.]*

9.79.170 Rape in the first degree. (1) A person is guilty of rape in the first degree when such person engages in sexual intercourse with another person not married to the perpetrator by forcible compulsion where the perpetrator or an accessory:

(a) Uses or threatens to use a deadly weapon; or
(b) Kidnaps the victim; or
(c) Inflicts serious physical injury; or
(d) Feloniously enters into the building or vehicle where the victim is situated.

(2) Rape in the first degree is a felony, and shall be punished by imprisonment in the state penitentiary for a term of not less than twenty years. No person convicted of rape in the first degree shall be granted a deferred or suspended sentence except for the purpose of commitment to an inpatient treatment facility: Provided, *That every person convicted of rape in the first degree shall be confined for a minimum of three years:* Provided further, *That the board of prison terms and paroles shall have authority to set a period of confinement greater than three years but shall never reduce the minimum three-year period of confinement nor shall the board release the convicted person during the first three years of confinement as a result of any type of automatic good time calculation nor shall the department of social and health services permit the convicted person to participate in any work release program or furlough program during the first three years of confinement. [1975 1st ex.s. c 247 § 1; 1975 1st ex.s. c 14 § 4.]*

9.79.180 Rape in the second degree. (1) A person is guilty of rape in the second degree when, under circumstances not constituting rape in the first degree, the person engages in sexual intercourse with another person, not married to the perpetrator:

(a) By forcible compulsion; or
(b) When the victim is incapable of consent by reason of being physically helpless or mentally incapacitated.

(2) Rape in the second degree is a felony, and shall be punished by imprisonment in the state penitentiary for not more than ten years. [1975 1st ex.s. c 14 § 5.]

9.79.190 Rape in the third degree. (1) A person is guilty of rape in the third degree when, under circumstances not constituting rape in the first or second degrees, such person engages in sexual intercourse with another person, not married to the perpetrator:

(a) Where the victim did not consent as defined in RCW 9.79.140(6) to sexual intercourse with the perpetrator and such lack of consent was clearly expressed by the victim's words or conduct, or

(b) Where there is threat of substantial unlawful harm to property rights of the victim.

(2) Rape in the third degree is a felony, and shall be punished by imprisonment in the state penitentiary for not more than five years. [1975 1st ex.s. c 14 § 6.]

9.79.200 Statutory rape in the first degree. (1) A person over thirteen years of age is guilty of statutory rape in the first degree when the person engages in sexual intercourse with another person who is less than eleven years old.

(2) Statutory rape in the first degree is a felony, and shall be punished by imprisonment in the state penitentiary for a term of not less than twenty years. No person convicted of statutory rape in the first degree shall be granted a deferred or suspended sentence except for the purpose of commitment to an inpatient treatment facility. [1975 1st ex.s. c 14 § 7.]

9.79.210 Statutory rape in the second degree. (1) A person over sixteen years of age is guilty of statutory rape in the second degree when such person engages in sexual intercourse with another person, not married to the perpetrator, who is eleven years of age or older but less than fourteen years old.

(2) Statutory rape in the second degree is a felony, and shall be punished by imprisonment in the state penitentiary for not more than ten years. [1975 1st ex.s. c 14 § 8.]

9.79.220 Statutory rape in the third degree. (1) A person over eighteen years of age is guilty of statutory rape in the third degree when such person engages in sexual intercourse with another person, not married to the perpetrator, who is fourteen years of age or older but less than sixteen years old.

(2) Statutory rape in the third degree is a felony, and shall be punished by imprisonment in the state penitentiary for not more than five years. [1975 1st ex.s. c 14 § 9.]

Notes

2. FACING THE FACTS

1. Federal Bureau of Investigation, *Crime in the United States 1976: Uniform Crime Reports* (Washington, D.C.: United States Government Printing Office, 1977).
2. Minnesota Department of Corrections, *The Sex Offender in Minnesota* (1964).
3. State of California, Subcommittee on Sex Crimes of the Assembly Interim Committee on Judicial System and Judicial Process, Preliminary Report (1950).
4. National Opinion Research Center of the University of Chicago. Survey reported in *President's Commission on Law Enforcement and Administration of Justice: The Challenge of Crime in a Free Society* (1967).
5. Metropolitan Washington Council of Governments, "The Treatment of Rape Victims in the Metropolitan Washington Area" (September 1976). Subcommittee of the District of Columbia City Council, "Report of the District of Columbia Task Force on Rape" (July 1973).
6. *Crime in the Nation's Five Largest Cities.* National Crime Panel Surveys conducted jointly by the National Institute of Law Enforcement and Criminal Justice, Law Enforcement Assistance Administration, U.S. Department of Justice, and the U.S. Census Bureau. Data gathered in 1972. (Advance Report, April 1974.) *Criminal Victimization Surveys in the Nation's Five Largest Cities* (Final Report, April 1975).
7. Richard Harris, "A Reporter at Large, Crime in New York," *New Yorker* (September 26, 1977).
8. Paul Gebhard, John Gagnon, Wardell Pomeroy, and Cornelia Christenson, *Sex Offenders: An Analysis of Types* (New York: Harper and Row, 1965).
9. Manfred S. Guttmacher, *Sex Offenses: The Problems, Causes, and Prevention* (New York: W. W. Norton, 1951).
10. E. G. Hammer and Bernard C. Glueck, Jr., "Psychodynamic Patterns in Sexual Offenders: A Four Factor Theory," *Psychiatric Quarterly* 31 (1957).

11. Ibid.

12. Manfred Guttmacher and H. Weihofen, *Psychiatry and the Law*, 375 (1952).

13. "The Sex Offender," *Police Chief* (December 1962).

14. Camille LeGrand, "Rape and Rape Laws: Sexism in Society and the Law," *California Law Review* 61 (May 1973).

15. Boston Women's Health Collective, *Our Bodies, Ourselves* (New York: Simon and Schuster, 1973).

16. Menachem Amir, *Patterns in Forcible Rape* (Chicago: University of Chicago Press, 1971).

17. Fritz Henn, Marijan Herjanic, and Robert Vanderpearl, "Forensic Psychiatry: Profiles of Two Types of Sex Offenders," *The American Journal of Psychiatry* 133 (1976).

18. Queen's Bench Foundation, *Rape Prevention and Resistance*, Law Enforcement Assistance Administration and the Office of Criminal Justice Planning (1976). The Queen's Bench Foundation, San Francisco, is a non-profit organization that first received LEAA funding for a *Rape Victimization Study* in 1974. This second study had matching funds from the Van Loben Sels Foundation, The Zellerbach Family Foundation, and Cowell Foundation.

19. Ibid.

20. Richard Rada, "Alcohol and Rape," *Medical Aspects of Human Sexuality* 9 (March 1975).

21. Ibid.

22. Gene Abel, David Barlow, Edward Blanchard, and Donald Guild, "The Components of Rapists' Sexual Arousal," *Archives of General Psychiatry* 34 (1977).

23. Joseph J. Peters, Linda Meyer, and Nancy Carroll, "The Philadelphia Assault Victim Study," Center for Rape Concern, Philadelphia General Hospital, Final Report R01MH21304 (1976). This project was funded by the National Institute of Mental Health.

24. Ibid.

25. Amir, op cit.

26. Thomas A. Giacinti and Claus Tjaden, "The Crime of Rape in Denver." A report submitted to the Denver High Impact Anti-Crime Council, Denver (1971).

27. Ed Jahn, "Portrait of a Crime, Cry Echoes Across Atlanta," *The Atlanta Journal* (March 25, 1974).

28. Jodi Tasso and Elizabeth Miller, "The Effects of the Full Moon on Human Behavior," *Journal of Psychology* 93 (1976).

29. "The Sexes," *Time* (July 22, 1974).

30. Jahn, op cit.

31. Duncan Chappell, Donna Schram et al. Battelle Memorial Institute Law and Justice Study Center, and Phillip Cohen, Ronald Sabo et al. National Legal Data Center, *Forcible Rape, A National*

Survey of the Response by Prosecutors, Prosecutors' Volume I. This joint project was funded by the National Institute of Law Enforcement and Criminal Justice, Law Enforcement Assistance Administration, U.S. Department of Justice (Washington, D.C.: United States Government Printing Office, 1977).
32. Amir, op cit.
33. James Selkin and Carolyn Hursch, *Fifth Quarter Report* (Denver: Rape Prevention Program, Violence Research Unit, Denver General Hospital, 1974).
34. Queen's Bench Foundation, op cit.
35. Peters, op cit.
36. FBI, op cit.
37. "Police Discretion and the Judgment that a Crime Has Been Committed: Rape in Philadelphia," *University of Pennsylvania Law Review* 117 (December 1968).
38. Ibid.
39. Ibid.
40. Ibid.
41. Susan Brownmiller, *Against Our Will: Men, Women and Rape* (New York: Simon and Schuster, 1975).
42. Ibid.
43. Lisa Brodyaga, Margaret Gates, Susan Singer et al. Center for Women Policy Studies, *Rape and Its Victims: A Report for Citizens, Health Facilities and Criminal Justice Agencies.* This project was funded by the National Institute of Law Enforcement and Criminal Justice, Law Enforcement Assistance Administration, U.S. Department of Justice (Washington, D.C.: United States Government Printing Office, 1975).
44. Grace Lichtenstein, "Rape Squad: Many Cases, Some Arrests, Few Convictions," *New York Times Magazine* (March 3, 1974).
45. Carol Eron, "Rape," *The Washington Post, Potomac* (July 15, 1973).
46. Peters, op cit.
47. Morris Ploscowe, *Sex and the Law* (Englewood Cliffs, N.J.: Prentice-Hall, Inc. 1951).
48. Guttmacher, op cit.; Guttmacher and H. Weihofen, op cit.
49. L. Eidelberg, *The Dark Urge* (New York: Pyramid Books, 1961).
50. Ralph Slovenko and C. Phillips, "Psychosexuality and the Criminal Law," *Vanderbilt Law Review* 15 (1961–62).
51. Ibid.
52. Louis Harris, "Public's Tough Line on Rapists," *San Francisco Examiner* (October 24, 1977).

3. CRY PAIN, CRY ANGER

1. Sharon L. McCombie, "Characteristics of Rape Victims Seen in Crisis Intervention," *Smith College Studies in Social Work* 46 (1976).

2. Ibid.
3. Ibid.
4. Sandra Sutherland and Donald Scherl, "Patterns of Response Among Victims of Rape," *American Journal of Orthopsychiatry* 40 (April 1970).
5. Ann Burgess and Lynda Holmstrom, *Rape: Victims of Crisis* (Bowie, Md.: Robert J. Brady, 1974). Burgess and Holmstrom, "Rape Trauma Syndrome," *American Journal of Psychiatry* (1974).
6. Joseph J. Peters, Linda Meyer, and Nancy Carroll, "The Philadelphia Assault Victim Study," Center for Rape Concern, Philadelphia General Hospital, Final Report R01MH21304 (1976). This project was funded by the National Institute of Mental Health.
7. Joseph J. Peters, "The Psychological Effects of Childhood Rape," *World Journal of Psychosynthesis* 6 (May 1974).

4. WOMEN'S WILES

1. Brown v. State, 50 Ala. (1973); Frank v. State, 150 Neb. (1949); Anderson v. State, 104 Ind. (1885); Lee v. State, 132 Tenn. (1915); to cite a few.
2. Vivian Berger, "Man's Trial, Woman's Tribulation: Rape Cases in the Courtroom," *Columbia Law Review* 77 (January 1977).

5. A CRUCIAL DECISION

1. Duncan Chappell, Donna Schram et al. Battelle Memorial Institute Law and Justice Study Center, and Phillip Cohen, Ronald Sabo et al. National Legal Data Center, *Forcible Rape, A National Survey of the Response by Prosecutors, Prosecutors' Volume 1*. This joint project was funded by the National Institute of Law Enforcement and Criminal Justice, Law Enforcement Assistance Administration, U.S. Department of Justice (Washington, D.C.: United States Government Printing Office, 1977).

6. MEDICAL MISMANAGEMENT

1. Lisa Brodyaga, Margaret Gates, Susan Singer et al. Center for Women Policy Studies. *Rape and Its Victims: A Report for Citizens, Health Facilities and Criminal Justice Agencies*. This project was funded by the National Institute of Law Enforcement and Criminal Justice, Law Enforcement Assistance Administration, U.S. Department of Justice (Washington, D.C.: United States Government Printing Office, 1975).

2. Joseph J. Peters, Linda Meyer, and Nancy Carroll, "The Philadelphia Assault Victim Study," Center for Rape Concern, Philadelphia General Hospital, Final Report R01MH21304 (1976). This project was funded by the National Institute of Mental Health.
3. A. Nicholas Groth and Ann Wolbert Burgess, "Sexual Dysfunction During Rape," *The New England Journal of Medicine* 297 (1977).
4. "Police Discretion and the Judgment That a Crime Has Been Committed: Rape in Philadelphia," *University of Pennsylvania Law Review* 117 (December 1968).

7. RAPED AGAIN

1. Federal Bureau of Investigation, *Crime in the United States 1976: Uniform Crime Reports* (Washington, D.C.: United States Government Printing Office, 1977).
2. Camille LeGrand, Jay Reich, Duncan Chappell et al. Battelle Memorial Institute Law and Justice Study Center, *Forcible Rape: An Analysis of Legal Issues.* This project was funded by the National Institute of Law Enforcement and Criminal Justice, Law Enforcement Assistance Administration, U.S. Department of Justice (Washington, D.C.: United States Government Printing Office, 1977).
3. Ibid.
4. Ibid.
5. Ibid.
6. Ibid.
7. Ibid.
8. Ibid.
9. Ibid.
10. Ibid.
11. Ibid.
12. Ibid.
13. Ibid.
14. Women Against Rape, *Stop Rape.* Pamphlet. (San Jose, Calif.: Santa Clara Valley Rape Crisis Center, 1974).
15. Susan Klemmack and David Klemmack, "The Social Definition of Rape," in *Sexual Assault,* edited by Marcia Walker and Stanley Brodsky (Lexington, Mass.: Lexington Books, 1976).
16. Harry Kalven, Jr., and Hans Zeisel, *The American Jury* (Boston: Little, Brown and Company, 1966).
17. Shirley Feldman-Summers and Karen Lindner, "Perceptions of Victims and Defendants in Criminal Assault Cases," *Criminal Justice and Behavior* 3 (1976).
18. UPI, "Judge Rips Jurors in Rape Case," *San Francisco Chronicle* (May 19, 1974).

19. Carol Bohmer, "Judicial Attitudes Toward Rape Victims," *Judicature* 57 (1974).
20. Ibid.
21. "A Study of Her Honor's Verdicts," *San Francisco Chronicle* (December 4, 1977).
22. LeGrand, op cit.
23. State v. Chaney, Alaska (1970).
24. Guy Wright, "Glickfeld's Friends," *San Francisco Examiner* (May 12, 1974).
25. Timothy Robinson, "Judge 'Sorry' in Jailing Attacker on D.C. Woman," *The Washington Post* (June 27, 1974).
26. Alan Sheehan, "Nine Life Terms Given to 3 Boston Men in Rape Case," *Boston Globe* (June 8, 1974).
27. "Rape and Culture, Two Judges Raise the Question of the Victim's Responsibility," *Time* (September 12, 1977).
28. "There Goes the Judge, Women Rout a Rape-Condoning Wisconsin Jurist," *Time* (September 19, 1977).
29. Pat Smyklo, "Hitchhiking: Ride or Rape?" *Plexus* 4 (September 1977).
30. Ibid.
31. Louis Harris, "Public's Tough Line on Rapists," *San Francisco Examiner* (October 24, 1977).
32. "Conviction of Forcible Rape of 15-Year-Old Daughter—Reversed: People v. McGillen, 220 N.W. 2d 677 (Michigan)," *Sex Problems Court Digest* 6 (1975).
33. "Rape and Sexual Assault Conviction Reversed: People v. Anderson, 314 N.E. 2d 651 (Illinois)," *Sex Problems Court Digest* 6 (1975).

9. ALTERNATIVE ANSWERS

1. Feminist Alliance Against Rape publication (July/August 1977) p. 6, and the National Committee to Defend Dessie Woods, P.O. Box 92084, Morris Brown Station, Atlanta, Georgia.

Bibliography

BOOKS AND PAMPHLETS

Amir, Menachem. *Patterns in Forcible Rape.* Chicago: University of Chicago Press, 1971.

Baughman, Laurance. *Southern Rape Complex.* Atlanta: Pendulum Books, 1966.

Boston Women's Health Collective. *Our Bodies, Ourselves.* New York: Simon and Schuster, 1973; Boston: Boston Women's Health Collective, 1971.

Brownmiller, Susan. *Against Our Will: Men, Women and Rape.* New York: Simon and Schuster, 1975.

Burgess, Ann Wolbert, and Holmstrom, Lynda. *Rape: Victims of Crisis.* Bowie, Md: Robert J. Brady, 1974.

Burton, Lindy. *Vulnerable Children.* New York: Schocken Books, 1968.

Csida, June Bundy, and Csida, Joseph. *Rape: How to Avoid It and What to Do About It If You Can't.* Chatsworth, Calif.: Books for Better Living, 1974.

DeFrancis, Vincent. *Protecting the Child Victim of Sex Crimes Committed by Adults.* Pamphlet. Denver, Colo.: The American Humane Association, Children's Division, 1965.

Edwards, Alison. *Rape, Racism, and the White Women's Movement: An Answer to Susan Brownmiller.* Pamphlet. Chicago, Ill.: Sojourner Truth Organization, 1976.

Gager, Nancy, and Schurr, Cathleen. *Sexual Assault: Confronting Rape in America.* New York: Grosset and Dunlap, 1976.

Goldsmith, Gloria. *Rape.* Beverly Hills, Calif.: Wollstonecraft, 1974.

Grimstad, Kirsten, and Rennie, Susan, eds. *The New Woman's Survival Catalog.* New York: Coward, McCann and Geoghegan/Berkeley, 1973.

Haskell, Molly. *From Reverence to Rape: The Treatment of Women in the Movies.* Baltimore: Penguin Books, Inc., 1974.

Horos, Carol. *Rape: The Private Crime, A Social Horror.* New Canaan, Conn.: Tobey Publishing Co., 1974.

Hursch, Carolyn. *The Trouble with Rape.* Chicago: Nelson-Hall, 1977.

Kalven, Harry, and Zeisel, Hans. *The American Jury.* Boston: Little, Brown and Company, 1966.

Lynch, W. Ware. *Rape! One Victim's Story: A Documentary.* Chicago: Follett Publishing Co., 1974.

268 : Fighting Back

MacDonald, John. *Rape Offenders and their Victims.* Springfield, Ill.: Charles C. Thomas, 1971.
MacKellar, Jean Scott. *Rape: The Bait and the Trap.* New York: Crown Publishers, 1975.
Medea, Andra, and Thompson, Kathleen. *Against Rape.* New York: Farrar, Straus and Giroux, 1974.
New York Radical Feminists. *Rape: The First Sourcebook for Women.* Edited by Noreen Connell and Cassandra Wilson. New York: New American Library, 1974.
Offstein, Jerrold. *Self-Defense for Women.* Palo Alto, Calif.: National Press Books, 1972.
Pekkanen, John. *Victims: An Account of a Rape.* New York: Dial Press, 1976.
Russell, Diana. *The Politics of Rape: The Victim's Perspective.* New York: Stein and Day, 1974.
Ryan, William. *Blaming the Victim.* New York: Pantheon, 1970.
Schultz, Gladys Denny. *How Many More Victims? Society and the Sex Criminal.* Philadelphia: J. B. Lippincott Company, 1965.
Tormes, Yvonne. *Child Victims of Incest.* Pamphlet. Denver, Colo.: The American Humane Association, 1968.
Walker, Marcia, and Brodsky, Stanley, eds. *Sexual Assault: The Victim and the Rapist.* Lexington, Mass.: Lexington Books, 1976.
Wood, Jim. *The Rape of Inez Garcia.* New York: G. P. Putnam's Sons, 1976.

Publications and Reports Funded by the National Institute of Law Enforcement and Criminal Justice, Law Enforcement Assistance Administration, U.S. Department of Justice, Washington, D.C. Copies available from the U.S. Government Printing Office, Washington, D.C. 20402.

Forcible Rape: Its Victims: A Report for Citizens, Health Facilities and Criminal Justice Agencies.
Forcible Rape: A National Survey of the Response by Police (Police Vol. I).
Forcible Rape: A Manual for the Patrol Officer (Police Vol. II).
Forcible Rape: A Manual for the Investigator (Police Vol. III).
Forcible Rape: Police Administrative and Policy Issues (Police Vol. IV).
Forcible Rape: Medical, Police and Legal Information for Victims, forthcoming, anticipated publication 1978.
Forcible Rape: A National Survey of the Response by Prosecutors (Prosecutors' Vol. I).
Forcible Rape: Prosecutor Manual for Filing and Trial (Prosecutors' Vol. II), forthcoming, anticipated publication 1978.
Forcible Rape: Prosecution Administration and Policy Issues (Prosecutors' Vol. III).
Forcible Rape: An Analysis of Legal Issues.

Articles

Abel, Gene et al. "The Components of Rapists' Sexual Arousal." *Archives of General Psychiatry* 34(1977):8.
Berger, Vivian. "Man's Trial, Woman's Tribulation: Rape Cases in the Courtroom." *Columbia Law Review* 77(1977):1.

Bienen, Leigh. "Rape II." *Women's Rights Law Reporter* 3(1977):3–4.
Bohmer, Carol. "Judicial Attitudes Toward Rape Victims." *Judicature* 57(1974):7.
Cohen, Laurie. "People v. Hood: the Admissibility of Rape Complaints as Spontaneous Declarations." *Illinois Bar Journal* 64(1976):6.
Eisenberg, Robert. "Abolishing Cautionary Instructions in Sex Offense Cases: People v. Rincon-Pineda." *Criminal Law Bulletin* 12(1976):1.
Giles, Linda. "The Admissibility of a Rape-Complainant's Previous Sexual Conduct: The Need for Legislative Reform." *New England Law Review* 11(1976):2.
Groth, A. Nicholas, and Burgess, Ann Wolbert. "Sexual Dysfunction during Rape." *The New England Journal of Medicine* 297 (1977):14.
Henn, Fritz et al. "Forensic Psychiatry: Profiles of Two Types of Sex Offenders." *The American Journal of Psychiatry* 133(1976):6.
Hernan, Lawrence. "What's Wrong with the Rape Reform Laws?" *The Civil Liberties Review* 3(1976/1977):60–73.
Hibey, Richard A. "The Trial of a Rape Case: An Advocate's Analysis of Corroboration, Consent, and Character." *American Criminal Law Review* 11(1973):2.
Holmstrom, Lynda, and Burgess, Ann. "Assessing Trauma in Rape Victims." *American Journal of Nursing* 75(1975):8.
Kardener, Sheldon. "Rape Fantasies." *Journal of Religion and Health* 14(1975):1.
Landau, Sybil. "Rape: The Victim as Defendant." *Trial* 10(1974):4.
LeGrand, Camille. "Rape and Rape Laws: Sexism in Society and the Law." *California Law Review* 91(1973):3.
McCombie, Sharon. "Characteristics of Rape Victims Seen in Crisis Intervention." *Smith College Studies in Social Work* 46(1976):2.
Peters, Joseph. "The Psychological Effects of Childhood Rape." *World Journal of Psychosynthesis* 6(1974):5.
Rada, Richard. "Alcohol and Rape." *Medical Aspects of Human Sexuality* 9(1975):3.
Roth, Edwin. "Emergency Treatment of Raped Children." *Medical Aspects of Human Sexuality* 6(1972):8.
Sasko, Helene, and Sesek, Deborah, "Rape Reform Legislation: Is It the Solution?" *Cleveland State Law Review* 24(1975):3.
Schiff, Arthur. "The New Florida 'Rape' Law." *The Journal of the Florida Medical Association* 62(1975):9.
Sgroi, Suzanne. "Sexual Molestation of Children: the Last Frontier of Child Abuse." *Children Today* 4(1975):3.
Symonds, Martin. "The Rape Victim: Psychological Patterns of Response." *The American Journal of Psychoanalysis* 36(1976):1.
Tasso, Jodi, and Miller, Elizabeth. "The Effects of the Full Moon on Human Behavior." *The Journal of Psychology* 93(1976):1.
Woods, Pamela Lake. "The Victim in a Forcible Rape Case: A Feminist View." *American Criminal Law Review* 11(1973):2.
Zonderman, Susan. "A Study of Volunteer Rape Crisis Counselors." *Smith College Studies in Social Work* 46(1975):1.

Index